Film Theory

What is the relationship between the cinema and the spectator? Renowned film scholars Thomas Elsaesser and Malte Hagener use this central question for film theory in order to guide students through all of the major film theories – from the classical period to today – in this brief, insightful, and engaging book. Every kind of cinema (and every kind of film theory) presupposes an ideal spectator, and then imagines a certain relationship between the mind and body of that spectator and the screen. Using seven distinctive configurations of spectator and screen that move from "exterior" to "interior" relationships, the authors retrace the most important stages of film theory from the 1920s onwards, with special attention paid to theories since 1945, from neo-realist and modernist theories to psychoanalytic, apparatus, phenomenological, and cognitivist theories, while also offering an incisive extension of film theory through the senses into the digital age.

Each chapter opens with a paradigmatic scene from a well-known film to introduce key concepts, and outlines the major schools of thought and theorists attached to a particular film theory. The films discussed combine classics of cinema such as *Rear Window* and *The Searchers* with contemporary films including *Donnie Darko* and *Eternal Sunshine of the Spotless Mind*. Film stills throughout provide a visual key to unlock challenging theoretical concepts.

Thomas Elsaesser is Professor of Film and Television Studies in the Department of Art and Culture at the University of Amsterdam. A renowned film scholar, he is the author and editor of many books, including *Weimar Cinema and After*, also published by Routledge.

Malte Hagener is Associate Professor of Media Studies at the Leuphana Universität Lüneburg. He has written *Moving Forward, Looking Back: The European Avant-garde and the Invention of Film Culture. 1919–1939* and edited many volumes, including

Film Theory

An introduction through the
senses

Thomas Elsaesser and
Malte Hagener

 Routledge
Taylor & Francis Group

NEW YORK AND LONDON

791. 4301 ELS

First published 2010
by Routledge
270 Madison Ave, New York, NY 10016

Simultaneously published in the UK
by Routledge
2 Park Square, Milton Park, Abingdon, Oxon OX14 4RN

Routledge is an imprint of the Taylor & Francis Group, an informa business

© 2010 Taylor & Francis

Typeset in Perpetua by Wearset Ltd, Boldon, Tyne and Wear
Printed and bound in the United States of America on acid-
free paper by Edwards Brothers, Inc.

Library of Congress Cataloging-in-Publication Data
A catalog record has been requested for this book

ISBN10: 0-415-80100-1 (hbk)
ISBN10: 0-415-80101-X (pbk)
ISBN10: 0-203-87687-3 (ebk)

ISBN13: 978-0-415-80100-3 (hbk)
ISBN13: 978-0-415-80101-0 (pbk)
ISBN13: 978-0-203-87687-9 (ebk)

Contents

Acknowledgments

This book originated in a series of seven lectures first given by Thomas Elsaesser at the University of Amsterdam in 2005–6 to the international M.A. students in Film and Television Studies. He was ably assisted by two of his PhD students, Marijke de Valck and Ria Thanouli, whose enthusiasm and valuable suggestions persuaded him that this might be a project worth pursuing further. The subsequent year, Patricia Pisters and Tarja Laine added their own perceptive layer of comments, and they have in the meantime built their own courses on the original model. The lecture notes and comments were sent to Malte Hagener, who translated them into coherent German, while giving the chapters shape and fleshing out the text with his own observations and analyses. The text then went back and forth a few more times in winter 2006–7, while Thomas taught a class of engaged and combative Yale undergraduates, whose mash-ups of films by Bergman, Tarkovsky, Sirk, Resnais, Mann and others opened up an altogether new possibility of how to make films think their own theory.

The German version was finally published in November 2007, greatly aided in the process by the critical-constructive support of Balthasar Haussmann and Steffen Herrmann. The overwhelmingly positive response encouraged us to have the German manuscript translated into English, not least because we found in Gabriele Stoicea an outstanding translator, whose dedication to the project went well past the call of duty. The fact that we eventually decided to rewrite almost every chapter, and add a new introduction and a concluding chapter on digital cinema and the senses, is entirely owed to the constructive criticism of the various anonymous Routledge readers, to whom we owe thanks, as well as to the team of sharp-eyed volunteer readers at Yale – Michael Anderson, Ryan Cook, Michael Cremer, Victor Fan, Seunghoon Jeong, Patrick Noonan and Jeremi Szaniawski. Ryan Cook deserves our special gratitude for his stellar work on finding appropriate illustrations, while Damian Gorczany and Patricia Prieto Blanco were instrumental in helping the new conclusion along. Other helpful comments on the English version came from Warren Buckland, Ria

Thanouli and Craig Uhlin. This, then, is a collaborative project in more ways than is signalled by the names of the two authors appearing on the cover, and while we are convinced it is a much better book for it, we readily accept that it is ultimately the readers and users who decide whether we have been successful in providing an introduction to Film Theory for the present.

Thomas Elsaesser, Amsterdam / Malte Hagener, Hamburg
September 2009

Introduction

Film theory, cinema, the body and the senses

I

Film theory is almost as old as the medium itself. The cinema developed at the end of the nineteenth century from advances in photography, mechanics, optics and the scientific production of serialized images (chronophotography), but also has its roots in centuries of popular entertainment, ranging from magic lantern shows and phantasmagorias, to large-scale panoramas, dioramas and optical toys. From the very beginning, inventors, manufacturers, artists, intellectuals, educators and scientists asked themselves questions about the essence of cinema: was it movement or was it interval, was it image or was it writing, was it capturing place or was it storing time? Besides its relationship to other forms of visualization and representation, the question was: was it science or was it art? And, if the latter, did it elevate and educate, or distract and corrupt? Discussions centered not just on the specificity of cinema, but also on its ontological, epistemological and anthropological relevance, and here the answers ranged from derogatory ("the cinema – an invention without a future": Antoine Lumière) to skeptical ("the kingdom of shadows": Maxim Gorki) or triumphal ("the Esperanto of the eye": D.W. Griffith). The first attempts to engage with film as a new medium took place in the early twentieth century, and two representatives whose work can lay claim to the title of "the first film theory" are Vachel Lindsay and Hugo Münsterberg. Film theory reached an initial peak in the 1920s, but it did not become institutionalized (e.g. find a home as part of the university curriculum) in the English-speaking world and in France until after World War II, and on a broader scale not until the 1970s. Other countries followed suit, but the debt to France and the head start of English language theorization has been a considerable advantage, ensuring that Anglo-American film theory – often showing strong "Continental" (i.e. French) influences – has been dominant since the 1970s. It is to this transnational community of ideas that the present volume addresses itself and seeks to contribute.

This already implies a first possibility of conceiving a new introduction to film theory for the twenty-first century, namely taking geographic provenance as the primary cue. One could distinguish, for instance, a French line of thought linking Jean Epstein, André Bazin and Gilles Deleuze, from a succession of English-speaking approaches, extending from Hugo Münsterberg to Noël Carroll. Initially, German-language film theory played a significant role, as the names of Béla Balázs, Rudolf Arnheim, Siegfried Kracauer, Walter Benjamin and Bertolt Brecht indicate, yet after National-Socialism and World War II, it lost its pre-eminent position in this international debate. The same could be said of Russian-language theory before and after Stalinism. Thus, the severity of certain historical breaks and political ruptures highlights two of the problems for a history of film theory based on geography and language. Moreover, a classification following national criteria would not only marginalize important positions elsewhere (Italy, the Czech Republic, Latin America and Japan, to mention just a few) and jettison the contribution of translation and migration, but it would also impose an external (national) coherence that hardly ever corresponds to the inner logic of theoretical positions, which are more often than not international in scope and universalist in intention.

On the other hand, geographic provenance can clarify the discursive logic of institutions, their strategies, their activities and publications: film theory often developed in close proximity to journals such as *Cahiers du Cinéma* and *Screen*, establishments such as the Cinémathèque française, the British Film Institute and the Museum of Modern Art, as well as in university departments and even around festivals and exhibitions. From this perspective, the translations, appropriations and transfers of film theoretical paradigms especially since the 1960s, such as semiotic, psychoanalytic or phenomenological film theory, would be subordinate to location, with so-called "creative clusters" determined by external factors, not by the internal dynamics of theory itself. Cities clearly play an important role in the formation of theory: Berlin in the 1920s and early 1930s, Paris in the 1950s and 1960s, London in the 1970s, but there is also Birmingham, UK, and Melbourne, Australia (for Film and Cultural Studies), and New York (for theories of avant-garde film and of early cinema). Universities not associated with major cities and still favorable to film theory in their time were the University of Iowa in the 1970s, the so-called "New Universities" in Britain in the 1980s, the University of Madison in Wisconsin since the 1980s (for neoformalism) and the University of Chicago in the 1990s (for theoretically informed film history). Often it is a combination of personal and institutional factors, but also intellectual fashions and trends that determine why or when a particular location is able to play the role of a "cluster"-site, successfully propagating certain theories, not least thanks to sending influential students into the academic world, hosting important conferences or by producing seminal publications.[1]

By far the most common way of building a classification system of theoretical approaches to the cinema has been to take the influential distinction between formalist and realist film theories as a starting point.[2] Whereas formalist theories look at film in terms of construction and composition, realist theories emphasize film's ability to offer a hitherto unattainable view onto (non-mediated) reality. In other words, "formalists" focus on cinema's artificiality, whereas "realists" call attention to the (semi-)transparency of the filmic medium, which ostensibly turns us into direct witnesses. According to this classification, Sergej Eisenstein, Rudolf Arnheim, the Russian Formalists and the American Neo-Formalists all advocate cinema's artificial construction (no matter whether they ground this construction in classical aesthetics, politics or cognitivism), whereas the opposite side would rally around Béla Balázs, Siegfried Kracauer and André Bazin under the banner of an "ontological" realism. The names already suggest that the debate is international and that it can be traced back at least to the 1920s, when questions about the specificity and nature of film as a medium, as well as about cinema's legitimacy as an art-form, were high on the agenda of a film and media avant-garde committed equally to theory and practice. Other distinctions, also organized in binary pairs, have been tried, such as normative versus descriptive, or critical versus affirmative.

Another, quite common approach sees film theory as a field of knowledge, which does not evolve its own object of study, but constantly adorns itself with borrowed plumes, and seems to owe its success to a kind of methodological opportunism, as well as to its mercurial adaptive abilities to new intellectual trends. Such an approach emphasizes the contextual embeddedness of film theory in larger developments pertaining to art history, literary theory, linguistics, to Cultural Studies and the social sciences, but it also highlights the trans-disciplinary tendencies, which have characterized the humanities in general at least since the 1980s. From this perspective, synchronic or diachronic schools of thought carry names like feminist (film) theory, (film) semiotics or cognitivist (film) theory.[3] As a further variation on this classification, one could subsume such theoretical positions under still-larger subject headings, in which case it makes sense, for instance, to separate psychological approaches from sociological ones, and contextual–anthropological ones from close textual or iconological ones.

More recent attempts to systematize film theories renounce these often polemical or normative classifications. Instead, they advocate a relay among successive individual standpoints.[4] As a result, film theory seems to advance teleologically toward perfection by virtue of the fact that each new theory improves upon the preceding one. At its worst, a revolving-door effect sets in, whereby one approach quickly follows another, without any of these schools or trends being put into perspective with regard to some shared or overarching question. In the former case, the individual perspectives exist only relative to one another, or primarily relative to some imaginary vanishing point, whereas in the latter case they exist more or less independently of, in parallel with or as swing-of-the-pendulum alternatives to one another. In order to sidestep both these problems, we have decided to organize our trajectory differently and instead of identifying schools and movements, we try to articulate film theory around a leading question. This allows us to bypass the simplistic listing of unrelated approaches, but also to avoid the evolutionary model, which projects an implicit goal according to a logic that is necessarily retrospective and thus must remain provisional. By proposing an explicit framework, we not only engage and challenge the existing theoretical positions, but also expect to take a stand ourselves within the field of scholarly debate, while acknowledging the historical situatedness of our own central question.

II

What is the relationship between the cinema, perception and the human body? Film theories, classical or contemporary, canonical or avant-garde, normative or transgressive, have all addressed this issue, implicitly framing it or explicitly re-focusing it. In *Film Theory: an Introduction to the Body and the Senses* we opt for making this our key concern: it provides the guiding concept to our historical-systematic survey and it gives the chapters their coherence.

Each type of cinema (as well as every film theory) imagines an ideal spectator, which means it postulates a certain relation between the (body of the) spectator and the (properties of the) image on the screen, however much at first sight the highlighted terms are "understanding" and "making sense", "interpretation" and "comprehension". What is called classical narrative cinema, for instance, can be defined by the way a given film engages, addresses and envelops the spectatorial body. Films furthermore presuppose a cinematic space that is both physical and discursive, one where film and spectator, cinema and body encounter one another. This includes the architectural arrangement of the spectatorial space (the auditorium with its racked seating), a temporal ordering of performances (separate sessions or continuous admission) and a specific social framing of the visit to the movie-theater (a night out with friends, or a solitary self-indulgence), the sensory envelope of sound and other perceptual stimuli, as well as the imaginary construction of filmic space through *mise-en-scène*, montage and narration. Likewise, bodies, settings and objects within the film communicate with each other (and with the spectator) through size, texture, shape, density and surface appeal, as much as they play on scale, distance, proximity, color or other primarily optical markers. But there are additional ways the body engages with the film event, besides the senses of vision, tactility and sound:

philosophical issues of perception and temporality, of agency and consciousness are also central to the cinema, as they are to the spectator. One of the challenges of our task was to tease out from formalist and realist theories their respective conceptions of cinema's relation to the body, whether formulated normatively (as, for example, in the approaches of both Sergej Eisenstein and André Bazin, however opposed they might be in other respects) or descriptively (more typical, at least in rhetorical strategy, of phenomenological and other contemporary theories).

This *leitmotif* of body and senses also communicates productively with the by-now widely used periodization of film history into early, classical and post-classical cinema, especially where these distinctions are based on the transformations of the cinema in its interrelation of (real) reception space and (imaginary) media space, from the fixed geometrical arrangement of projector, screen and spectator, to the more fluid and informal viewing conditions in front of the television screen or the laptop monitor, and extending to the mobile screens on hand-held devices, which explicitly invite new modes of bodily engagement in their hand–eye coordination.

This is why our model also tries to re-articulate in a theoretically pertinent manner the spatio-temporal relations between the bodies and objects depicted in a film, and between film and spectator. Crucial in this respect is the dynamics connecting the diegetic and the non- and extra-diegetic levels of the "world" of the film and how they intersect with the "world' of the spectator. The concept of diegesis (derived from the Greek "diegesis", meaning narration, report or argument, as opposed to "mimesis", meaning imitation, representation) was originally used in narrative theory to distinguish between the particular time–space continuum created by narration and everything outside it. For instance, jazz music in a nightclub scene is diegetic, when the film includes shots of the musician or band, whereas the background strings heard but not seen in a romantic tête-à-tête, are usually non-diegetic (i.e. referring to elements made meaningful within the film but located outside its story world). Whenever the camera independently closes in on an object carrying considerable narrative weight (for instance the revelation at the end of CITIZEN KANE that "Rosebud" is a sled), one speaks of a non-diegetic camera movement, even though the object itself is diegetic. Given that today's films tend to carry with them also extra-diegetic materials, such as DVD bonuses and commentary, and that spectators watching films "on the go" increasingly inhabit two worlds (the cinematic universe, the diegesis, and their own physical environment and ambient space), suspending one in favor of the other, or shuttling between them, a new definition of the concept of diegesis will play an important part in our overall argument.[5]

The different forms that this relation takes between cinema, film, sensory perception, physical environment and the body might be pictured as a series of metaphors, or paired concepts, which can be mapped on the body: its surfaces, senses and perceptive modalities, its tactile, affective and sensory-motor faculties. Yet the semantic fields thus staked out also take into account physical, epistemological and even ontological foundations of the cinema itself, emphasizing its specific properties and key elements. We have chosen seven distinct pairs that describe an arc from "outside" to "inside", and at the same time, they retrace fairly comprehensively the most important stages of film theory roughly from 1945 to the present, from neo-realist and modernist theories to psychoanalytic, "apparatus", phenomenological and cognitivist theories. Using the seven configurations as levels of pertinence as well as entry-points for close analysis, we noted that earlier film theories, such as those from the "classical" period during the 1920s and 1930s, also respond to such a re-organization, suggesting that our outline – however schematic or provisional at this stage – can eventually lead to a more nuanced and thorough re-classification of the cinema's many contact points with the human senses and the body of the spectator.

While relevant to film theory as hitherto understood, our conceptual metaphors neither amend previous theoretical models nor do they form a succession of independent or autonomous units: despite covering core arguments from very disparate and seemingly incompatible theories, the chapters – on window/ frame, door/screen, mirror/face, eye/gaze, skin/touch, ear/space and brain/ mind – nonetheless tightly interlace with each other. We are not proposing a Hegelian synthesis, but neither do we stand outside the fray – this would be, in a nutshell, our methodological premise on the issue of the historicity of theory itself. A new approach (implicitly or explicitly) tackles questions which a preceding theory may have brought to light but which it could not explain in a satisfactory manner. But, by the same token, each new theory creates its own questions, meaning that it can find itself once more confronting the same issues, which a previous theory had counted as resolved. For instance, one explanation for the surprising revival since the mid-1990s of André Bazin's theories, after one thought his theory of realism had been laid to rest in the 1970s (when realism was widely seen as an ideological characteristic of bourgeois art) is the fact that the transition from analog to digital media again raises, albeit in a new form, Bazin's central question concerning the "ontology of the photographic image".[6] The revival of Bazin (but also that of Kracauer, Epstein, Balázs and Arnheim) proves that the history of film theory is not a teleological story of progress to ever-more comprehensive or elegantly reductive models. Generally speaking, a theory is never historically stable, but takes on new meanings in different contexts. If, as already indicated, film theory is almost as old as the cinema, it not only extends into the future, but also the past, as witnessed by the renewed interest in seventeenth- and eighteenth-century scientific treatises on the theory of motion in images. Similarly, the new dialog between the hard

Application of old theory to modern cinema

sciences and the humanities around cognitivism has given Hugo Münsterberg's *The Photoplay: a Psychological Study* (1916) a new topicality as "predecessor", which suggests that the history of film theory extends into the future, which is to say, it is liable to change, because every new present tends to rewrite its own history.

To return to our central question: the individual chapters not only stand in a particular relation to the history of film theory, but also to the forms of cinema prevalent in a given period, since the evolution of theory and the changes in film-making and cinema-going are mutually influencing factors. Besides a historical–analytical overview of many important *theoretical* positions (from André Bazin and David Bordwell, to Gilles Deleuze and Laura Mulvey), our project also involves the beginnings of a re-classification of *film history* (around pre-cinema and early cinema, but also from the 1940s to the present), based on the premise that the spectator's body in relation to the moving image constitutes a key historical variable, whose significance has been overlooked, mainly because film theory and cinema history are usually kept apart. Consequently, more is at stake than presenting film theory from an objective perspective, treating it as a closed universe of discourse that belongs to history. Rather, we want to probe the usefulness of the various theoretical projects of the past for contemporary film and media theory, in the hope of re-conceptualizing theory and thus of fashioning, if not a new theory, then a new understanding of previous theories' possible logics.

But such a history is in any case not at the forefront of our study, because diachronic overviews have never been in short supply. What we aim for is a comprehensive and systematic introduction, underpinned and guided by a specific perspective opened up when raising a different set of questions about old problems. Our mission – to condense a hundred years of history with thousands of pages of theory – necessarily involves losses, biases and omissions, but on the whole we hope to achieve an effect similar to that of a concentrate: the volume decreases, the liquid thickens, but important flavors and the ingredients linger. The distinctiveness, sometimes to the point of incompatibility, among theories should not disappear or be disavowed.

Each chapter also opens with a paradigmatic scene from a film, capturing in a nutshell a central premise, highlighting one of the levels, and introducing the main proponents (schools, concepts and theorists). The films selected combine well-known classics of the cinema, such as REAR WINDOW (1954, Alfred Hitchcock) and THE SEARCHERS (1956, John Ford) with more recent titles, such as CRASH (2004, Paul Haggis) and ETERNAL SUNSHINE OF THE SPOTLESS MIND (2004, Michel Gondry). The period of the films we draw on does not necessarily coincide with the date of the respective theories, for although our seven-tier model develops roughly along chronological lines, it does not purport to trace an exact one-to-one fit between the history of cinema and film theory. Therefore, the emblematic film scenes should not be understood as "examples" or "illustrations", but rather as an opportunity to think with a given film (not just about it), as Gilles Deleuze has so emphatically proposed and attempted to do in his cinema books.[7] Moreover, in every chapter we return time and again to specific examples, which do not serve as evidence for independently existing theories, but rather want to offer food for thought and an opportunity to re-acquaint oneself with films and theories. We hope that readers will feel inspired to bring their own film-culture and cinema-experience to bear on this theoretical knowledge, not in the sense of "applying" one to the other, but rather as an act of inference or even interference: a meditation on the ways cinema builds on theory, and theory builds on cinema. Many contemporary films, from blockbusters to art-house fare and avant-garde statements, seem to be acquainted with advanced scholarly positions and want to be taken seriously also on a theoretical level, sharing a certain knowingness with the spectator as part of their special reflexivity.

III

In concluding this introduction, a brief overview of the seven following chapters can hopefully clarify our methodological aims and assumptions. The first chapter is dedicated to "window and frame", and it deals with the framing of the filmic image as its essential element. Various approaches, such as André Bazin's theory of filmic realism or David Bordwell's examination of staging in depth, have promoted the concept of the cinematic image as offering a privileged outlook onto and insight into a diegetically coherent, but separate, universe. By contrast, other authors, such as Rudolf Arnheim and Sergej Eisenstein, have emphasized the principles of construction governing the image's composition within the frame-as-frame. We argue that these two positions, often opposed as realist and formalist, resemble each other more than is generally assumed. In both cases, perception is treated as almost completely dis-embodied because of its reduction to visual perception.[8] This is where Chapter 2 picks up by focusing, under the heading of "door and screen", on positions that seek to describe the transition from the spectator's world to the world of the film. In this chapter we concentrate both on physical entry into the cinema and imaginary entry into the film, examining the approaches put forward by narrative theory, i.e. narratology, when dealing with the question of spectators' involvement in the processes of filmic narration, such as focalization, identification, engagement and immersion. This field of research comprises formalist theories, as well as (post-)structuralist positions, but also models, which interpret the relationship between spectator and film in dialogic terms, such as those drawing on Mikhail

Bakhtin. Underlying this interpretation is the idea of the spectator as a being who enters an unfamiliar/familiar world and thereby is "alienated" from his/her own world (in the sense of the *ostranie* that Russian Formalists use), in order to better, or wiser, return to it.[9]

The third chapter stands under the motto of "mirror and face", and explores the reflective and reflexive potential of cinema. On the one hand, this allows us to talk about self-referentiality as exemplified by the modernizing movements in European cinema from the 1950s through the 1970s (the so-called "New Waves"). On the other hand, the mirror has come to occupy a central position in psychoanalytic film theory, according to which looking into the mirror implies not just confronting oneself, but also turning this gaze outward, i.e. transforming it into the gaze of the Other. Cinema's fascination with the *Doppelgänger* motif – stories of doubles and identity-switches, linking German Expressionist films from the 1920s with Japanese ghost stories of the 1970s and South Korean horror films from the 1990s – is as important in this context as questions of identification and reflexivity. An often discussed, highly ambivalent yet nonetheless theoretically still under-explained topic is the effect of mimesis and doubling between film and spectator. We ask if it is founded on similar mechanisms of confusion between Self and Other as are being discussed in the recent neurobiological literature on mirror-neurons in the human brain. We also review in this chapter those theoretical approaches that focus on the central role of the close-up and the human face, each being a version of the other, while every face-to-face is, of course, also a moment of mirroring.

The look into the mirror already implies a certain spatial arrangement, on which the cinematographic gaze might be said to have been modeled. This is discussed in greater detail in Chapter 4, dedicated to the "eye and look", referring chiefly to a series of positions developed in film theory during the 1970s. On the one hand, these were strongly influenced by Jacques Lacan's poststructuralist re-formulation of Freudian psychoanalysis and, on the other hand, they drew on Michel Foucault's theory of the panopticon as a model for social relations based on vision and control. Particularly feminist theory has worked with gendered, a-symmetrical schemata of look and gaze (as they are structuring and structured in a film, circulating between the camera and the characters, as well as between spectator and film). This school of thinking implies that a certain distance is maintained between spectator and film, which manifests itself in the field of vision as a form of pathology ("voyeurism", "fetishism") and mistaken perception ("miscognition", "disavowal").

The situation of distance is almost the opposite in the approaches discussed in Chapter 5 under the heading of "skin and touch" which – premised on proximity – could be seen as a reaction or backlash against the "scopic regime" of previous theories. There have always been attempts to conceptualize the cinema as an encounter of sorts, as a contact space with Otherness, or as an occasion to bring faraway places closer and render them physically present. These correspond with theories based on the assumption that skin is an organ of and touch a means of perception, from which follows the understanding of cinema as a tactile experience, or conversely, one that grants the eye "haptic" faculties, besides the more common "optic" dimension. This simultaneously interpersonal, trans-cultural and – in its philosophical assumptions – phenomenological school corresponds to a fascination with the human body, its surfaces and fluids, its softness and vulnerability, but also its function as carapace or protective shield.

Such a focus on material nuance, texture and touch leads directly to the approaches presented in Chapter 6, which, under the title "ear and sound", also emphasize the importance of the body to perception and to three-dimensional orientation, further undermining the previous theories' almost exclusive concentration on visual perception, whether two-dimensional or three-dimensional. From skin and contact we thus turn our attention to the ear as an interface between film and spectator, an organ that creates its own sonorous perceptual envelope, but also regulates the way that the human body locates itself in space. For, unlike previous understandings of the spectator as someone defined by ocular verification and cognitive data processing, these newer approaches draw attention to factors such as the sense of balance or equilibrium, organized not around the frame, but around duration, location, interval and inter-action. The spectator is no longer passively receiving optical information, but exists as a bodily being, enmeshed acoustically, senso-motorically, somatically and affectively in the film's visual texture and soundscape. Technological developments such as the advances in audio engineering since the 1970s (the various Dolby formats) relate directly to theoretical advances in psychoanalysis, aesthetics and sound studies.

Finally, the seventh conceptual pair can best be typified with Gilles Deleuze's motto "the brain is the screen". One the one hand, film inscribes itself in the spectator's innermost being, stimulating synapses and affecting brain functions. The moving image and sound modulate neuronal pathways and affect nerves, they incite bodily reactions and involuntary responses, as if it was the film that "directs" the body and mind, creating an entity ("mind") that produces the film at the same time as it is produced by it ("body"). Such ideas of a fusion between the pre-existence of a cinema running in the mind, and mental worlds morphing into or taking shape as observable material realities, underlie numerous films from the past 15 years, where the diegesis – the spatio-temporal "world" of a film – turns out to be a figment of the protagonist's imagination, no longer obeys the laws of nature, or is explicitly created so as to deceive or mislead the spectator. Cognitive narratologists find here a confirmation of their theses, and films like The Sixth Sense, Fight Club, Eternal Sunshine of the Spotless Mind have elicited lively discussions around "complex storytelling" and "forking path narratives". Deleuze, on the other hand, would regard such narratological analyses as beside the point, since for him there is no "mind" that sits in the brain and is "in control" of input and output, so that the problems these films pose to the spectator, are situated differently. The chapter on "mind and brain" addresses radical versions of constructivism and epistemic skepticism, giving the word to Deleuze, but also asking how cognitivists have responded to the challenges implied by mind-game and time-warp films, in order to understand such tendencies in contemporary film-making not just sociologically, as competing in the marketplace with video-games and computer simulations, but also epistemologically as philosophical puzzles.

The idea of the body as sensory envelope, as perceptual membrane and material–mental interface, in relation to the cinematic image and to audio-visual perception, is thus more than a heuristic device and an aesthetic metaphor: it is the ontological, epistemological and phenomenological "ground" for the respective theories of film and cinema today. This process of examining the different film theories in light of their philosophical assumptions, and evaluating both across the touchstone of the body and the senses, finds further support in the (non-teleological) progress that our conceptual metaphors chart, from the "outside" of window and door, to the "inside" of mind and brain. We could also call it a double movement: from the disembodied but observing eye, to the privileged but implicated gaze (and ear); from the presence of the image as seen, felt and touched, to sense organs that become active participants in the formation of filmic reality; from the sensory perceptual surface of film that requires the neurological brain, to the unconscious that registers deep ambivalences in the logic of the narrative, where rational choice or rational agency theories see merely an alternating succession of action and reaction. At the limit, film and spectator are like parasite and host, each occupying the other and being in turn occupied, to the point where there is only one reality that *un*folds as it *en*folds, and vice versa.

The focus on the body, perception and the senses thus not only cuts across formalist and realist theories, or tries to close the gap between theories of authorship and reception. Cautiously formulated in our concluding chapter is the hope that it can also bridge the divide between photographic and post-filmic cinema, not by denying the differences, but by re-affirming both the persistence of the cinema experience and reminding ourselves of the sometimes surprising and unexpected, but welcome complementarity among the seemingly contending theoretical approaches across the cinema's first 100-year history.[10]

Commensurate with the importance that the moving image and recorded sound have attained in the twenty-first century, there is, finally, another possible consequence of concentrating on the body and the senses: the cinema seems poised to leave behind its function as a "medium" (for the representation of reality) in order to become a "life form" (and thus a reality in its own right). Our initial premise of asking film theory to tell us how film and cinema relate to the body and the senses thus may well lead to another question (which we shall not answer here), namely whether – when putting the body and the senses at the centre of film theory – the cinema is not proposing to us, besides a new way of knowing the world, also a new way of "being in the world", and thus demanding from film theory, next to a new epistemology also a new ontology. This, one could argue, is quite an achievement, when one considers how film theory might be said to have "started" in the seventeenth century as a technical description of movement in/of images, and now – provisionally – ends as a form of film philosophy and in this respect as a general theory of movement: of bodies, of affect, of the mind and the senses.

Chapter 1

Cinema as window and frame

A man, immobilized in a wheelchair, observes, as a way to pass the time and entertain himself, through a rectangular frame the human dramas that unfold before his eyes. He is capable of alternating his visual field between a wide panorama and a closer view for detail. His position is elevated and privileged, while the events seem to unfold independently of his gaze, yet without making him feel excluded. This is one way to summarize the basic tenets of Alfred Hitchcock's REAR WINDOW (US, 1954), which has become an exemplary case study in film theory precisely because the film's point of departure is often held to figuratively re-enact the specific viewing situation of classical cinema:[1] Having suffered an accident, photographer L.B. Jefferies (James Stewart) is confined to a wheelchair with his leg in a cast. A pair of binoculars, as well as the telephoto lenses of his camera, allow him to switch between long shots of the back yard onto which his window opens and close shots of individual apartments and their residents. Two basic principles, according to the school of theory that considers the cinema as window/frame, can be derived from this situation: Jefferies' *seemingly* privileged perspective as onlooker and (to a lesser degree) as listener, and second, his distance from the events. The film even provides an answer to the question formulated in the introduction – whether the film is outside or inside in relation to the spectator: as long as Jefferies keeps his distanced role of observer, the events cannot harm him. Not until he – or, rather, his girlfriend Lisa Carol Fremont (Grace Kelly), instigated by him – transgresses this threshold does the world "outside" pose a threat to the one "inside". However, REAR WINDOW does not resonate in film-theoretical space solely through its emphasis on visibility and distance:

> The title REAR WINDOW, apart from the literalness of its denotation, evokes the diverse "windows" of the cinema: the cinema/lens of camera and projector, the window in the projection booth, the eye as window, and film as "window on the world."[2]

These and some other key aspects of the first ontological metaphor will be examined and discussed in this chapter.

As we will be arguing, the concepts of window and frame share several fundamental premises, but also exhibit significant differences. Let us start with the similarities: first of all, the cinema as window and frame offers *special, ocular access* to an event (whether fictional or not) – usually a rectangular view that accommodates the spectator's visual curiosity. Second, the (real) two-dimensional screen transforms in the act of looking into an (imaginary) three-dimensional space which seems to open up beyond the screen. And, third (real and metaphorical) distance from the events depicted in the film renders the act of looking safe for the spectator, sheltered as s/he is by the darkness inside the auditorium. The spectator is completely cut off from the film events, so that s/he does not have to fear his/her direct involvement in the action (as in modern theater) nor does s/he feel any moral obligation to intervene (as in real life). In other words, the cinema as window and frame – the first of our seven *modes of being (in the cinema/world)* – is ocular–specular (i.e. conditioned by optical access), transitive (one looks at something) and disembodied (the spectator maintains a safe distance).

Even though both concepts meet in the compound "window frame", the metaphors also suggest somewhat different qualities: one looks *through* a window, but one looks *at* a frame. The notion of the window implies that one loses sight of the framing rectangle as it denotes transparency, while the frame highlights the content of the (opaque) surface and its constructed nature, effectively implying composition and artificiality. While the window directs the viewer to something behind or beyond itself – ideally, the separating glass pane

Figure 1.1 REAR WINDOW: space cropped and at a safe distance.

completely vanishes in the act of looking – the frame draws attention both to the status of the arrangement as artifact and to the image support itself: one only has to think of classical picture frames and their opulence and ornaments, their conspicuousness and ostentatious display. On the one hand, the window as a medium effaces itself completely and becomes invisible, and on the other, the frame exhibits the medium in its material specificity.

Both window and frame are well-established notions within film theory, yet when seen in historical context, their differences become more pronounced. Traditionally, the frame corresponded to film theories called *formalist* or *constructivist*, while the model of the window held sway in *realist* film theories. For a long time, the distinction between constructivist (or formalist and formative) and realist (or mimetic and phenomenological) theories was believed to be a fundamental distinction. Siegfried Kracauer's elaborated it in his *Theory of Film* and as taken up and refined by Dudley Andrew in *The Major Film Theories*, it has proven to be widely influential.[3] In such a classificatory scheme Béla Balázs, Rudolf Arnheim and the Russian montage theorists stand on one side, contrasted with Bazin and Kracauer on the other. The first group focuses on the alteration and manipulation of filmic perception, distinct from everyday perception by means such as montage, framing or the absence of color and language. The second group defines the essence of cinema in terms of its ability to record and reproduce reality and its phenomena, including aspects which are invisible to the naked human eye.

There exist, however, a series of links between these two seemingly opposed poles. Both tendencies aim at enhancing the cultural value of cinema, i.e. to put

Figure 1.2 REAR WINDOW : Jefferies as spectator.

it on a par with the established arts. The idea of window and frame is helpful in this respect because historically it answered to a felt inferiority complex of film vis-à-vis its older and more established siblings – theater and painting – that rely upon the assumption of a spectator distanced from the object and scene. The humanistic, Renaissance ideal of art appreciation – marked by individual immersion and contemplation of the work as opposed to the collective and distracted experience of early cinema – requires distance and therefore framing. For constructivists as well as for realists, perception is limited to the visual dimension, the sense and data processing are thought of as highly rational while the primary goal is to consciously work through what is being perceived. In this respect Balázs and Bazin, Eisenstein and Kracauer all conceptualize the spectator–film relationship along similar lines, even though Kracauer and Eisenstein were sensitive to the "shock" value and somatic dimension of the film experience.[4]

A further affinity between the metaphors of window and frame has been identified by Charles F. Altman: "Though the window and frame metaphors appear diametrically opposed, they actually share an assumption of the screen's fundamental independence from the processes of production and consumption."[5] Both models, frame and window, postulate the image as given and view the spectator as concentrating on how most fully to engage with the work and its structures, making wholeness and (assumed) coherence the focus of the analysis. If only by default, they tend to overlook the potentially contradictory processes of production (be they technological or institutional) that are also leaving traces on the films; nor do they give due weight to the freedom but also constraints which differences in human perception, cultural conditioning and cognition bring to the reception of films. The spectator thus conceptualized is not only disembodied, but exists mostly for the benefit of the theory he or she is supposed to exemplify.

The distinction between "open" and "closed" forms of cinema allows for another perspective on the window/frame divide.[6] Following Leo Braudy,[7] the term "closed" refers to films in which the universe depicted in the film (its diegesis) closes in upon itself in the sense that it contains only elements which are necessary because internally motivated: Georges Méliès' films, which experiment with cinematic techniques and trick shots while constantly referring back to themselves, belong in this category, as do the carefully constructed worlds of Fritz Lang, Alfred Hitchcock and David Fincher, in which everything seems to have its predetermined place following the dictates of some invisible, but omnipresent hand or elaborate master plan. Furthermore, whatever exists "on-screen" stands in a relationship of mutual dependence but also tension with what lies outside the frame, creating a potent dynamic between on-screen and off-screen space. By contrast, open films offer a segment, a snapshot, or a fragment from a constantly flowing and evolving reality. The films of the Lumière brothers have often been cited (not always convincingly) as the prototypical example for this type of cinema. Other important cases are the films of Jean Renoir with their long, flowing camera movements and large cast of characters, the Neorealist films of Roberto Rossellini as well as the Dardenne brothers' recent works balancing the fine line between documentary and fiction. The diegetic world appears as if what it depicts might continue in much the same way even if the camera were turned off, and life would continue to ebb and flow beyond the limits of the frame. The closed form by contrast is centripetal, oriented inwardly; the totality of the world is contained within the image frame (which, by definition, includes off-screen space). The open form, on the other hand, is centrifugal, oriented outwardly. Here the frame (as mobile window) represents a changeable portion of a potentially limitless world:

> The difference may be the difference between finding a world and creating one: the difference between using the preexisting materials of reality and organizing these materials into a totally formed vision; the difference between an effort to discover the orders independent of the watcher and to discover those orders the watcher creates by his act of seeing. Voyeurism is a characteristic visual device of the closed film, for it contains the proper mixture of freedom and compulsion: free to see something dangerous and forbidden, conscious that one wants to see and cannot look away. In closed films the audience is a victim, imposed on by the perfect coherence of the world on the screen. In open films the audience is a guest, invited into the film as an equal whose vision of reality is potentially the same as that of the director.[8]

The difference between closed and open film form can thus also be seen as a reformulation of the difference between window and frame: the window

Figure 1.3 La Grande Illusion (FR, 1937, Jean Renoir): reality flowing freely in and out of the frame.

offers a detail of a larger whole in which the elements appear as if distributed in no particular way, so that the impression of realism for the spectator is above all a function of transparency. By contrast, foregrounding the frame shifts the attention to the organisation of the material. The window implies a diegetic world that extends beyond the limit of the image while the frame delineates a filmic composition that exists solely for the eyes of the beholder.

The concepts of window and frame, based as they are on managing the complex relations of distance and proximity between film and viewer, come together in a cinematic style generally known as "classical". Classical cinema keeps its disembodied spectators at arm's length while also drawing them in. It achieves its effects of transparency by the concerted deployment of filmic means (montage, light, camera placement, scale, special effects) which justify their profuse presence by aiming at being noticed as little as possible. A maximum of technique and technology seeks a minimum of attention for itself, thereby not only masking the means of manipulation, but succeeding in creating a transparency that simulates proximity and intimacy. This paradox, namely that the effect of an unmediated view (the window) requires elaborate means and codified rules (the frame), may be what makes this specific style so dominant, which is to say, so attractive to viewers and so expensive to producers. For those film industries that could afford it, this classical style, perfected for the first time in Hollywood in the late 1910s, remained internationally prevalent at least until the late1950s.[9] Although the terms "Hollywood" and "classical" are often used interchangeably, most forms of popular cinema in whatever country and whatever period have broadly adhered to its rules, sometimes with local or national modifications: we find its norms upheld in the films of the Nazi period and those of Socialist Realism, even in many films of Italian Neorealism and of British "kitchen-sink" realism. Most contemporary made-for-television films are still classical at least in the sense that they try to make the medium and its artificiality disappear.

In the classical cinema the spectator is an invisible witness – invisible to the unfolding narrative that does not acknowledge his/her presence, which is why neither direct address nor the look into the camera are part of the classical idiom, and instead – as in the French *Nouvelle Vague* – signal a deliberate departure or break from its normativity. Interestingly enough, the same tension arises within the different styles of documentary, where the notion of cinema as window and frame can also be found, and where certain styles of documentary (direct cinema, or the "fly-on-the-wall" approach in which crew and technology try to stay invisible both to the spectators of the film and to the subjects being filmed) offer the spectator a seemingly transparent view on an unmediated reality, while other styles, notably *cinéma vérité*, want to get close to the world

Figure 1.4 Caspar David Friedrich: *Frau am Fenster* – window framing a view.

(and traverse the frame) without trying to create the illusion of transparency (the window) by consciously utilizing the camera as a catalyst to provoke (re) actions. The spectator figures either as an invisible witness, or is invited as a virtual participant of events taking place independently of him/her, yet happening in a shared world (outside the cinema).[10] There is thus in the dynamic of window and frame, an inherent split between passive and active, between manipulation and agency, between witnessing and voyeurism, between irresponsibility and moral response that REAR WINDOW brilliantly enacts in all its dramatic potential and terrifying consequences.

This tradition of visual representation characterized by managing distance and privileging apperception principally through the disembodied eye did not emerge with the cinema, but originated in the central perspective used in classical painting since the Renaissance. Stephen Heath, along with many others, has traced the development of camera perspective in cinema back to the discovery of central perspective in fifteenth-century Italy:

> What is fundamental is the idea of the spectator at a window, an "*aperta finestra*" that gives a view on the world – framed, centered, harmonious (the "*istoria*") [. . .] The conception of the Quattrocento system is that of a scenographic space, a space set out as spectacle for the eye of a spectator.[11]

Yet, there remains a tension between perspective as technique and perspective as symbolic form. As technique, the single vanishing point and the respective implications of size and scale ensure that a three-dimensional reality is reduced to a two-dimensional surface, which is organized in such a way as to simulate another three-dimensional reality. This might be experienced either as another world (an imaginary universe) or as a continuation of the spectator's own three-dimensional world – a persistent legend claims that Lumière's film of the arrival of a train sent people in panic who allegedly imagined the locomotive was about to enter the auditorium space, while Lucas' introduction of Dolby sound in STAR WARS gave spectators the sense that they occupied the same (aural) "space" as the spaceship (see Chapter 6). As symbolic form, perspective embodied the belief of Western humanism in a world "centered" on the single individual, whose frame of perception is aligned or equated with an act of possession,[12] and in which the window on the world can become either a safe in the wall or the shop window on a world of objects and people as commodities. Film-makers have often tried to play on these contradictory features of seeing the "surface of things" and "seeing through things", by either "flattening" the image (e.g. Jean-Luc Godard in PIERROT LE FOU [FR, 1965]) or de-centering the frame (Jean-Marie Straub and Danièle Huillet in NICHT VERSÖHNT/NOT RECONCILED [GE, 1965]).

As this brief historical survey and the film examples try to suggest, it may be necessary to dismantle the longstanding, deeply entrenched opposition between the analytical models of window and frame, if understood as lining up realists against constructivists. To that end we let three theoreticians who are usually believed to stand on different sides of the divide speak for themselves. From the

Figure 1.5 PIERROT LE FOU: flattened image and skewed perspective.

ways they conceptualize cinema, Rudolf Arnheim and Sergej Eisenstein are constructivists, who accentuate the frame and with it the creative intervention in the filmic world, whereas André Bazin, commonly seen as a realist because he focuses on the transparency of the filmic medium, has nonetheless important things to say about the frame, which in turn help to highlight what is distinctive in the positions of the other two, also with respect to transparency and medium-specificity.

Rudolf Arnheim developed his film theory while working as a film critic for *Die Weltbühne*, a journal of the non-partisan Left in the Weimar Republic.[13] Arnheim graduated with a degree in psychology, having specialized in both critical sociology and Gestalt theory. This seemingly incompatible background is put to good use in his main contribution to film theory, which appeared in 1932 under the title *Film as Art*.[14] In this book Arnheim starts out from "the basic elements of the film medium" and from this vantage point postulates some fundamental differences between "film and reality", i.e. between the way in which cinema presents the visible world to the spectator and everyday human perception. It is the oscillation between the impression of reality and ordinary perception that is central to Arnheim's theory: "Film pictures are at once plane and solid" (20). Arnheim's conclusion is that cinema does not copy or imitate reality, but that it creates a world and a reality of its own:

> Thus film, like the theater, provides a partial illusion. Up to a certain degree it gives the impression of real life [...]. On the other hand, it partakes strongly of the nature of a picture in a way that the stage never can. By the absence of colors, of three-dimensional depth, by being sharply limited by the margins on the screen, and so forth, film is most satisfactorily denuded of its realism. It is always at one and the same time a flat picture post card and the scene of a living action.
>
> (31)

The innate mental capacities of human beings to discern forms and to create patterns, to develop an inner organisation from outer sense perception are, according to Gestalt theory, the prerequisites for filling in such a "partial illusion". It is the viewer's aptitude of creating a *Gestalt* (to assemble a number of disconnected sense impressions into a whole that is larger than the sum of its parts) that endows film with the status of art, but also what gives it realism. Put differently: the cognitive act of combining disparate data and sensations from within a shared frame is the fundamental premise for our understanding of film. Here the frame is more a perceptual constraint and cognitive task than a transparent plane giving access to the world.

This position puts Arnheim firmly in the mainstream of theoreticians of the 1920s and 1930s who saw film's specificity and artistic merits not in its capability to show the world outside, i.e. its purported realism, but rather in the distance between everyday perception and filmic perception. If film were to affect the spectator in the same way as a complete sensory encounter with the world, i.e. spatial, colorful and acoustic, then it could not be distinguished from reality itself and would amount to no more than its mechanical double. This duplication could not attain the status of art because art – this was the common argument of the time – presupposes active human involvement and cannot be generated by a machine. In this perspective, film as art depends on the creative intervention of an artist, with mechanical duplication merely serving as its means of production. For Arnheim (and others at the time) it was precisely the lack and absence (of color, of naturalistic sound, of three-dimensionality) that posed the artistic challenge of the new medium.

Consequently, Arnheim remained skeptical vis-à-vis the sound film that emerged in the late 1920s. As long as this new technological addition was overwhelmingly used in a naturalistic way (as it was in the "talkies"), it moved film merely toward a reproduction of reality. Not surprisingly, Arnheim addressed the topic of cinema only sporadically, after he had fleshed out his rejection of sound cinema in a series of essays published around 1930, a good example of which is the programmatically entitled "Silent Beauty and Noisy Nonsense".[15] In his view, sound film was the result of an unacceptable compromise between two incompatible art forms (silent film and radio drama), a position he summarized in his theoretical cornerstone article, "The New Laocoon".[16] For the remainder of his long productive life, Arnheim concentrated on radio, photography and the psychology of visual perception in the arts. While Arnheim thus accentuated the frame as an element of abstraction from everyday perception, another theoretician who was also a practicing film-maker used the frame to promote his concept of montage: Sergej Eiseinstein.

With films such as Bronenosez "Potemkin" (SU, 1925, The Battleship Potemkin), Oktjabr (SU, 1927, October/Ten Days That Shook the World) or IVAN GROZNY (SU, 1943/6, two parts, IVAN THE TERRIBLE), Eisenstein became one of the most important directors of world cinema, but he also bequeathed an extensive if unsystematic theoretical oeuvre that would prove enormously influential over the years. In keeping with the views of the revolutionary avant-garde, Eisenstein along with his Soviet colleagues Dziga Vertov and Vsevolod Pudovkin did not distinguish between the practical work of making a film and the theoretical work of writing a text: theory and practice complement and condition each other: they are conceivable only in terms of a dialectical unity. Following this precept, Eisenstein invested a considerable amount of energy in teaching at the Moscow film school, the first of its kind in the world. Eisenstein was a universal genius who spoke half-a-dozen languages fluently, took an equally active interest in Kabuki theater and Marxist dialectic, and was well versed in both quantum mechanics and psychoanalysis. In addition to having to master these wide-ranging references, what complicates any engagement with Eisenstein's ideas is the fact that they cannot be easily summarized or pressed into a coherent and self-consistent theory.[17] Instead of a clearly-structured theoretical edifice with a foundation based on a few axioms, his thinking resembles a labyrinth of multiple dimensions in which one can suddenly lose one's way, as in a short story by Jorge Luis Borges or a drawing by M.C. Escher. And yet, at least in posterity's eyes, Eisenstein's (film theoretical) meditations are associated with a single concept, namely that of montage.[18] The fact that this concept has taken on numerous nuances which were initially disconnected, if not outright contradictory and mutually exclusive, should not come as a surprise in the case of such a baroque thinker who recorded his ideas on slips of paper, who constantly revised his texts and thereby generated the largest individual collection in the Moscow State Archive.[19] Given that Eisenstein himself could offer plenty of material for an introduction of his own, we shall single out only a few moments which are of particular interest from the point of view of framing.[20]

For Eisenstein, the frame as the boundary of the image and the depicted object stand in a productive tension to each other: "The position of the camera represents the materialization of the conflict between the organizing logic of the director and the inert logic of the phenomenon in collision, producing the dialectic of the camera angle."[21] In this respect his thinking evolves less from the Renaissance perspective, but is inspired by very different cultural traditions such as the pictorial language and forms of representation prevalent in Japanese culture, at least as Eisenstein understood it. He objected to the Western "scenic" method of staging for the camera where the frame appears to be both artificial and given, and instead advocates the Japanese method of using the frame to choose a detail from a totality (a landscape or scene), allowing the camera to appropriate the world by setting up a part–whole relationship. This leads

Eisenstein to reclaim for himself a method, where the director is "cutting out a piece of reality by means of the lens".[22] This formulation, in turn, seems more committed to the revolutionary pathos of Marxism than to the Japanese wood-block artists, from whom Eisenstein nevertheless retains the conviction that in montage the important elements must remain implicit if the spectator is to become active. What the camera lens must capture is the complex totality of

Figure 1.6 Japanese *ukiyo-e*: an example of montage within the frame.

the world which cannot be caught in the long takes of, say, the Lumière films, but only as a collision of shots extrapolated from this totality. A long take or sequence shot, because its framing is solely determined by the scale and orientation of the human body and its visual sense, means for Eisenstein a "cage" as it is incapable of representing the historical forces (implicit in the Marxist–Leninist logic of history) that exceeds any aesthetics derived from the individual's standpoint. Of course, Eisenstein cannot avoid using the rectangular shape of the frame,[23] but he made every effort to fully exploit the compositional possibilities for dynamism contained within this rectangle, such as the use of diagonals, a-symmetries and parallels.

Once the framing has been decided upon, the task of the director is to select and arrange these entities (shots) into sequences, i.e. montage. It would be a misconception to assume that this term, initially borrowed from the Fordist assembly line mode of (industrial) production and the modular principles of the construction industry, draws a direct parallel with the building of a house (brick by brick) or assembling a car, out of ready-made parts. Instead, for Eisenstein, the shot is a cell, and just like a living organism, it is a self-contained part that nonetheless fulfills a specific function within a larger whole: "The shot is by no means a montage *element*. The shot is montage cell. [. . .] What then characterises montage and, consequently, its embryo, the shot? Collision. Conflict between two neighbouring fragments."[24] Following this idea of the conflict as the fundamental relation between shots, Eisenstein – basing himself on experiments conducted under the guidance of the theatrical innovator V.E. Meyerhold – developed in the mid-1920s his seminal concept of the "montage of attractions". In line with other popular forms of entertainment like the circus, the fairground and the vaudeville, cinema was to combine attractions, i.e. short fragments (shots or scenes), in such a way as to have a specific effect on the audience. According to a behavioristic concept of human nature popular at the time (Pavlov's "conditional reflexes" were highly influential in the young Soviet Union's attempt to increase its industrial productivity), Eisenstein assumed that certain stimuli, in this case shots or scenes, elicit certain responses in the spectator which can be investigated scientifically and reproduced at will. A film aims at "influencing this audience in the desired direction through a series of calculated pressures on its psyche".[25] Such statements make it clear that Eisenstein was by no means interested in a mimetic reproduction of reality, but rather in the constructivist constitution of a distinctive experience which can only be imparted through artistic means, themselves based on "scientific" principles, and inflected toward a particular purpose:

An attraction [. . .] is in our understanding any demonstrable fact (an action, an object, a phenomenon, a conscious combination, and so on) that is known and proven to exercise a definite effect on the attention and emotions of the audience and that, combined with others, possesses the characteristic of concentrating the audience's emotions in any direction dictated by the production's purpose. From this point of view film cannot be a simple presentation or demonstration of events: rather it must be a tendentious selection of, and comparison between, events, free from narrowly plot-related plans and moulding the audience in accordance with its purpose.[26]

Thus, the body and the senses do not disappear, but change places: from being the subject in realist theories, they become the object in constructivist theories. Eisenstein's ideas about the role of the spectator as well as of the collective reception which is the auditorium space evokes the normal conditions of cinema in his time. But a cultural form, often assumed to be based on the reproduction of reality or on its spectacular display, is given by Eisenstein a distinct performative (or, as he might say: "dialectical") turn: now it is the dynamic interaction of film and spectator, when mutually constructing each other that constitutes the cinematic event.

By the late 1920s Eisenstein had further developed his montage schema by distinguishing among several forms. Thus, in the wake of his STAROE I NOVOE/ GENERAL'NAJA LINIJA (SU, 1926–9, OLD AND NEW/THE GENERAL LINE) Eisenstein formulated a typology of five varieties of montage.[27] *Metric montage* is a purely temporal measurement and based on "the absolute length of the shots" (186). *Rhythmic montage* creates a relation between the length of individual shots and their content. As an example, Eisenstein uses the famous Odessa steps sequence from POTEMKIN in which the movement of the soldiers coming down the stairs affects the tempo of montage: "There the 'drum-beat' of the soldiers' feet descending the steps destroys all metrical conventions. It occurs outside the intervals prescribed by the metre and each time it appears in a different shot resolution."[28] The next two steps – *tonal* and *overtonal montage* – are constituted from movements, forms and intensities within the shot. In explaining rhythmic montage Eisenstein referred to movement as such, while tonal and overtonal montage relates to "vibrations", an umbrella term meaning specific cases of image composition (diagonally floating sail boats), qualities of brightness and shading, certain combinations of geometrical forms (peaked elements pointing upward under a curved arc) and even the emotional content of shots. While tonal montage refers to the dominant qualities of the "vibrations", to "*all sorts of vibrations* that derive from the shot" (188), overtonal montage by contrast refers to marginal or variable elements of the shot.

This set of four types of montage functions like a trigger in a Pavlovian stimulus–response scheme, an assembled arsenal of specific techniques, to fashion

Figure 1.7 BATTLESHIP POTEMKIN (SU, 1925, Sergej Eisenstein): the drum-beat of the soldiers' feet descending.

or produce certain emotions. It is the combination of these different but com-plementary forms of montage that creates a truly great film, according to Eisen-stein's normative scheme: "They become a *montage construction* proper when they enter into conflicting relationships with one another . . ." (191), i.e. when the discrete forms are not combined harmoniously, as in theories of classical cinema, but when the spectator is conditioned by consciously generated con-flicts to grasp a pre-ordained idea or experience a desired effect. The fifth level, *intellectual montage*, transcends Pavlov's stimulus–response schema and moves to more intricate conceptual forms: Eisenstein wanted to open up for cinema such complex mental structures as metaphors, comparisons, synecdoches and other tropes, normally limited to communication based on language. While the montage of attractions is mainly aimed at the affective control of the audience, the intellectual montage asks the spectator to follow a specific train of thought (presented through images). Here Eisenstein alludes to what happens when physiological stimuli generate effects directly in the brain (a "cognitivist" point once more made topical by Gilles Deleuze to which we shall return in Chapter 7): "provoked by an intellectual stimulant combined differently, produces an identical reaction in the tissues of the higher nervous system of the thought apparatus" (193). The prime example for this form of montage is a sequence in OKTJABR in which the diegetic slogan "For God and Fatherland" (under which the counter-revolutionary forces fight against the Bolshevik) initiates a brief non-diegetic reflection on the nature of religion and nationalism. A rapid suc-cession of iconic images, a sort of visual-anthropology essay, is meant to activate the spectator into apprehending the vacuous idolatry of the concepts. Even though it is the film that directs the thinking, it is nevertheless dependent on the cognitive, moral and affective associations the spectator invests, as film and mind are short-circuited in this memorable sequence.

André Bazin is in many respects an antipode to Eisenstein; this antagonism might be most apparent in Bazin's programmatically entitled essay "Montage interdit" in which the term "montage" indirectly alludes to Eisenstein.[29] Also in political terms, Bazin's Catholic humanism is a far cry from Eisenstein's revolutionary communism. Thus, Bazin's commitment to Italian Neorealism was motivated not only aesthetically, but equally by socio-political sympathies with a movement that grew out of Catholics and Communists making common cause against fascism: writing as he did in desolate post-war Europe and facing the almost incomprehensible horror of genocide and mass annihilation, Bazin recognized in the early works of Roberto Rossellini, Vittorio de Sica and Luchino Visconti the rejection of a film style which, according to many contemporaries, had been compromised by lending itself to being used (and abused) by totalitarian regimes.[30] Cinema as a mass medium and as a means of mobilization played a central part in the official propaganda of Nazi Germany, Fascist Italy and Stalinist Soviet Union, thereby forfeiting the revolutionary fervor that constructivist montage had been invested with in the 1920s and 1930s by Leftist authors like Walter Benjamin, Bertolt Brecht and Siegfried Kracauer.[31] The film movement that grew in Italy out of the dereliction left behind by Fascism assumed the moral right to redeem this fallen art form. Neorealism wanted to reclaim and

Figure 1.8 ROME, OPEN CITY: Neorealism as a political and ethical cinema of action.

re-appropriate the cinema in order to renew the faith in the medium's capability to show reality as it is before it presumed to change it. Politically, it was the first of a series of modernist cinema movements of renewal that, under the name of "new waves", would shape European cinema well into the 1980s, even when its aesthetic precepts were not always followed.

Bazin believed that by placing the camera in the right position and letting it register what is before it, film could show the world as it was, but contrary to general belief, he did not rule out all forms of montage, trick shots and cuts. Editing that manipulated a found reality or transformed it in order to yield a particular message were suspect to him, not merely for political reasons but because they violated one of the truly unique aspects of the cinema, precisely the mechanical recording of reality without human intervention. To reinstate this capacity of the cinema seemed to him both eminently political ("revolutionary") and purposively ethical ("humanist"). As a warning against what he saw were the new divisions, he began, from 1947 onwards, to champion Italy and its cinema:

> In one sense Italy is only three years old [. . .]. In a world already once again obsessed by terror and hate, in which reality is scarcely any longer favored for its own sake but rather is rejected or excluded as a political symbol, the Italian cinema is certainly the only one which preserves, in the midst of the period it depicts, a revolutionary humanism.[32]

It would, however, be fundamentally wrong to locate Bazin within the realm of a traditional film aesthetics of psychological realism. On various occasions Bazin attacked an uncritical application of the realist conventions which emerged in nineteenth-century French literature (primarily in the works of Gustave Flaubert or, under the label of Naturalism, also in those of Emile Zola): "Against this he affirmed a realism of perceptual experience wherein the daily life habit of apperception, recognition, and mental elaboration is structurally reproduced in the cinema."[33] Already the quotation above suggests that, for Bazin, realism is always a question of being grounded not only in a perceptual but also in a specific social reality. In other words, realism for Bazin is not so much a style that one can apply or an effect induced in the spectator, but rather an attitude or stance that the film-maker adopts vis-à-vis his material:

> If the word [Neorealism] has any meaning – whatever the differences that arise over its interpretation, above and beyond a minimal agreement – in the first place it stands in opposition to the traditional dramatic systems and also to the various other known kinds of realism in literature and film with which we are familiar, through its claim that there is a certain "wholeness" to reality [. . .]. Neorealism is a description of reality conceived as a whole

by a consciousness disposed to see things as a whole. Neorealism contrasts with the realist aesthetics that preceded it, and in particular with naturalism and verism, in that its realism is not so much concerned with the choice of subject as with a particular way of regarding things. [. . .] neorealism by definition rejects analysis, whether political, moral, psychological, logical, or social, of the characters and their actions. It looks on reality as a whole, not incomprehensible, certainly, but inseparably one.[34]

This idea of reality as an "inseperable whole" is used by Bazin repeatedly and means that the things embraced by a film – the "fact", as Bazin calls it – possess an ontological unity which film has to respect. The smallest unit of filmic construction is therefore not the shot or the scene (as Eisenstein or analytical montage would have it), a technical quantity derived from production, but the "fact", a given and pre-existing element which overrides technique and technology. For Bazin, cutting was not forbidden, but in contrast to montage theories the meaning of a film does not arise from a collision and cohesion of elements, but from the ontological presence of the things themselves ("reality conceived as a whole") filtered through the film-maker's sensibility ("a consciousness disposed to see things as a whole"). A conventional (non-neorealist) film creates things and facts, while a neorealist film subordinates itself to these. Ideally, it is

Figure 1.9 BICYCLE THIEVES: ontological unity of reality.

a window on a given reality or a specific milieu – as in LADRI DI BICICLETTE (IT, 1948, Vittorio de Sica, BICYCLE THIEVES) or in LA TERRA TREMA (IT, 1948, Luchino Visconti) – or a specific historical situation – as in Roberto Rossellini's ROMA CITTÀ APERTA (IT, 1945) or PAÍSA (IT, 1946). Brought logically to its conclusion, the vanishing point of Bazin's theory is the disappearance of the medium and its artificiality as formulated hyperbolically in a discussion of LADRI DI BICICLETTE (IT, 1948, Vittorio de Sica, BICYCLE THIEVES): "No more actors, no more story, no more sets, which is to say that in the perfect aesthetic illusion of reality there is no more cinema."[35] An example that realised at least some of Bazin's aspirations was a scene in UMBERTO D. (IT, 1952, Vittorio de Sica) in which the morning routine of a housemaid is shown almost in what today we would call real-time.[36]

Bazin compares traditional Realism with bricks produced for the specific purpose of building a bridge, whereas Neorealism resembles more readily the boulders in a river: one can use them to cross the river but they were not made specifically for this purpose. Consequently, their "stony reality" will not be altered by their use:

> If the service which they have rendered is the same as that of the bridge, it is because I have brought my share of ingenuity to bear on their chance arrangement; I have added the motion which, though it alters neither their nature nor their appearance, gives them a provisional meaning and utility. In the same way, the neorealist film has a meaning, but it is *a posteriori*, to the extent that it permits our awareness to move from one fact to another, from one fragment of reality to the next, whereas in the classical artistic composition the meaning is established *a priori*: the house is already there in the brick.[37]

Accordingly, Bazin wants "neorealist" to be understood solely as an adjective, since only certain elements of a film can conform to this aesthetic. In a Bazinian perspective, Neorealism can therefore hardly be conceived of as a movement.

But Bazin did not become a key figure in film theory solely by virtue of his writings, richly suggestive though they remain. He also presided over an influential network of people who contributed to *Cahiers du Cinéma*, the film magazine co-founded by Bazin and arguably the most important publication of film criticism over the past 50 years. Bazin also took on the role of a godfather for the French *Nouvelle Vague*: he was a surrogate father to François Truffaut, who had been uprooted from his family at a young age and expressed his gratitude to Bazin by publishing a posthumous edition of the latter's works; Bazin also helped Eric Rohmer and Claude Chabrol with their early publications on cinema, opening opportunities that would eventually lead to their becoming film directors, and Jean-Luc Godard's masterpiece LE MÉPRIS (FR/IT, 1963, CON-TEMPT) is prefaced with a (mis-appropriated) quotation from Bazin. However, Bazin did not live to see this generation of young French talents blossom in the 1960s, as he died in 1958 at age 40.[38] Bazin's method of writing can also be seen as paradigmatic for film theory: he produced primarily essays and reviews; a systematic theory was something that had to be derived inductively from his prolific output of short to medium-length writings.[39] To this day there are few contributions to film theory that could be said to meet the standards of academic philosophy. Most of these contributions, professional philosophers will argue, qualify at best as approaches and *aperçus*. Yet again, the fact that much of film theory consists of creative tinkering and bricolage, of hybrid texts and an ad-hoc mixture of polemics and reflection, prescription and description, also contains the possibility of transcending conventional boundaries and of creating something radically new.

With the significant differences of emphasis and nuance mentioned above, Arnheim, Eisenstein and Bazin nonetheless implicitly accepted the cinema as a window on the world and as a frame on a pre-constituted reality. While no synthesis of their positions is either needed or desirable, a way of rethinking their options from a single vantage point can be found in the work of David Bordwell, who is as familiar with classical Hollywood cinema as with the works of Eisenstein and Ozu.[40] Bordwell, inclined to reclaim Arnheim's moderate constructivism, takes neither Bazin's ontological realism nor Eisenstein's types of montage as his point of departure, but rather, a special kind of spatial composition, the *staging in depth*, which he traces through the entire history of cinema and which, according to him, has challenged generations of directors to make stylistic choices that can be implemented not only in completely different ways, but interpreted across seemingly incompatible ideologies.[41] Bordwell argues that, for most directors, treating the frame as window does not have any kind of pre-determined ideological or symbolic function; its purpose is to make the spectator understand a story's temporal unfolding through the organization of space and the compositional constellation of the characters. In this context deep space and depth of field make it possible for different image planes to be played off against one another, or for a person in the background to gain particular dramatic importance when the "normal" hierarchy is inverted. While this covers much the same ground as Bazin had in his famous analysis of deep focus and the long take in William Wyler's THE BEST YEARS OF OUR LIVES (1946),[42] the fact that "continuity editing" can serve this purpose as easily as the long take is proof for Bordwell that in Hollywood a "pragmatic" view prevails about the meaning of stylistic devices: they are subject to the principle of "functional equivalence", i.e. style is often a matter of several techniques coming together to fulfill certain expressive functions.

However detailed and historically informed Bordwell's argument is, it stays within the overall framework according to which there are, in practical terms, few alternatives to the "classical" form of representation, where window and frame have a centripetal pull, gathering narrative and compositional energies inward and backward, so to speak. In an approach no less art historical than Bordwell's, Jacques Aumont has developed a more inclusive and diverse pictorial genealogy for the cinematic image, reviving the legacy of Eisenstein in this respect, and making more room for de-centered images, off-screen space, two-dimensionality and abstraction, developing aspects of Bazin's legacy that have come to the fore in film-making since the 1960s.[43]

The window as legacy of the Renaissance and metaphor for one of the "ontologies" of cinema has also been interpreted quite differently, namely as an imaginary curiosity cabinet or urban shop window. Cinema as a medium has, since its inception, been closely associated with the highlighting of objects and the selling of merchandise: product placement, the star system, and various points of contact with other forms of promotion and display, such as exhibitions and fairs, have always been typical of the cinema as a self-consciously modernizing medium.[44] It was especially in the 1980s that film theory, focusing more insistently in the wake of feminism on the role of the spectator and recipient, began to situate cinema firmly within broader tendencies of consumerism and advertising, seeing it as part of an individualized service industry oriented toward images as commodities. Besides acting as a window onto the real world, cinema – as display window onto the world of commodities – helps to "virtualize" this world, making it stand for something else, whatever this "else" might be, while opening up the spectator to desire and fantasy.[45] Here the metaphor of the window, in the sense of contemplating an external reality from a safe distance, converges or morphs into that of the mirror, as the display of imaginary objects reflects back on a desiring subject, enticing him/her into phantasmagoric projection and illusory acquisition/appropriation. A logical step is to align the cinematic experience with "window shopping", making the imagined spaces of consumer-oriented films overlap with the real, though equally image-conscious spaces of the shopping malls, where multiplex cinemas seamlessly extend the experience of consumption, blending shopping, tourism and the taste of the exotic.[46]

If in the 1980s the idea of cinema as a transparent window onto reality was considered obsolete and Bazin chided for his supposedly naive realist ontology, charitably put down to his Catholic worldview, his thoughts on the nature of cinema have seen a surprising comeback in the past decade, not least thanks to Gilles Deleuze, to whom we shall return later, and who took up some central tenets of Bazin's ontology without confining them to idea of the photographic–indexical realism. Moreover, it is the digital revolution itself, and the increasing ubiquity of "flat" computer monitors as display surfaces, which has advanced the window to the status of a leading cultural metaphor: the paradoxical connections linking Alberti and Brunelleschi, the "fathers" of single point perspective as "the open window", to Bill Gates' Microsoft "Windows" and Steve Jobs' touch-screens is too enticing not to have attracted scholarly commentary.[47] Yet does this genealogy that leads from a graphic method of representing three-dimensional space on a two-dimensional surface to today's Graphical User Interfaces enhance the windows metaphor or merely reduce it to an ironic, but misleading euphemism? Have we not reached the endpoint of "the window" with "Windows"? What needs to be borne in mind with respect to the digital (or virtual) window is that the (material) screen functions as a (metaphorical) window onto an imaginary (cyber) space, which is the ultimate negation of space.

Chapter 2

Cinema as door
Screen and threshold

As the film begins, a shining rectangle illuminates the darkness of the cinema auditorium that, were it to be horizontal rather than vertical, might be the light-reflecting silver screen itself. This gleaming shape turns out to be a door, which opens onto a – if not *the* – quintessential North-American landscape: Monument Valley, made immortal as the setting and backdrop of numerous Westerns. The camera follows a woman, at first only a silhouette against the bright light, crossing the threshold along with her onto the porch, leaving the darkness inside behind. From far away a man walks toward the settlers' cabin, a man who is as mythical in Hollywood cinema as the distinctive landscape with the bizarre mountain formations from which he emerges: John Wayne as Ethan Edwards. The motif of entering and leaving, of traversing and crossing – because crossing a threshold always implies leaving a space and entering another – is central to THE SEARCHERS (US, 1956, John Ford). The film is constructed around a series of crossings and transgressions, and it involves a constant change of places, both literally and metaphorically: it oscillates between familial and racial affiliation, between nature and culture, between wilderness and garden, between convictions and actions. The film ends with a mirror-like repetition of the opening sequence: Edwards/Wayne leaves the house and in the glowing sunlight walks off into the distance while the rectangular, illuminated doorway gently closes, plunging the spectator into the same darkness of the auditorium from which the film had picked him/her up in the beginning. The bright rectangle of the doorway corresponds to the "dynamic square"[1] of the cinema screen and points indirectly also to the artificial and constructed nature of the film's panoramic views. The shock of this transition is almost as unexpected as the shot–countershot sequence in Luis Buñuel's UN CHIEN ANDALOU (FR, 1929) in which a woman opens a door and leaves a room, only to be shown standing on the beach in the very next shot.

This opening sequence of THE SEARCHERS focuses on the threshold; the film is reflecting on itself as it highlights a moment that one can find in almost any film: the passage from one world to another which presupposes the co-existence

of two worlds, separated as well as connected by the threshold. For the spectator, it is the threshold between her/his world and that of the film; for the film
it is the threshold between myth and reality, and for the actor, it is the threshold
between role and image (John Wayne will always evoke certain ideas of American masculinity, of US politics and Hollywood cinema, even before we know
anything about the role he plays in a given narrative). The Western, as a quintessential American genre, tends to charge with mythological significance
several kinds of spatial markers and points of crossing, and especially the fundamental threshold that makes possible the West(ern) as a cultural category in the
first place: the "frontier", that borderline between "civilized land" and "the wilderness" which in the nineteenth century relentlessly pushed from East to West
across the North-American continent.[2] This story of conquering and subjecting
the vast expanses of land was then repeated over and over again in twentieth-
century art and popular culture: the United States fashioned from it its own
myth of self-creation, of which it constantly reminds itself and the world. In
film, this myth is based upon an underlying binary opposition of nature/culture:
the garden versus the wilderness, cowboys versus Indians, but also cattle barons
versus homesteaders (the former has cowboys wandering about with the herd,
the latter are settling down as farmers), the law of the gun versus the law of the
book, the saloon singer versus the teacher, etc. The Western constantly stages
and affirms the frontier as a demarcation and its (necessary) transgression as the
basis of US popular culture as the nation's mythology.[3]

Figure 2.1 THE SEARCHERS: John Wayne at the threshold.

As the first chapter detailed, the cinema keeps the spectator visually at arm's length while nonetheless drawing him/her in emotionally, by deploying window and frame as mutually regulating conceptual metaphors for looking at a separated reality that nonetheless exists for our benefit. This chapter, by contrast, deals with the different ways the spectator enters into this world, physically as well as metaphorically. We will discuss numerous separations and thresholds between the universe of the film and the "real world": spatial, architectural, institutional, economic and textual. After some introductory remarks on the real and imaginary thresholds of the cinema, an etymological derivation will support the claim we make in this chapter. The main part will deal with narratology, an approach that revolves around the question of how the spectator enters the story of the film; we will present two models, one neoformalist, one post-structuralist. Initially though, we want to try to designate more precisely the kinds of threshold between spectator and film that need to be traversed.

A threshold always points in two directions, because it simultaneously connects and separates – a border can be crossed precisely because a division always implies spatial proximity. As Niklas Luhmann, among others, reminds us, we make distinctions, by dividing something into two parts, or by designating a marked and an "unmarked space" (George Spencer Brown). It follows that the border(line) always derives from an observation (in order to look at something, we have to be able to distinguish it from its surroundings) without which knowledge would not be possible at all.[4] For film theory, then, the question arises as to where exactly the limit or threshold of film lies. What is film, what is not, where do film and cinema begin (and end)? These questions are not trivial because a film is both more than and different from its material basis, the celluloid strip. Film theories have always attended to drawing such distinctions, and here we attempt to theoretically grasp the distinction film/not-film/not-yet-film/no-longer-film, by focusing on the entrance of the spectator into the diegetic world, but also into the commercial machinery of mass entertainment, and into the imaginary reality of projection and identification.

If one conceptualizes the cinema experience as the entrance into another world, then the distance that was at the basis of the idea of the cinema as window and frame diminishes. The spectator finds him/herself between two poles, projection and identification: pointing outward, projection allows the spectator to plunge into the film, to temporarily dissolve part of his/her bodily boundaries and give up his/her individual subject status, in favor of a communal experience and a self-alienating objectification; and, pointing inward, identification means the spectator can absorb the film, make it his or her own, i.e. incorporate the world and thereby constitute him-/herself as an "imaginary" subject. The anthropologist and sociologist Edgar Morin has based his classic study *The Cinema, or The Imaginary Man* on the polymorphous oscillation between these

two positions.[5] He emphasizes that the fictional characters on the screen function as "Doppelgänger" or doubles for the spectator; this, on the one hand,
confers upon them the status of a projection interface through which one can
enter the film and, on the other, it gives them an uncanny quality, as if these
characters were the embodiment simultaneously of what is all-too-familiar and
yet all-too-feared in ourselves – hence the pertinence and prominence of the
"uncanny" and the "return of the repressed" (Freud) in certain film theories (as
well as the renewed theoretical interest in the horror film). The positions
described in this chapter share at least one basic assumption: they all try to conceptualize a liminal situation, a not-quite-here but also a not-quite-there configuration, an in-betweenness of sorts in which film functions as a threshold and
space of passage, or – to use an expression from anthropology and Cultural
Studies – as a "liminal space".[6]

The real interface in the auditorium, the material border between spectator
and film, is the screen. A brief etymological–archaeological overview of the
word itself will help us to get a clearer grip on the frame of reference in operation when we use the term. The word "screen" developed in the early four-
teenth century from the old Germanic term "scirm" which opens up a rich
semantic field. A "scirm" acts like a shield and protects us from enemies or
adverse influences (such as the heat from a fire or the weather), thus allowing us
to get closer. Yet again, a screen also denotes an arrangement that hides something or someone by dividing a space (e.g. by putting up a paravent). In this
sense, the screen can mean the exact opposite of displaying something, making
something visible or bringing something closer, but refers instead to keeping a
safe distance.

A further meaning of screen as a protective filter or coating is that of a curtain
restraining sunlight and thus protecting light-sensitive persons or objects. This
attribute is also linked to visibility and light, but in contrast to the screen in the
cinema auditorium it does so in a negative sense. By way of analogy, the word
can furthermore denote an object that is being used with the purpose of protecting, hiding or blocking, also implying a division or filter. The first known
occurrence of the word "screen" as a designation of a surface that can be used to
depict an image or object was in 1864. The proverbial "silver screen" was used
in the projection of Laterna Magica-images, one of the predecessors of the
cinema as popular entertainment, while the projection technology of the phan-
tasmagoria introduced the term "smoke screen", because the images were not
projected on a material carrier, but reflected–refracted on smoke or fog: the air
itself was made intransparent, so that light and shadow no longer passed through
it, but make it appear "material" and physical, perceived as a division or
obstacle.

Even such a partial account of the etymology and range of meanings given to the word clarifies that a number of features and attributes of the "screen" stand in a relation of tension, if not outright opposition, to each other: screens hide and protect, but they also open up and reflect. Screens are (semi-permeable) membranes through which something might pass, but they can also keep something out: they act as sieve and filter. They are rigid and solid, but they can also be movable and flexible. Screens are in effect something that stands between us and the world, something that simultaneously protects and opens up access, and it is in this sense that this chapter revolves around questions of door and screen. Given the multitude of meanings and uses, the cinema screen is an unusual or at least ambivalent screen and would appear as the exception rather than the rule. The cinema screen is solid and clearly bounded, it emanates and makes visible instead of shielding and protecting. It brings something close and makes something present instead of filtering, screening and separating.

It may seem a truism that when we see a film, we always cross a border and enter another world that is different from ours. Yet besides the physical markers of difference, there are semantic and symbolic thresholds that have their own way of encoding and addressing the spectatorial experience: as an unusual economic exchange (one pays in order to gain a view of something), as a social institution (which has often been attacked for its anti-social consequences) and as a cultural phenomenon (which undermines the separation between art and commerce). Depending on one's perspective, these demarcations will vary considerably in the significance we attribute to them. Later on we will return to the quintessential role of the screen, especially in films in which the screen itself is thematized as a semi-permeable membrane: from UNCLE JOSH AT THE MOVING PICTURE SHOW (US, 1902, Edwin S. Porter) to SHERLOCK JR. (US, 1924, Buster Keaton) all the way to PURPLE ROSE OF CAIRO (US, 1985, Woody Allen) and LAST ACTION HERO (US, 1993, John McTiernan). But we want to begin with the more common forms of entrance into the cinema, as they enforce or blur the conventional limits and delimitations of what is (part of) film and what it is not, starting with the rectangular frame of the image constituted by the cache of black material surrounding the screen, or vice versa, if we think of the white screen as removing the film visually from the ambient engulfing darkness.

Consider the cinema as a material–immaterial architectural ensemble: even if one describes a visit to the cinema as a social and phenomenological event, one can still find many markers that make this visit equivalent to crossing several borders: the façade of the movie palace, for instance, which used to fashion itself in an exotic (Egyptian or Chinese) garb, present itself as ultramodern (the ocean liner motif) or adopt a playfully modern (art nouveau, art deco) look, in order to set itself apart from the street; once past the lobby (another transitional space marked as such) one sits in front of a sumptuously decorated frame surrounding (in older cinema halls) not the screen itself, but its red velvet curtain;

Figure 2.2 THE PURPLE ROSE OF CAIRO (US, 1984, Woody Allen): the fiction entering the world of the spectators through the screen as semi-permeable membrane.

a further temporal marker and threshold was the stroke of the gong, as an acoustic signal, before a program of advertisements and coming attractions introduces additional elements of transition, presented with the lights half-dimmed, to underscore their liminal status.

In English, which is not only the lingua franca of economic and cultural globalization but, thanks to Hollywood, also the language of film, the common expression for designating the arrival of a film in cinemas is to say that a film "opens" at a cinema. According to this figure of speech, the opening of a film requires the cinema as its site. Upon closer inspection, however, it turns out that the cinema is not the only point of entry into a film. There are many other openings through which a film tries to enter into the awareness of its potential audience: there is the title, which either draws on an already introduced and familiar "property" (book, comic, video game, TV series, historical event) or which announces the promise of action (SPEED, DIE HARD, LAST ACTION HERO, THE FAST AND THE FURIOUS), suspense (WHAT LIES BENEATH, THE SIXTH SENSE) or sex (FATAL ATTRACTION, SHOWGIRLS, STRIPTEASE). Then there is the poster (in the format of a door, not of a window), which tries to condense the essence of the film into a single image, similar to the "tag line" or advertising slogan.[7] On the way from the lobby to the cinema, one used to encounter, as if in a stations-of-the-cross dramatization of Christ's Calvary, or in the way Giotto sequenced Church history, large displays and specially made stills, depicting characters or scenes from the movie. One can even enjoy thematically appropriate refreshments while being entertained, prior to the actual film, by trailers for other films in which the main attractions (stars, genre, storyline, special effects) are condensed into two or three minutes.[8] Finally, the film begins with a sort of transition from the world of the spectator into the filmic universe; after the logo

Figure 2.3 GOLDFINGER: the autonomous title sequence as literal and figurative point of entry.

of the distribution and production company comes the so-called "credits sequence". Nowadays this sequence is in fact often a mini-film, a small graphical work of art or even an abstract poem in images and sounds. Ever since Saul Bass and Maurice Binder laid the foundations for this art-form in the 1950s through the credits they created for Alfred Hitchcock and Otto Preminger (Bass) as well as for James Bond (Binder), the title sequence has developed into a quasi-autonomous genre with an art scene of its own, to which specialized companies and celebrated people belong such as Kyle Cooper, famous for his credit scene in David Fincher's SE7EN (1995).[9]

How does all this connect with the film as door and screen as opening? It suggests that a film has many more points of entry than merely the screen on which the diegetic world unfolds. But in addition, as our previous remarks about cinema architecture, its façade, lobby and foyer as well as the various means of advertising indicate, cinema is an experience that unfolds in time and space, which begins to "work" on the spectator long before the filmic narration sets in. How can we define this "work" more specifically? Various models lend themselves to explaining the smooth transition from outside to inside, between the physically present spectator and the imaginary event as well as between text and context, sight and site. The literary scholar Gerard Genette has discussed texts which surround another text, attach themselves to it, occupy it in a parasitical way but also help and support it, calling them "paratexts", which position themselves between inside (text) and outside (non-text) and create a space of transition and transaction.[10] These paratexts address an audience, they pre-structure horizons of expectation and call forth promises of identification, but they might also, like a virus or bacteria, affect a text by opening up a semantic field of association not intended by the producers of the text. Paratexts thus indicate the semantic instability and tectonic shifts and turbulence of texts, as inside and outside are never quite stable and fixed and their boundaries become fuzzy or jagged. A famous example of context taking over text is provided by THE ROCKY HORROR PICTURE SHOW (1975, Jim Sherman) which was planned as an innocuous parody of 1950s science-fiction films and which on its initial release gained only a limited success. The community that gathered weekly at a New York cinema turned the film (without the knowledge or intention of the producers) into a "cult film" until this phenomenon was noticed by the press and spread to other places (and became a genre: the "Midnight Movies").[11] As a consequence, the film was marketed differently, demonstrating how unstable the meaning of a text can be, once its boundaries shift. Paratexts, therefore, mediate between the actual text and what lies outside it (its audience, other texts, institutions); they also mark the threshold – i.e. the point of entrance and exit – and forge a "communicative contract" between spectator and text as described by semio-pragmatics.[12]

The opening of the actual filmic narration introduces a similar threshold situation as the paratexts. The question that film theory needs to answer in this respect is: how does one guide the spectator into the film? What visual stimuli, affective surprises and cognitive promises does a film have at its disposal in order to draw the spectator into the diegetic universe and captivate him/her (or, as the avant-garde would argue, how does one free the spectator from too routinized a form of specular seduction or sedation)? Here, one can enlist the help of narrative theory (or "narratology") which investigates, theorizes and systematizes the mechanisms and dynamics of filmic narration. Film beginnings play a key role in this context because it is at this point in any film that several functions overlap: a film's beginning must lure the audience, i.e. it must prompt the necessary attention and suspense, it must plant important information, but also set the tone and atmosphere that prepares for the film to come. Accordingly, the classical, closed film form usually introduces in the first few minutes either an enigma to be solved in the rest of the film, or a deadline that communicates to the spectator from the very beginning at what point in (diegetic) time the story will come to its narrative climax. Either way, the film puts (some of) its cards on the table from the very start, exposing its rules, or to change the metaphor: staking out its goal, and mapping its playing field. Other film forms, like the European art cinema, consciously do not adhere to this unspoken contract between spectator and film, but create their own rules: in Michelangelo Antonioni's L'AVVENTURA (IT/FR, 1960), one of the characters, Anna, disappears early on in the film on a deserted island; the other characters start a searching expedition for her, but Anna's fate drifts into the background and is never resolved in the film as a romance develops between boyfriend and best friend of the missing Anna.

Narrative theory has developed and expanded into a transdisciplinary venture – first in literary and media studies, but also in psychology, history and other disciplines – since the 1970s. Roughly speaking, one can distinguish a cognitive and (neo-)formalist school from a (post-)structuralist tendency; even though there are encounters and exchanges between both camps, they sometimes seem to oppose each other in irreconcilable differences. Neoformalist and cognitive theories of narration tend to emphasize rational-choice scenarios and logical information processing, while post-structuralist and deconstructive approaches focus on the instability of meaning. The former believes in a fair and free relationship between spectator and text, the latter is rather more interested in power structures and unconscious processes. We will now briefly introduce both approaches, using our initial example of a late classical Hollywood film – THE SEARCHERS.

For neoformalists, a film consists mainly of audio-visual "cues", which the spectator perceives and processes accordingly: "In the neoformalist approach, viewers are not passive "subjects" [. . .]. Rather, viewers are largely active, contributing substantially to the final effect of the work."[13] These cues lead to the creation of hypotheses and schemata, a process which is to no small measure possible because the spectator can draw on familiar experiences with similar works. These mental preconstructions are especially important for the comprehension of narratives. Neoformalist theories assume that the spectator compiles and assembles the experienced film (i.e. what spectators discuss upon leaving the cinema) in a process of active construction. From the raw material of the "plot" (or the "syuzhet", as the Russian Formalists originally called it) spectators derive the "story" (or "fabula").[14] The plot is "the structured set of all causal events as we see and hear them presented in the film itself" (38f.), i.e. the succession of actions as presented in the film. It is often characterized by spatial and temporal ellipses (cut from a character to another at a different place, i.e. in a phone conversation; a time lapse ranging from seconds as in a jump cut to millennia as in the famous cut in 2001: A SPACE ODYSSEY in which the first tool, a bone, becomes, via a match cut, the latest, a space ship), by temporal rearrangements (flashbacks and flashforwards), and by material or information not belonging to the diegetic world (credits, extra-diegetic music). The "mental construction of chronologically, causally linked material" (39), the creation of a causal, temporal and spatial coherence, produces the story. To give an example of how plot and story relate: the plot of PULP FICTION (1994, Quentin Tarantino) presents its narrative material in a-chronological order, while MEMENTO (1999, Christopher Nolan) is narrated "backwards": in each case (and to different degrees) the spectator creates the story by ordering the events in such a way that the individual actions flow forward in time and follow a causal–sequential logic. The three attributes of knowledgeability, self-consciousness and communicativeness help to describe the narrative style more closely: does the story "know" every fact about the narrative world (for example, is the camera present at a place even before something happens?) or is the narration limited to the level of knowledge of a specific character? Does the film foreground the act of narration itself by zooming in or singling out details in a self-conscious fashion? Are important pieces of information consciously held back by the film such as when we see the murder take place, but the murderer's face is withheld from us, as in MILDRED PIERCE (1945, Michael Curtiz)?

When it comes to openings, a neoformalist might argue that they create a set of expectations that the film will be measured against by the spectator: "Concentrated, preliminary exposition that plunges us *in medias res* triggers strong first impressions, and these become the basis for our expectations across the entire film."[15] With this basic premise in mind, let us turn to THE SEARCHERS to examine what expectations the opening calls forth. Initially, a conflict between two brothers is indicated, the homesteading Aaron (Walter Coy) and the roaming Ethan (John Wayne), who is moreover secretly in love with Aaron's wife Martha (Dorothy Jordan). This tension will come to also dominate the relation between Ethan and Martin Pawley (Jeffrey Hunter), Aaron's step-son: the nomadic lifestyle of Ethan makes him a typical relic of the old West; Martin by contrast wants to settle down like his step-father. Besides, Ethan's pathological hatred of Native Americans is already focused in the opening. From these "cues" in the first scenes, the spectator constructs a double plot line that will structure the rest of the film: on the one hand, the film revolves around the fate of Debbie, Aaron's younger daughter, who has been abducted by Indians; on the other hand the love story between Martin and Laurie (Vera Miles) provides the action-packed search and rescue mission with a second plotline as its emotional sounding board. Both plot lines converge in the fact that Ethan Edwards openly exhibits his racial hatred of Native Americans, rejecting both the "half-breed" Martin (who is one-eighth Cherokee) and Debbie who has, in his mind, turned Indian by living among them for such a longer period of time. Typically, classical films operate with a double plot line – one concerns a task that has to be accomplished, the other is a (heterosexual) love story – which are initially set apart, but become intertwined in the course of the film, so that closure is achieved when both are resolved: one by means of the other. From a neoformalist–constructivist perspective, a film is classical in its generation of meaning when an analysis allows one to understand the activity of the spectator as following through the initial "cues" laid out to him/her. To a certain sense, such a film functions like an algorithm that, once understood, the spectator reproduces, giving rise to the possible charge that any activity on the part of the spectator is little more than a reordering of preordained tasks.

Cognitive, constructivist and neoformalist theories of narrative have developed into various differentiated and diverse sub-questions. Edward Branigan, for instance, has advanced a model of seven "levels of narration" which adapt Gerard Genette's theory of narrative perspective ("focalization") to feature film analysis. Revising previous debates around "subjective" versus "objective" shots and refining his own discussion of point of view in the cinema, Branigan now identifies many more distinct levels and perspectives, ranging from an omniscient narrator outside the diegetic universe to the adoption of the restricted perception of a character inside the story world.[16] From being concerned with "comprehension", this school of narratology has been increasingly concerned with developing a cognitive model for the emotional entanglement of the spectator in the film.[17] Extending the scope beyond the classical film in both period and geography, Kristin Thompson has presented a number of studies into historically diverse forms of narration ranging from Ernst Lubitsch's style in Germany and the US to contemporary Hollywood films.[18]

Post-structuralist or deconstructionist theories of narrative take their starting point from one of the central premises of structuralism, primarily the thesis that language and its logic play a constitutive role for cultural processes of any kind, including narrative, whose logics are based on the generation and permutation of difference. In contrast to structuralism, however, which – in the work of A.J. Greimas, the early Roland Barthes and Christian Metz – had hoped to arrive at a comprehensive inventory of narrative types and moves, by adhering to a set of strictly defined rules of universal validity, post-structuralism acknowledges that meaning may be inherently unstable, that the process of signification is unlimited and that differences reproduce themselves indefinitely. Not unlike Gregory Bateson, who famously defined "information" as the "difference that makes a difference", suggesting not a relation of binary opposition but of levels and meta-levels, post-structural narratology puts the emphasis on the inherent incompleteness of narratives. By shifting the focus from the idea of structures as objectively given and "out-there", and envisaging narratives as processes of open and indeterminate exchange between reader or viewer and text or sound-and-image track, post-structuralist thinking is not only on its guard against totalizing or centralizing theories of meaning, but also concerned to give the recipient or narratee a more active, intervenionist or inter-active role. Proponents of this type of narrative theory – which include the later Roland Barthes, Julia Kristeva, Jacques Derrida and Michel Foucault – have often referred themselves to Mikhail Bakhtin, notably to his work on Dostoevsky and Rabelais from the 1930s and 1940s.

A Russian literary theorist and cultural critic, Bakhtin maintained that any utterance – be it of a purely linguistic nature or, like verbal or filmic narrative, made up of different, interwoven symbolic codes – presupposes and refers to other utterances, i.e. it simultaneously represents an offer (inviting a response) and an answer (to an implied question). Every text (in the sense of the Latin *textum* – "texture") is thus not only complex in its semiotic structures but "dialogical", in that it binds, in the case of narrative, the narrator and narratee into a discursive situation of question and answer, of expectation and its fulfillment, including the suspension, frustration or subversion of such expectation and dialog. What Bakhtin called "unfinalizability" also has a temporal dimension, in that an act of speech or of narration presupposes past utterances and anticipates future ones: "every utterance is emitted in anticipation of the discourse of an interlocutor."[19] This polyphonic quality of the work, where many "voices" speak, Bakhtin has termed "heteroglossia". It extends also to the reader–spectator, who becomes part of a chorus in the act of perception–reception–participation. The transitional or in-between spaces that earlier we described as "thresholds" can in Bakhtin's sense also be understood as moments of hesitation that invite new openings that need to be activated and performed by the spectators. In this perspective, text, context and paratexts function as so many passages or portals through which energies circulate that implicate the spectator and respond to his/her particular input.[20] Among film scholars, Raymond Bellour, Stephen Heath and Colin MacCabe can be said to have made the transition from structuralism to post-structuralism, while Robert Stam has been Bakhtin's most eloquent advocate and disciple in the English-speaking film-studies community.[21]

From a post-structuralist perspective, to return to our example of film openings in general and that of THE SEARCHERS in particular, an opening is less a matter of being plunged in the middle of an ongoing action, but rather the beginning of an encounter, where one partner or party has yet to make their entry, or – to use a different vocabulary – it is a metatext disguising itself as an action *in medias res*. Thus, THE SEARCHERS begins not simply by introducing the fundamental, binary conflict between culture and nature, between soldier (hunter/gatherer) and settler (homesteader/farmer), but it comments on the genre of the Western not least by the very hyper-realism of its opening sequence. The fact that the dark rectangle directly leads onto Monument Valley and the appearance of John Wayne draws attention to two central myths of the genre. As spectators, our view is initially framed by the darkness of the doorway (doubling the darkness of the auditorium), thus underlining the distance that separates us in both time and space from this West, a wholly mythologized past which now comes to us through such highly self-reflexive reconstructions as John Ford, his cinematographer and screenwriter give us. In a way, the film itself deconstructs the genre's previous construction of the West; it is post-classical in the way it cites the mythology, especially when it highlights through Ethan's rantings against American Indians the Western's usually much more covert racism and implicit colonialist subtext. Along with THE MAN WHO SHOT

LIBERTY VALANCE (1962) and CHEYENNE AUTUMN (1964), THE SEARCHERS invites a sort of Bakhtinian dialog with its audience, as Ford's cinematic perspectivism brings many more "voices" into the debate about the foundations of America's frontier identity. No wonder that few other films have elicited as many readings as has this late work from one of the great Hollywood auteurs.[22]

Multiple decodings of opening sequences, along with studies of credits, trailers and other meta- and paratextual materials, have become quite common in recent years. A particularly sophisticated post-deconstructionist take on the topic is Garrett Stewart's *Framed Time: Toward a Postfilmic Cinema*, where he proposes a new approach to film narratology which he calls "narratography". It is defined as "a reading of the image and its transitions for their own plot charge" rather than as bearers of narrative meanings already established. By paying attention to moments where the visual, material and graphic elements of image and sound body forth their own dramas of conflicting sensations, he sees their (photographic but also digital) textures and surfaces take on the kind of narrative weight usually invested only in the characters. As to the privileged status of openings, Stewart argues that "the sponsoring first image graphs its own optic means into the open before being assimilated by the story's drive toward closure".[23] Rather than follow Stewart into his explorations of contemporary cinema, we want to return to a theorist to whom we owe two ground-breaking analyses of film openings, Thierry Kuntzel, who went on to a remarkable career as a video and installation artist. In a two-part essay from 1972 and 1975 entitled *Le Travail du film*, Kuntzel dissected the openings of Fritz Lang's well-known masterpiece M (GE, 1931) and of THE MOST DANGEROUS GAME (US, 1932, Ernest B. Schoedsack and Irving Pichel), a Hollywood B-film that had previously received little or no critical attention in film theory.[24]

Kuntzel's textual analysis of THE MOST DANGEROUS GAME is exemplary in this sense, not only by its careful and multi-dimensional attention to the opening scenes, but because it offers an overview and primer of the formal analysis of classical narratives as a dynamic process, which he labels "the work of film". While at first glance it may seem as if Kuntzel remains fully within the narratological framework of French Structuralism (in the 1970s led by Claude Levi-Strauss' dialog with Vladimir Propp and Roland Barthes' programmatic "Structural Study of Narrative" and "Myth Today"), his multi-faceted and stereometric approach to narrative gave the films he analyzed both "body" and "volume", quite different from the powerfully reductionist models of formal logic promoted by Greimas' semiotic square. Kuntzel begins by identifying the importance of the motif of the door in THE MOST DANGEROUS GAME: "Openings and closings of doors punctuate the film. [. . .] Narrative trigger, gauge of suspense, dramatic emphasis: the association of doors with fade-ins at the beginning of the film and with fade-outs at the end is not gratuitous."[25] This hermeneutic dimension, in which to open or close a door, to enter or cross a space, produces specific meaning, but also acts as a punctuation mark or a shift of register, constitutes for Kuntzel the first, linear level of the film. Yet Kuntzel finds a second dimension, beyond plot and story, where we discover "how the [door, as] passage through the mystery leads, in the end, to nothing other than the original *void*".[26] Emptiness or absence represents the second central motif, in keeping, perhaps, with the psychoanalytic belief that (primordial) lack always functions as catalyst and stimulus. The paradoxical motif of absence as a *perpetuum mobile* explicitly harks back to Sigmund Freud and his idea of dreamwork, from which Kuntzel borrows his title as well as other key concepts such as condensation, displacement and secondary revision. Kuntzel's ambition was to show how the entire film is folded or condensed into the opening scenes, at once prefiguring what follows in a kind of mini-narrative, and anticipating it in condensed and encrypted form, by exploiting to a maximum the "polysemic", ambiguous nature of words, such as "game", of gestures of welcome or entry, and even of acts and actions, such as rescue and shelter.

Kuntzel's analysis further encouraged a tendency – reflecting the entry of Film Studies into the university syllabus – toward close textual analysis of films, not in the manner of literary "new criticism", but with a special sensitivity to the different intensities and textures of filmic signification. The idea that an entire

Figure 2.4 THE MOST DANGEROUS GAME: condensation effect.

film might already be prefigured in its opening, while indebted to Freud's interpretation of dreams, also showed the way toward a new understanding of the
rhetoric and figurative language typical even of "realistic" cinematic narratives.
For formalists, mental and emotional engagements are a matter of carefully
feeding information to the spectator or withholding it at certain points, to
create suspense, fright or mystery. The "film-work" of the post-structuralists
also requires the spectator to be fully engaged, but the information s/he receives
is present in often coded form that requires special interpretative keys, such as
linguists and rhetoreticians like Roman Jacobson or psychoanalysts like Sigmund
Freud provide. Puns and semantic play occupy an important role in this process
because they allow for a measure of compression and disguise, without blocking
comprehension outright. To their detractors, this method merely licences the
interpreter to freely associate, because "anything goes", but the close analyses
and detailed readings by theorists such as Raymond Bellour's of particular
scenes in Hitchcock films, Stephen Heath's examination of TOUCH OF EVIL and
a collectively authored text by the editors of *Cahiers du Cinéma* on John Ford's
YOUNG MR. LINCOLN (1939) proved enormously influential and formative for
an entire generation of scholars.[27]

A challenge and dilemma for structuralist and post-structuralist film theory
is that it risks being seen as exterior, as well as superior, to the films it analyzes,
i.e. that it operates on the assumption that it can tell films (and their spectators)
what they hide or "really" (mean to) say. What has been termed the "hermeneutics of suspicion" (Paul Ricœur) may regard films as seemingly innocuous
vehicles of pernicious ideologies, as covertly enforcing normativity or as a
patient suffering from "symptoms" but it can also use films as portals (or back-
doors) to insights about the workings of our social institutions and cultural value
systems. Film Studies (and its sister-discipline, Cultural Studies) have been at
the forefront of the "culture wars" for much of the 1980s and 1990s, but there
is a sense that the hermeneutics of suspicion may now be breaking down doors
that are wide open. The countervailing tendencies are to try to let films speak
for themselves – in the form of a "historical poetics" (David Bordwell[28]) or, as
in our case, to allow theory to restore to films a "body" and its "senses", with
many different openings and passages, where meaning and aesthetic presence
become two-way processes. To paraphrase Gilles Deleuze: theory's task is less
to discourse *about* films, but to speak with (and through) films.

In this sense, the door as a central motif of cinema is useful in that it evokes
a number of visual and conceptual terms that bring to the fore a film's spatial
and narrative logics. Yet it also adds a rich field of metaphoric associations: a
door can hide and conceal but it can also reveal and open, or do both at the same
time, echoing the features of the screen that we discussed in our etymological
sketch above (pp. 38–9). The door can also function quite literally as a "dramatis

persona" in a film. Examples can be found in the keyhole films of early cinema[29] and in Ernst Lubitsch' preference for stagings that make doors a central dramatic element (LADY WINDERMERE'S FAN, US, 1925; TROUBLE IN PARADISE, US, 1932; ANGEL, US, 1937; TO BE OR NOT TO BE, US, 1942) not forgetting many of Hitchcock's films, such as VERTIGO (US, 1958) or PSYCHO (US, 1960), which often hide a "secret behind the door" (see below, p. 52). This configuration may be more typical of classical cinema, but it can also be found in contemporary films, for instance in BLUE VELVET (US, 1986, David Lynch) or PANIC ROOM (US, 2002, David Fincher). In sound films, the door can also foreground the difference between acoustic and visual perception, as for instance in Roberto Rossellini's ROMÀ, CITTÀ APERTA (IT, 1945, ROME, OPEN CITY), where in the Gestapo Headquarters the interrogation room is located directly adjacent to an office and a parlor. During the torture of prisoners, optical and acoustic relays link the separated rooms into constantly changing spatial configurations. Finally, a door or a gate can also block access, as in the opening of CITIZEN KANE, when the camera defies the "No Trespassing!" sign by flying over the fence and thus setting the film in motion by a flagrant act of transgression.

The door not only signals the crossing from one physical space into another, but it also invokes the transport from one ontological or temporal realm to another. As we saw in THE SEARCHERS, the doors at the beginning and the end open and close not only onto a real landscape but also onto the myths of the American West. In the romantic comedy SLIDING DOORS (US, 1998, Peter Howitt), the hydraulic sliding doors of a subway dictate fate: the door through

Figure 2.5 BRANDED TO KILL: revealing view through the keyhole.

which the protagonist Helen (Gwyneth Paltrow) manages to slip in the first version of the story, but not in the second, determine her future life. Doors, therefore, can generate alternative universes. Doors are deeply rooted as metaphors in our cultural consciousness: a door can open onto a brighter future or be slammed shut, one can have a foot in the door or lock the stable door after the horse has bolted. The gates of Heaven play a decisive role in such different films as LILIOM (FR, 1934, Fritz Lang), LEAVE HER TO HEAVEN (US, 1945, John M. Stahl), and A MATTER OF LIFE AND DEATH (GB, 1946, Michael Powell, Emeric Pressburger), while the animation film MONSTERS INC. (US, 2001, Pete Docter) deploys the concept of the door as a zone of transition and liminality for the Internet age (see the Conclusion, p. 180). These examples illustrate that the door as motif cannot be separated from its narrative function – and that its use in turn seems to favor certain theoretical models. The act of creating worlds (SLIDING DOORS), the autonomous transgression of borders (CITIZEN KANE), the clandestine observation of others (BLUE VELVET), the surprising confrontation of different spaces (ROME, OPEN CITY) are equally designating the functions of doors as well as highlighting structures of narrative progress and delay that conduct the spectator into and through the film.

With Aldous Huxley's book title *The Doors of Perception* (a term he borrowed from William Blake, and which Jim Morrison took in turn from Huxley for the name of his rock band), we are in the realm of promised lands and the stimuli that unlock completely different (internal) worlds. Since the 1960s, the idea of cinema as a trip (into another world, into the self, into an artificial paradise or a synthetic hell) has inspired many films, notably THE TRIP (US, 1967, Roger Corman), 2001: A SPACE ODYSSEY (GB/US, 1968, Stanley Kubrick), EASY RIDER (US, 1969, Dennis Hopper), TRAINSPOTTING (GB, 1996, Danny Boyle) and FEAR AND LOATHING IN LAS VEGAS (US, 1998, Terry Gilliam).

Figure 2.6 MONSTERS INC. (US 2001, Pete Docter): the door as portal: unlimited access in the Internet age.

Doors have a special significance in the genres of classical cinema that focus on women's role in the domestic sphere, i.e. in the Gothic romances such as REBECCA (US, 1940, Alfred Hitchcock), GASLIGHT (US, 1944, George Cukor) or SECRET BEYOND THE DOOR (US, 1947, Fritz Lang), in the horror–thriller originating with Hitchcock and his successors, including THE BIRDS (US, 1963, Hitchcock), ROSEMARY'S BABY (US, 1968, Roman Polanski) or THE EXORCIST (US, 1973, William Friedkin), as well as in the family melodrama, especially in Douglas Sirk's films, such as ALL THAT HEAVEN ALLOWS (US, 1955) or WRITTEN ON THE WIND (US, 1956). Instead of analyzing the function of doors in these films, we can point to a compilation film that condenses precisely the physical effect and emotional impact of the door (and window) motif in these "women's genres". Matthias Müller's "found footage" experimental short HOME STORIES (GE, 1990) is a seamlessly edited collage of short (television) clips from Hollywood melodramas of the 1950s and 1960s. The recurring motifs of door and window graphically evoke the suspense and cliché situations of the plots, telling in their repetition and combination a single, relentless story with different protagonists going through the same motions: restless sleep, awakening, eavesdropping at the door, switching on lights, surprise, anxiety, mostly conveyed through opening and closing doors. In the originals these moments – and women – become sleepwalking yet susceptible, numbed yet hyper-alert embodiments of an "unconscious" or a "symptom" that their male counterparts surreptitiously or sadistically try to keep in check. In Müller's work, however, the motivating narratives have dissolved, and invested these reactive women with a new kind of agency, making the compulsive repetition of the stock situations and the architecture of their surroundings vibrate with a palpable sense of anticipation and imminence. Müller's insistent use of frames within frames – doors, windows, staircases, beams and mirrors crowd the compositions – emphasizes

Figure 2.7 WRITTEN ON THE WIND (US, 1956, Douglas Sirk): the motif of the door in the domestic sphere.

the inner turmoil pounding against a keen sense of visual confinement. The framing allows women to come into focus, but only to enforce their own (sense of) captivity.

All these films are united by the plurality of meaning generated within the semantic field of door, threshold, passage and screen. Moreover, the complementary (i.e. overlapping but also contradictory) effects of these elements highlights some of the constitutive components in the configuration we conveniently unify under the name of cinema. In fact, the cinema as apparatus and *dispositif* is made up of discrete parts that are in tension to each other even as they work together, and which – at a conceptual level – may well stand in opposition to each other. For instance, the projector and the frame are in productive but unresolved competition: the projector disperses (scatters) light, which the screen needs to "mask" (or gather), by surrounding it with a black border, in order to generate from the diffusion of light a clearly delimited and focused image. The same holds true for the productive tension between the screen as window (transparent) and the screen as filter (opaque), which can also be construed as incompatible concepts (unmediated, direct access versus mediated, constructed representation). The discussion in contemporary (digital) media theory, around the layering practice of superimposition, video overlay, and the presence of multiple images of different intensity and contours within the same frame, comes much closer to the old concept of the screen as sieve and filter than it is to the idea of the screen as window or door. A film like THE MATRIX (US, 1999, Andy and Larry Wachowski) very accurately registers these changes in the function of doors, windows, filters, screens and passageways once life takes place in the digital domain.

As a final illustration of what is at stake, we will briefly look at those films where the screen functions as a semi-permeable membrane, already cited at the beginning:[30] In SHERLOCK JR., Buster Keaton plays a film projectionist who falls asleep on the job and literally enters the on-screen world where the normal rules of physics are replaced by the capricious rules of film editing. The film literalizes the "entry" of the spectator into the film and at the same time illustrates what spatial and temporal non-sequiturs are elided or hidden by montage, since Keaton's appearances visualize the impossible space between the cuts, as well as the desires that make us complicit in their elision. Editing, which so often is primarily discussed as standing in the service of making the narration smooth and fluent, here foregrounds the logical paradoxes of the spectator being "woven" into the narration, a problem that film theory knows as "suture" and that we will explore in the next two chapters in more detail.

THE PURPLE ROSE OF CAIRO, which tells the story of Cecilia (Mia Farrow), who takes refuge in cinema from the beatings and infidelity of her husband Monk (Danny Aiello), reverses this relationship of inside and outside. Cecilia falls in love with a film that she watches over and over again, THE PURPLE ROSE OF CAIRO, until during her fifth viewing, the protagonist Tom Baxter (Jeff Daniels), turns toward the audience and starts talking to Cecilia. He tells her that he noticed her at the film screenings, then walks off the screen into "her" reality. No sooner is he in the "real world" than he encounters difficulties in adapting himself to the harshness of life during the Great Depression. But likewise, "in" the film, difficulties arise from the fact that the leading man is now missing, and the secondary characters are left to their own devices. Hollywood cannot let this happen, so the studio sends out Gil Shepherd, the actor who plays Tom Baxter on-screen (also Jeff Daniels), in order to capture the escaped "role" and bring it back into the film. The film thus wittily balances itself on the thin line between two kinds of (incompatible) fiction, as the cinema allows our fantasy and imagination to escape from the demands of reality into the realm of wish-fulfillment, while both sides, as it were, are having to pay a price for conniving in this flight. Here, it is not a matter of a spectator entering into the fictional world of the film, but a figure from a fictional universe stepping into extra-filmic reality – which reminds us of the "reality" we are prepared to invest in a star's image, as well as demonstrating the rich "ontological" potential of the liminal spaces constituted by the cinema auditorium and the social act of "going to the movies".

Summing up the idea of cinema as door and screen, we can say that it is a bodily concept indicating crossing or transgression: the spectator enters metaphorically "another world" or experiences his/her own world as foreign and strange, while retaining an awareness of entry and transition, rather than remaining in the state of witnessing a display, an exhibition and an unveiling. This movement passage, transport and transposition, though, is relativized by the (literal as well as etymological and metaphorical) fixity and immobility of the components of the cinema. While the window underlines the distance and disembodiedness (weight, matter, gravitation and physicality are suspended) in favor of pure visibility, the door and screen, acting as sieve and filter, draw our attention to the partial permeability of the image. Therefore, they are concepts of exchange and even dialog, a fact that becomes palpable in the paradoxical nature of the film experience: on the one hand, the film supports bodily orientation, physical presence and the referentiality of place, on the other hand it remains highly abstract, artificial and is self-enclosed. The entanglement between door and screen allows us to map a common field of reference for these polarities. At the same time, their single but contradictory spatial configuration already prefigures the paradigms that will occupy us in the next chapters, also relying on specific spatial arrangements: mirror and eye.

Chapter 3

Cinema as mirror and face

We see glimpses of a small film projector, running; followed, in a rapidly edited sequence, by an image strip made up of old silent films, children's hands, a lamb being slaughtered, nails driven into hands, a scorpion, trees in dirty snow, the corpses of two elderly people, a child in bed, the same child trying to touch the large, blurry face of a woman with alternately open and closed eyes. By making the projector and the film strip visible, the opening sequence of Ingmar Bergman's PERSONA (SE, 1965) draws our attention to the fact that we are about to see a film: a technology and an artifact which should not be mistaken for real life. Furthermore, the close-up of the woman's face projected onto a translucent surface and tentatively touched by the boy pictures an archetypal relation enacted by the cinema: that of serving as a mirror. The many ways of theorizing this moment, when we are confronted with an image as if with our own reflected self, will be the focus of this chapter.

PERSONA, a film in which the mirror motif is intensely deployed, revolves around the emotionally fragile actress Elisabeth Vogler (Liv Ullmann) who, after having suffering a nervous breakdown on stage, finds herself placed in the care of nurse Alma (Bibi Anderson). The ensuing rapprochement and eventual closeness between the two women gives rise not only to intimacy, but also to tensions and conflict, depicted as a temporary blurring of their identities: to such a degree that even the spectator can at times no longer be sure to tell them apart. At one point, a composite face is generated by combining one half of each actress' face, looking into a mirror – or is the face looking at us?[1] When studying Bergman's filmography, one realizes that several film titles announce the centrality of mirror and face in his oeuvre: ANSIKTET (SE, 1958, THE FACE), SÅSOM I EN SPEGEL (SE, 1961, THROUGH A GLASS DARKLY), ANSIKTE MOT ANSIKTE (SE, 1976, FACE TO FACE), KARINS ANSIKTE (SE, 1986, KARIN'S FACE).[2] But what exactly are the implications of the spectator looking into the eyes of a face that is larger-than-life? Should it be interpreted in terms of phenomenology, psychoanalysis or neuroscience? Approaches from all these disciplines have been brought to bear on the question.

Figure 3.1 PERSONA: mirroring as confrontation with the human face.

From the 1960s to the mid-1970s film theory, under the sign of mirror construction or *mise-en-abyme*, highlighted the reflexive potential of cinema. Self-reference of different kinds became an integral part in the stylistic arsenal of various European New Waves, itself reflected in turn by film theory.[3] Immersion into the fiction suddenly seemed to become impossible. As discussed in the previous two chapters, entering into the diegetic world through window and door was a matter of keeping one's distance, however "close" one was, or of crossing thresholds and traversing liminal spaces. Now the metaphor of the cinema as mirror blocks this passage to any world clearly labeled either "outside" or "inside", rendering the relationship of spectator and screen considerably more complicated. Some of the most influential theories, for instance, would claim that any engagement with a film is predicated on an act of identification that is – inevitably and fatally – based on a mis(re) cognition. After transparency and permeability, which were the hallmarks of window and door, theories predicated on the notion of mirror have to grapple with a special kind of framed view, at once transparent and opaque, permeable and closed off. A look into the mirror necessitates a confrontation with one's own face as the window to one's own interior self. Yet this look at oneself in the mirror is also a look from outside, a look that no longer belongs to me, that judges or forgives me, criticizes or flatters me, but at any rate has become the look of another, or "the Other".[4] In addition, cinema's fascination with stories of *Doppelgängers* and exchanged identities has always implicitly acknowledged the problematic dynamic of identification and self-estrangement, fleshing out into narrative terms or turning into allegory the spectator's own uneasy or uncanny awareness of the characters as his or her delegates and doubles, ideal selves or dreaded alter egos. Moreover, and aligned to the mirror, the close-up and/or the image of the human face have entailed film theoretical positions of great subtlety and recurring topicality. Whereas, for instance, the close-up held a special fascination for film theory in the 1920s, the metaphor of the mirror gained prominence at a time when the cinema as window came under ideological scrutiny. Dudley Andrew has trenchantly described this moment:

> [I]n classical film theory two metaphors of the screen had vied for suprem-
> acy. André Bazin and the realists championed the notion that the screen
> was a "window" on the world, implying abundant space and innumerable
> objects just outside its border. But to Eisenstein, Arnheim, and the formal-
> ists, the screen was a frame whose boundaries shaped the images appearing
> on it. The frame constructed meaning and effects; the window displayed
> them. [. . .] Jean Mitry holds that cinema's particular advantage and appeal
> lies in maintaining the implications of both these metaphors. The cinema is
> at once a window and a frame.
>
> Classical film theory could go no further. Only by shifting the discourse
> to another plane and invoking another system could modern theory
> develop. A new metaphor was advanced: the screen was termed a
> *mirror*.[5]

When the cinema as mirror had seemingly exhausted its cognitive possibil-
ities in the mid-1980s, the interest in the close-up, in the face and in detail staged a return in film theory. As a distinctive focus of film theory, the look into the mirror – and, by extension, the face and the close-up – is older than its more fashionable conceptualization in the psychoanalytically inspired theories of the 1970s. To take the link between cinema, face and close-up first: it can be traced back to the earliest days of moving pictures, became prominent in think-ing about D.W. Griffith,[6] but was popularized especially with the face of (Maria) Falconetti in Carl Theodor Dreyer's LA PASSION DE JEANNE D'ARC (FR, 1928, THE PASSION OF JOAN OF ARC). The first fully articulated theory of the close-up, however, we owe to Béla Balázs, a screenwriter and director as well as a critic and theoretician. Already in 1924 Balázs emphasized the importance of the close-up and the face: "In a truly artistic film the dramatic climax between two people will always be shown as a dialogue of facial expressions in close-up."[7]

Figure 3.2 Vivre sa Vie (FR, 1962, Jean-Luc Godard): Anna Karina (as Nana) mirroring Maria Falconetti's (as Jeanne d'Arc) tears on the screen.

Balázs was born in 1884 in the Hungarian town of Szeged. After the collapse of the short-lived Soviet republic led by Béla Kun in 1919, during which Balázs had been appointed minister of education, he fled to Vienna where he worked as a writer, translator and film critic, and soon also as a scriptwriter.[8] Balázs' *Der sichtbare Mensch/The Visible Man* (1924), from which we just quoted, grew out of these manifold interests and activities.[9] In three prefaces Balázs addresses respectively the judges of art (i.e. classical, philosophical aesthetics), the practitioners (i.e. the film industry) and the audience (i.e. public opinion), in order to nip in the bud any possible objections against his theoretical efforts to establish the grounds for cinema as an art form. Having in this way protected himself on two flanks against accusations of populism (i.e. of engaging with a popular medium solely for the purpose of gaining support) and elitism (i.e. of ennobling an inferior form through a superior theory), Balázs describes in a short passage of a few pages the main aspect of his film theory: to make the human being and his world (once more) visible.[10] For Balázs, culture was, until the invention of the printing press, primarily visual; it transformed under the influence of books, leaflets, brochures etc. into a culture based on writing. Implicitly, writing is associated here with an alienation from immediate (facial and bodily) expression, whose return, thanks to the cinema, Balázs associates with momentous changes in human civilization:

> The discovery of printing has gradually rendered the human face illegible. People have been able to glean so much from reading that they could afford to neglect other forms of communication. [. . .] Well, the situation now is that once again our culture is being given a radically new direction – this

time by film. [. . .] The whole of mankind is now busy relearning the long-forgotten language of gestures and facial expressions. This language is not the substitute for words characteristic of sign language for the deaf-and-dumb, but the visual corollary of human souls immediately made flesh. Man will become visible once again.[11]

The visuality of silent cinema in the mid-1920s, developing a form of communication not based on language or writing, thus establishes a connection to the age of cathedrals and of the great pictorial tradition of religious art works. Yet when read today, passages from *The Visible Man* also seem to anticipate the more recent "visual turn", the re-instatement of iconicity, figuration and Griffith's "Esperanto of the eye"[12] as it is being championed by art historians as well as proponents of the new digital media.[13]

In Balázs' view, cinema stands for the return to an age when (written) language had not yet positioned itself between (human) existence and (face-to-face) communication. But, at the same time, film is not a return to some pre-lapsarian "golden age", but the re-assertion of an expressive realm via wholly modern, technological means. While the cinema's special kind of non-mediated presence is communicated through actions and gestures, bodies and movements, it is most fully evident in the close-up, which consequently moves to the center of Balázs' film theory. Close-ups enable the spectator not only to see (aspects of) the world in a previously unknown light, but also to look at him/herself as if in a mirror, since the close-up typically shows a face, or gives the world the ability to look back at us. If the unique expressivity of the human face derives from the fact that emotions and affects do not manifest themselves consecutively in a succession of expressions but, rather, present a simultaneity of concurrent and even contradictory affective states and their metamorphoses, then the same principle holds true for the close-up, which joins the phenomenology of pure appearance with the necessity to render legible both a multiplicity and a latency of meanings. Balázs writes:

> Since film permits of no psychological explanations, the possibility of a change in personality must be plainly written in an actor's face from the outset. What is exciting is to discover a hidden quality, in the corner of the mouth, for example, and to see how from this germ the entire new human being grows and spreads over his entire face.
>
> (101)

With this observation Balázs outlines a crucial distinction between "to-be-looked-at-ness", or "spectacle" and "progress-through-juxtaposition", or "narrative" (an opposition which was to become so important in feminist film theory of the 1970), while he also points to another constant tension that has haunted film theory ever since, namely an oscillation between mimetic–phenomenological and semiotic–symbolic approaches. Balázs, who wrote his first film-theoretical work without having seen the films of Sergej Eisenstein or Georg Wilhelm Pabst and before the great works of Friedrich Wilhelm Murnau or Fritz Lang were made, found the ultimate embodiment of this ambivalence in the actress Asta Nielsen, whom he eulogizes in his final chapter. Of central significance here is the concept of physiognomy, which Balázs applies to objects and landscapes as well as to the human figure; physiognomy reveals itself to the eye and exceeds intention and communication in its pure visuality. Physiognomy often manifests itself as gesture, even as mass gesture, i.e. the movement of larger groups of people, exemplified in Ernst Lubitsch's direction of crowds for his grand-scale historical films from the early 1920s, which he had learned from Max Reinhardt's theatrical stagings.[14] Even if Balázs' initial contention that printing had rendered the human face illegible cannot be supported in this sweeping formulation, when we think of the rise of portraiture since the Renaissance, his cultural thesis of a new faciality-in-motion coming into being with the cinematic close-up rightly introduces the idea of the spectator confronting a mirror, seeing him/herself anew with every single close-up in the cinema – monumentally big as well as intimately small.

As already hinted at, Balázs' film theory in general and his thoughts on the close-up in particular have recently made a comeback and received fresh impetus. For Gilles Deleuze the "movement-image" (hence also the title of the first volume of his cinema books) is characterized by three dominant articulations: perception-image, action-image and affection-image. While the former two interlock in the typical chain of narrative events – the perception of a situation leads to a (motivated) action which in turn entails a new situation that can be perceived and followed by another action – the affection-image holds another quality: "*The affection-image is the close-up, and the close-up is the face. . . .*"[15] By directly tying the larger-than-life face of cinema projection to the affection-image, Deleuze explicitly harks back to the views of Balázs, particularly the latter's idea of the image as a spatio-temporal abstraction.

> As Balázs has already accurately demonstrated, the close-up does *not* tear away its object from a set of which it would form part, of which it would be a part, but on the contrary *it abstracts it from all spatio-temporal co-ordinates*, that is to say it raises it to the state of Entity. The close-up is not an enlargement and, if it implies a change of dimension, this is an absolute change: a mutation of movement which ceases to be translation in order to become expression.
>
> (96, emphasis in original)

For Deleuze, the affection-image is at the same time "a reflecting and reflected unity" (87), i.e. a mirroring surface which constitutes the image that it reflects and the image itself.

Ever since Gilles Deleuze assigned a pioneering role to Balázs in his books on cinema, a lively discussion about the face and the close-up has been ensuing, in which film-makers like Pascal Bonitzer and critics such as Philippe Dubois and Jacques Aumont are as involved as American (James Naremore) and German scholars (Wolfgang Beilenhoff). Aumont, in his wide-ranging and comprehensive study, distinguishes between the face as a hermeneutic enigma, i.e. as a surface for the expression of some hidden interiority, as Balázs tended to see it, and a view of the face that emphasizes its function as both a pure "phenomenal" presence, and a "text" to be deciphered. What the face and the close-up share is that both present "a surface that is sensible and legible at the same time, which produces, as Deleuze says, an Entity".[16] Contemporary research on this topic has since diversified in so many directions that the face today can be considered a multifunctional "medium" in its own right, which cuts across traditional visual arts (cinema, television, painting, advertising, fashion, video and installation art) in order to find its own encoding and formal language, creating its own research areas, for instance as in the examination of the affective structure of film, of the "faciality" of the close-up or of the use of the face in early cinema.[17]

Turning to the "cinema as mirror" instantly evokes a much older tradition in Western aesthetics. Already Plato formulated the difference between an artist and a craftsman in terms of the former creating an object according to an inner image or an ideal type whereas the latter has a material prototype whose mirror image he fashions or reproduces. In the argument whether the cinema is an art or a craft, the fact that film reproduces what is in front of the lens seemingly without human intervention has tended to make the mirror-function of photography count against the cinema's claim to artistic autonomy. In our discussion of self-reflexivity we will see how this function of the cinema can be also employed to mirror the spectator's look back onto him/herself, thereby complicating any clear-cut relationship. The mirror, which both distances and objectifies, but also reveals an (unpalatable) truth, is a traditional motif in the visual arts, often associated with the sin of "vanitas" (vanity). It always retains a double meaning, signifying a split personality, as in the fantastic novels of E.T.A. Hoffmann, E.A. Poe, Robert Louis Stevenson or Oscar Wilde, who in turn inspired so much of German Expressionist cinema and the Hollywood horror genre. These outer/inner readings of the mirror are important from a cultural–historical perspective: they constitute the basis for the distinction between the classical and the romantic aesthetic, thereby modifying Plato's opposition into alternate versions of the artistic vocation. In *The Mirror and the Lamp*, M.H.

Abrams contrasts two complementary metaphors of mind, one likening the mind to a reflector of external objects (in classicism), the other to a radiant projector that changes the appearance of the object it perceives (in romanticism).[18] The former is based on a concept of representation, whereas the latter gives priority to the idea of imagination – a contrast that frequently re-appears in film theory as well, notably when opposing narrative and realism in mainstream cinema to imagination and illumination in avant-garde "pure cinema" or poetic film.

How inherently complex the notion of representation (as mirroring reflection) can be, even without being juxtaposed to imagination, is amply demonstrated in painting, not least since Michel Foucault's discussion of Diego Velasquez's *Las Meninas*, a justly famous painting of the Spanish Royal Family, in which complex mirror relations and viewing axes destabilize the fixed position of the spectator, becoming shifting and unstable, pulling the very ground of "representation" from under us.[19] Similarly, in Eduard Manet's *A Bar at the Folies Bergères*, the man reflected in the mirror either has to stand right in front of us or he has to be us as spectator, doubting the space of our own observational position.

As we hope to show, many of these philosophical and aesthetic questions are also relevant to film theory, even if their terminologies (and "solutions") take off from a different problematic, or borrow less from classical or post-structuralist

Figure 3.3 Edouard Monet: *A Bar at the Folies Bergères* (1882) – mirror as a disorienting effect.

philosophy and more from literary hermeneutics, Marxism and psychoanalysis. One can heuristically distinguish three paradigms which belong to the semantic field of the mirror and its metaphoric connotations. First of all, there is the dominant notion – and a common trope in much of classical cinema – which regards the look into the mirror as a window on the unconscious, referring to a surplus or excess of Self, which the mirror is capable of disclosing. Second, the mirror metaphor in the cinema points to a reflexive doubling of what is being seen or shown: such moments tend to signify in film theory a distancing and estranging effect rather than disclosing deeper meaning. It shows how modern cinema knows about its own history as a medium of appearances and deceptions, whose "illusionism" has to be foiled, blocked or fragmented by mirror images and multiple reflections. The mirror as reflexive–reflective doubling, stopping a narrative in its tracks, and – as in Bergman's PERSONA – referring us back to our situation as viewers of an artifact, is typical of the auteur cinema and the New Waves of the 1960s. Finally, the mirror in the cinema can also refer to the mirror of the other as identified by anthropologists as a component of human identity, agency and intersubjective communication. In this respect, the cinema may play an important part in human cognitive evolution, when it comes to the origins of empathy, sympathy and affective interaction with others, hinting at a connection between the debate around mirror, face and close-up in Film Studies and scientific discussions of the so-called mirror neurons, a phenomenon recently discovered in apes by evolutionary (neuro-)biologists and heavily debated among behavioral theorists.

The idea of the cinema as a mirror became a central paradigm of film theory from the mid-1960s to the mid-1980s. Two possible articulations sometimes overlap and are not always easily separated: on the one hand, Sigmund Freud's theories of the unconscious inspired Jean-Louis Baudry to develop his notion of the "cinematic apparatus" and le dispositif as modeled on the human psyche, and on the other hand, Christian Metz borrowed from Jacques Lacan's concept of the unconscious as a language, to speak of the "imaginary signifier", which aligns the cinema with several key notions in structural linguistics. While Baudry sees a relation between film technology and the psyche, Metz argues that the filmic image refigures an absence as a presence and thus "signifies" through a dynamic process of substitution, whereby the spectator is "captured" by an imagined or projected presence, similar to Freud's example of the "fort-da" game. Metz further complemented this theory of narrative cinema as a chain of substitutions ("metaphors") and displacements ("metonymies") with another Lacanian notion: that of the mirror stage as a key moment in the formation of human subjectivity, which in turn became conflated with some of Baudry's speculations.[20] While the details of this mirror stage will be taken up below (pp. 64–7), and once more – especially in its implication for the question of gender in the cinema – examined in the subsequent chapter on "eye and gaze", one should note at this point that these psychoanalytically informed approaches share the idea that in the cinema body and mind "regress" to an earlier stage of psycho-physiological development. In the darkened environment of the cinema auditorium, one's grip on reality is loosened, facilitating through the external, optical projection also different kinds of internal, psychic projections, and bringing about a fusion of the interior "dream screen" with the actual screen in the cinema. Hence the comparison of certain stylistic figures and tropes with the mechanisms identified by Freud as "dream work", already touched upon in the previous chapter in connection with Thierry Kuntzel's detailed analyses – "the work of film" – of opening sequences.

As one of the most important successors – and critical antagonists – to André Bazin (discussed in Chapter 1), Christian Metz (1931–93) necessitates further comment. Arguably the leading figure in Film Studies during the 1970s, Metz taught for most of his career at the École des Hautes Études en Sciences Sociales in Paris, where he gathered around him a growing number of younger scholars, not only from France. Through (summer) courses held in English, and rapid translations of his work, Metz was also able to attract a wide Anglo-American public who helped to spread his ideas in England and the United States.[21] Metz's thinking can be broadly divided into two parts: an early, structuralist phase during which Metz systematically tried to establish the similarities and differences between cinema (as a "language") and human language, as described by structural (or Saussurean) linguistics.[22] In other words, Metz took literally one of the recurring metaphors of film theory since the montage theories and practices of Soviet directors during the 1920s: in what sense one can speak of a "language of film", and by extension, in what way can a seemingly arbitrary succession of images be said to convey a precise (i.e. verbalizable and syntactically correct) meaning? Metz concluded that cinema was a language only in a restricted sense ("a language without a language system") and he began to formulate the problem more generally, by setting out "to understand how films are understood".[23] It is this question which eventually led him to partially abandon any strictly linguistic analogy and pursue a more psychoanalytically inflected theory of the spectator, as the origin and construer of meaning.

This insight initiated a second phase in his work, culminating with the publication of Le signifiant imaginaire: psychanalyse et cinema, a collection of essays written between 1973 and 1975.[24] There, Metz argued against the common analogies between cinema and dream, elaborating instead the structural similarities between cinema and mirror. He pointed to the apperceptive richness of both types of visual perception (plenitude of details, similarity between the represented world and the real one) as well as the unreality of the image (only light and shapes projected onto a flat surface), but he also drew on Lacan's "mirror stage". The Imaginary Signifier thus shifts attention away from film as text, language and narration to film as an imaginary support for the fragmented perception of the viewing subject and to cinema as a "mental machine" (apparatus) that allows the spectator to perceive himself [sic] as "self-present" and to experience as whole and unified a succession of seemingly disconnected shots and sequences. Nevertheless, there are for Metz also some crucial distinctions between the mirror image and the film image:

> But film is also different from the natural mirror in one important respect: although everything can reflect just as well in the former as in the latter, there is one thing that will never find its reflection in film, namely the spectator's body. From a certain point of view, then, the mirror suddenly becomes opaque.[25]

This passage marks a key moment in this phase of film theory: the identification of the spectator who watches a film is always a construction, filling an opaque spot or a perceptual hole. The look into the mirror of the screen no longer resembles – as was still the case with Balázs – the recognition of a human being *through* another. Rather, what takes place is an act of false recognition or miscognition, as if one were to recognize another as oneself, or conversely, (mis-) perceive oneself *in and as* another.

Essential for this "identification through miscognition" as constitutive of the cinema is Jacques Lacan's theorization of the "mirror stage" (*stade du miroir*), a complex and contested notion, but crucial because of its central role in the film theory of an entire generation.[26] The mirror stage describes a phase in the development of infants between the ages of six and eighteen months. At this (st)age, the child is not yet able to control motor-coordination and bodily movements to such an extent as to function as an autonomous being, but s/he can recognize his/her image in the mirror. This sudden recognition which is acted out through mimicry and situational apperception involving the maternal presence, does not, however, exhaust itself in a pure perceptual effect as in the case of primates, but, rather, marks according to Lacan, the nascent human being's entrance into the symbolic order, i.e. into social structures, such as laws, prohibitions and rules of proper behavior, as well as language. On the one hand, the child perceives herself/himself from the outside as complete and self-contained, thereby objectifying and alienating itself in the act of becoming "image" for itself. But if "[t]he child identifies with itself as an object",[27] it also projects agency in excess of its physical capabilities into this image, thus identifying with its image as an idealized self, giving rise, according to Lacan, to both an "ideal ego" (idealized self-projection) and an "ego ideal" (ideals projection from another onto the self), whose contradictory dynamics form the basis for all subsequent identifications, self-images and love objects:

> This jubilant assumption of his specular image by the child at the *infans* stage, still sunk in his motor incapacity and nursing dependence, would seem to exhibit in an exemplary situation the symbolic matrix in which the *I* is precipitated in a primordial form, before it is objectified in the dialectic of identification with the other, and before language restores to it, in the universal, its function as subject.[28]

Underlying every affective relationship according to this model would be some kind of projective miscognition or narcissistic self-delusion, implying, for instance, that desire is not only based on a (perceived) lack within the self, but also finds itself always mediated by someone else's (imagined) desire.

Film theorists, such as Metz and Baudry recognized in this apparently so abstruse and far-fetched model of human development, a powerful concept that unified many of their partial or contradictory efforts in explaining the fascination that cinema inspires in its spectators. Not only did the (two-dimensional) mirror provide a better visual analogy for the framed picture plane of the screen than the window, by inscribing the viewer as in some sense active; Lacan's theory also accommodated the idea of cinema inviting "regression" and the relaxation of self-control. For, similar to Freud's thinking about the subsequent and complementary phases of human development (oral, anal, oedipal), Lacan proposed that issues pertaining to earlier developmental stages were never fully dealt with or settled; they consequently remain present at all times as traces or residual layers, so that the possibility of regression is always given.

Yet equally crucial for the adoption of the "cinema as mirror" paradigm was the peculiar spatial geometry of idealization (self/other) and the temporal structure of anticipation inherent in the Lacanian mirror-phase. It seemed to explain the iterative, compulsive and highly narcissistic pleasures associated with narrative cinema, irrespective of whether style and genre were "realist" or "fantasy". Identification in the cinema would thus be contingent upon establishing with the moving image not a relation of appearance versus reality, or fiction versus truth, but an imaginary relationship internal to the spectator: similar to the one underlying the coming into self-awareness of an infant, even though this similarity remains concealed, and "must no longer be presented to the spectator formally on the silver screen, as in the mirror of his childhood".[29]

Metz specifies this imaginary relation by drawing a distinction between primary and secondary identification: the latter is the one we usually have in mind when we speak of "identifying" with a character in a film, while the former is the (unconscious) identification with the (absent) look of the camera. This primary identification is both more foundational and more concealed than the identification with the characters. Foundational because it makes the fiction and narration of successive images possible in the first place; concealed because in classical cinema the camera's look is folded into our look, giving us the illusion of visual mastery, when in fact we are being led and mastered by the camera: "In short, the spectator *identifies with himself* as a pure act of perception (astute and alert): as a condition for the possibility of the perceived object, hence also as a kind of transcendental subject who precedes any *There is*."[30] Primary identification, in other words, is a theoretical construct which is meant to explain several features of cinema: it accounts for why we normally do not notice (consciously) that the images we see have been recorded by a camera – specifically *for us*; it suggests why images – even when not marked as "point of view" shots – can have a strong "subjective" feel or impact, and it introduces, via the philosophical concept of the "transcendental subject", the problem of how something can be both "imaginary" and "foundational", as well as both cause and effect.

With this theoretically sophisticated but metaphorically also elegant cinematic mirror phase, one of the most thorny and intractable issues in film theory could be tackled afresh: the question of realism, which especially in its Bazinian formulation had irked even many of his followers, since it seemed to privilege only one form of cinema, namely neorealism, but excluded both Hollywood and abstract or avant-garde cinema. It was Jean-Louis Baudry who fully elaborated the consequences of this shift in focus from window to mirror, by succeeding to explain why "realism" (as an aesthetics) is a style and thus a construct, and why even "illusionism" (as practiced by Hollywood) can have such a strong "reality effect". This was because all "reality effects" are first and foremost "subject effects", i.e. require the construction of a ("transcendental") subject, before a representation is perceived as "realistic", i.e. as recognizable by a spectator as concerning (or addressing itself to) him or her. Baudry's immense influence on the development of film theory (based as it was on only two articles) was due to an astute combination of three types of knowledge: a new technological account of cinema; the psychoanalytic theories of Freud and Lacan (as elaborated by Metz); and a philosophically more informed grasp of the relevant issues, combining Plato's idealist theory of perception and reality with Kant's epistemological skepticism about the possibility of objective knowledge.

Rather than beginning with the idea of cinema as a representation of reality or as a storytelling medium, Baudry used the technological genealogy of the cinema in Renaissance perspective, the camera obscura and Cartesian optics, for an ideological critique of its subjective effects, arguing that the peculiar spatial organization of the different elements in the cinema, i.e. the alignment of projector, spectator and screen, constituted what he called "a basic cinematic apparatus" which in and by itself already predicated and circumscribed the effects it could have on the spectator. It confirmed that this apparatus imitated at the physical level what bourgeois individualism sought at the ideological level and monocular perspective accomplished at the perceptual level: the "centering" as well as "pinning down" or "capturing" of the single individual as the locus of consciousness and coherence, giving the impression of mastery when such mastery was the mere effect of the respective machineries – optical, ideological, narrative, specular – put in place by the bourgeois–capitalist world picture. The sense of self, produced by the cinema, was thus both illusory and real. Unable to take control of the forces that manipulate or guide perception, the spectator nonetheless experiences such strong (and often pleasurable) subject-effects of address and interpellation that a heightened sense of presence is the result, making the "dispositif cinema" a perfect synthesis of Western ideal-ist philosophy and Freudian accounts of the psyche.[31]

We have already discussed how the psychoanalytic configuration highlights the cinema's mirroring function. The philosophical dimension takes its cue from Plato's parable of the cave: trying to explain why perception of real objects cannot grasp these objects in their essence, Plato compares human beings to prisoners in a cave who are chained in such a way that they can only look in one direction. A fire burns behind them, and between the fire and the prisoners is a walkway along which puppeteers can move. These puppeteers, who are outside the prisoners' field of vision, carry objects which cast shadows onto the wall that the prisoners are facing. While the prisoners have no reason to believe they are perceiving anything but the "real" objects, the spatial arrangements make it clear to anyone "outside" or "transcending" these limiting conditions that what is on view is a secondary reality however much the effect or impact on the spec-tators is real and immediate. Plato's allegory corresponds, in Baudry's view, with uncanny prescience, to the spectator's situation in cinema:

> It is therefore their motor paralysis, the impossibility to go away from where they find themselves, that makes a reality check impossible in their case, thereby beautifying their misapprehension and causing them to confuse the representational for the real – or, rather, the image of the former and its projection onto the screen for which the cave wall before them stands and from which they cannot turn (their eyes) away. They are glued, tied, chained to the projection surface – a relationship, a prolonga-tion between it and them that is interdependent on their inability to break free from it. This surface is the last thing they see before they fall asleep.[32]

In the cinema, the specific set-up of projection, screen and audience, together with the "centering" effect of optical perspective and the focalizing strategies of filmic narration, all ensure or conspire to transfix but also to transpose the spec-tator into a trance-like state in which it becomes difficult to distinguish between the "out-there" and the "in-here". Thus, apparatus theory – as this amalgam of technical, psychoanalytic, art-historical, philosophical and ideological critique has come to be known in the Anglo-Saxon world – seemed, across the metaphor of the mirror, to offer a multi-dimensional model with an interlocking set of concepts for mapping the relationship between cinema, film and the spectator's senses and consciousness, the body and the unconscious:

> This is a return to a relative narcissism and, even more obviously, to a form of reality reference which could be described as enveloping and in which there are no clear-cut boundaries between one's own body and the outside world. In this way one can arrive at an understanding of how strong the connection of the subject to the image and to the identification cultivated in cinema really is. Return to a primordial state of narcissism through a regression of the libido [. . .]; non-delimitation of the body, transposing of the internal into the external [. . .].[33]

Ingenious though it may have been at the time, when its very difficulty made it seriously persuasive to a new academic elite, apparatus theory was not without its critics. One series of objections came from the emerging field of feminist Film Studies, where its gender-blindness and "fetishistic" approach to technology was challenged, notably in two articles by Constance Penley, who claimed that even though apparatus theory seemed to validate non-narrative, experimental or "materialist" films as progressive and critical deconstructions of the inherent idealism of this apparatus, the filmic avant-garde was still caught in its own imaginary, constructing a kind of "bachelor machine" (Marcel Duchamp) of failed male control: in other words, more toys-for-the-boys.[34] Seen from this vantage point, apparatus theory merely adds another layer of (self-)deception to the almost tragic efforts of 1970s theory to extricate itself from its own entrapment by the lure of the moving image, in both its reality-effects and its subject-effects.

Second, apparatus theory not only relied on the (controversial) mirror stage postulated by Lacan and a radical, anti-ideological reading of Renaissance central perspective, from which the monocular view of cinema is said to be the direct descendant, it also offered an all-too-streamlined and monolithic version of film history. While the genealogy of cinema deriving from monocular perspective was challenged by the art historian Jonathan Crary,[35] historians of early cinema and pre-cinema also cast doubt on the idea that the moving images' first spectators were even metaphorically "chained" to their seats. Instead, the ranked auditorium seating as we know it from classical movie houses resulted from an intriguingly protracted process of "disciplining" the audience, transforming them from a noisy and often unruly collectivity into the individualized, silenced and captivated spectator: a figure which, paradoxically, began to make way for more mobile viewers in front of all kinds of screens, just about the time when

Baudry formulated his famous theory.[36] The impact of early cinema studies and so-called "revisionist" film history on psychoanalytically inspired film theory was considerable. Condensing a ten-year debate about the nature of early cinema into a single, easily graspable formula, Tom Gunning proposed a "cinema of attractions" as typical of cinema's initial mode of display and address. Its success further weakened the grip of apparatus theory, since it suggested that, throughout film history, there existed an alternative model of picturing the relation between screen, spectator and the moving image: that of loosely connected, semi-autonomous "attractions", directly appealing to the viewer in a gesture of overt performativity, rather than any reality effect, wrapped up in a subject effect or owed to disavowed voyeurism.[37]

The (ideological) split in early cinema is somewhat different. On the one hand, early cinema does exhibit an undercurrent of latent anxiety concerning the integrity of the human body and shows a fear of its fragmentation through the technique of editing. Well-known is the story about the resistance to the close-up that D.W. Griffith and his cameraman Billy Bitzer first encountered when breaking up the frame into partial views. Linda Williams, from a feminist perspective, went back to chronophotography and Eadweard Muybridge to locate this ambiguous fascination with the (naked, gendered) body in mechanical motion ("animal locomotion"), attempting to reconcile the mirror stage with the new film history.[38] On the other hand, as Lucy Fisher and Noel Burch among others discovered, a great number of films do feature dismemberment as both terrifying and comic situations, in short as "attractions".[39] They single out many Méliès films (e.g. Dis-locations Mystérieuses [The Clown with the Movable Body, FR, 1901], Le Bourreau Turc [The Terrible Turkish Executioner, FR, 1903]) or How It Feels To Be Run Over (GB, 1900), as well as films that purport to show spectacular accidents (Explosion of a Motor Car [GB, 1902]). Burch argued that these films were attempts to come to terms with the progressive disintegration of the body's wholeness, brought into the culture by the invention of cinema (as well as modern regimes of mechanized labor and assembly-line production methods). The variable size of the image in the cinema, and the general issue of scale and detail, already discussed earlier around the close-up and the human face, underlines the importance of proximity or distance of the camera from the action and of the spectator from the screen. It is to these body-based anxieties and perceptual dislocations that "classical" cinema responded and reacted in the late 1910s with a process of "re-centering" and "re-calibration" around the human figure as the norm of spatial relations of scale and proportion. What in apparatus theory figures as "cause" and origin, namely classical cinema, can now be seen more properly as effect and counter-move, in a process that has alternated or oscillated ever since.

Following this line of thinking, it makes sense that one of the few European attempts to break the hegemony of classical Hollywood storytelling in the

1920s, namely German Expressionist cinema, resorted to skewed perspectives and odd angles, and also played a profuse variety of turns on the motif of the double, the mirror and the lost shadow[40] – taken from the Romantic literature of the nineteenth century and given renewed urgency by the mechanized and quasi-automatic mirroring function of the cinema.

If one agrees with Gunning that early cinema demonstrates a self-reflexive orientation toward performative display, one will want to attach a different meaning to the alternately uncanny and playful use of close-ups, or shifts in scale and perspective. Rather than looking for how they can be (re-)integrated into the surrounding action, they should be read as performative turns, as "insert shots", and not as close-ups in a gradual process of intensified proximity. A good example is a film like GRANDMA'S READING GLASS (1900), whose close-up can be interpreted as either motivated by a coherent, if rudimentary, narrative frame (a little boy finds his grandmother's magnifying glass on the table and points it successively at various objects), or as merely the narrative excuse for an alternating series of homely and unsettling close shots: familiar images (canary, kitten) and unfamiliar ones (close-up of a clockwork mechanism, the punishing eye of the grandmother) sustain a certain ambivalence: the spectator cannot be sure what attitude to adopt vis-à-vis this new sudden immediacy of the world, paradoxically feeling distanced and dislocated by their very proximity and

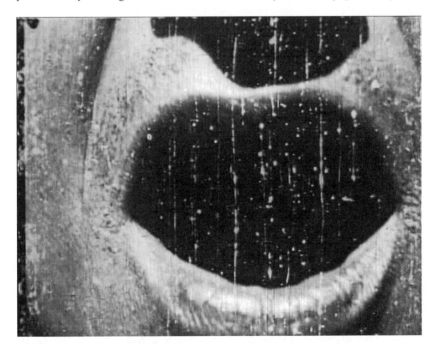

Figure 3.4 THE BIG SWALLOW: proximity as dislocation.

unusual scale (see Chapter 1). The unsettling effect is even stronger in THE BIG SWALLOW (1901), about a man protesting about being filmed. Instead of avoiding the intrusive camera, he moves closer and closer to it – and us – until, mouth wide open, he swallows the camera along with the cinematographer, smacking his lips in pleasure. What is comical about the film is its frightening impossibility: at the critical moment, the giant mouth filling the screen transgresses the normally invisible "space in front" and must have unsettled a contemporary spectator's viewing position almost as drastically as the mouth coming out of the television set does in David Cronenberg's VIDEODROME (1983).

Since the close-up in cinema combines the attention to detail that we are used to from miniatures and models with the monumentality we know from public memorials and statues, there is always a tension, not to say contradiction, between the desire to get even closer, and the opposite, to move away in order to retain a proper perspective. A monument usually comes with its own spatial coordinates – an empty square, the vista of an avenue, a hilltop – that allow us to approach it at a pace that adjusts to its size. In cinema, where we cannot move our bodies to adjust scale, a close-up is always in some fundamental way transgressive of the human scale: at once too big and too close, a fact which is normally negotiated by narrative motivation, but which in the case of certain directors – foremost among them Alfred Hitchcock and Fritz Lang – remains an option for a radical critique of cinema's realist ontology.[41]

With respect to unsettling the viewer's sense of safe distance, THE BIG SWALLOW also bears striking similarity to the credit sequence of LE MEPRIS (CONTEMPT, FR, 1963, Jean-Luc Godard) in which we witness the shooting of the very film that we are watching. In the opening scene, a camera, behind which one can recognize the film's cinematographer Raoul Coutard, tracks from a distance slowly but relentlessly toward our vantage point, filming the script girl Francesca who, alongside the camera, walks toward us. As she and the camera come close to the point from which we see the scene, the diegetic camera (the camera that we see) pans and the spectator finds him/herself gazing into the gaping abyss of the hooded lens. With LE MEPRIS, we arrive – after a brief detour to insert shot, close-up and direct address in early cinema – at the second aspect of the mirror paradigm: modernist self-reflexivity. Typical for the New Waves of the 1960s and 1970s, from the French Nouvelle Vague to the New German Cinema, LE MEPRIS focused attention on the function of *reflexive doubling*. Along with representative work by Bergman, Fellini and Antonioni, Godard's film takes a distance from itself and comes closer to us, while it observes itself in the process of its own making.

If one surveys some of these directors' canonical works of the 1960s European art cinema, one common denominator of the modernist turn in film emerges. Recall that our first two paradigms – the step across a threshold (the door) or the look through a transparent divide (the window) – were essentially enacting or specifying the ground-rules of a contract between spectator and film. But as the cinema begins to lose its audiences to television, and becomes unsure of what sort of audience it can count on, its makers turn their regard upon themselves, or – through the return of the look and the mirroring of the face – try to decipher the look of the other. It therefore does not come as a surprise that many of these films attempt to come to terms with the creative process itself: the protagonists of four key films from the period are all practicing artists. In LE MÉPRIS, Michel Piccoli plays the screenwriter Paul Javal, in Ingmar Bergman's PERSONA cited at the outset, Liv Ullman portrays the actress Elizabeth Vogler, in Michelangelo Antonioni's BLOW-UP (UK/IT, 1966) David Hemmings is the photographer Thomas, and finally Marcello Mastroianni in Federico Fellini's 8½ (IT, 1963) takes on the role of the film director Guido Anselmi. All four characters face a creative crisis that revolves around the relationships to their means of artistic expression and to the world: Javal fears that he has sold out to capital, Vogler goes mute on stage, Thomas believes to have discerned the scene of a murder in one of his photographs, and Anselmi is incapable of completing his film. Inasmuch as these films thematize the creative act and its conditions of possibility, they reflect or enfold the process of their own making.

On the one hand this can be seen as a doubling and thus an enrichment of the world they depict, but at the same time it entails also a hermetic closing off that destabilizes the role the spectator is meant to assume, unsure on which side of the mirror to locate him/herself at a given moment. In fact, it is not only the

Figure 3.5 BLOW-UP: Thomas acts out his creative crisis.

creative process that is rendered problematic; the characters' sense of identity falters, often signaled by the border between reality and fantasy becoming blurred. In all these instances, cinema's reflexive turns approach an act of self-effacement, in the sense that the various *mise-en-abyme*-constructions resemble looks into the mirror: suggesting that the modernist European art cinema doubts the conditions but also the justifications of its own existence. In the films this self-questioning is thematized as a crisis affecting a close and intimate relationship: "contempt" for the other among a couple, in the battle of the sexes (CONTEMPT), the ricochet or pendulum effects in the mutual over-identification of two characters who can no longer be separated (PERSONA), a radical calling into question of the trust one has in one's own perception (BLOW-UP), or a creative identity crisis, as the demands of the outside world and one's own inner demons conspire to sap all energies and make either cynicism or retreat into the past the only possible responses (8½).

The development toward reflexive cinema originated from a number of sources. Initially Italian Neorealism had promoted a direct access to reality through the medium of film (see Chapter 1), but it was already clear from the "*temps mort*", or "dead time" – the seemingly plotless stretches of inaction in the early films of Michelangelo Antonioni (for example, STORY OF A LOVE AFFAIR [CRONACA DI UN AMORE, IT, 1950]), which would later become a signature element of his style – or from the aimlessly wandering protagonists in Roberto Rossellini's VOYAGE TO ITALY (VIAGGIO IN ITALIA, IT, 1954) that such a depiction of (the characters' inner and psychological) reality would make the classically constructed narrative, driven by clear goals and single-minded objectives, fragment and disintegrate. Second, in the 1960s the media theory and theatrical practice of Bertolt Brecht became a major cultural force. One of Brecht's central aims was to make the spectator active as a critical judge, distrusting a realism that took phenomenal appearance or psychological motivation as its measure of truth. Third, critical reflexivity in the cinema was – by the end of the 1960s – also nourished by a general movement toward political action through revolutionary aesthetics, often understood as a way of deconstructing phenomenal realism, which made appear as "second nature" what was the result of specific historical power-relations of oppression or injustice. The various struggles of liberation (women, gay and lesbian, black, third world and post-colonial, etc.) eagerly took up this aesthetic model of challenging, subverting or deconstructing classical narrative.[42]

The modernist reflexive aesthetic also claimed for itself another of Brecht's theories, that of distanciation, which wanted to break the mutually complicit contract of "make-believe" between the spectator and the theatrical stage play. In the cinema, as we have seen, such effects of doubling, mirroring and the play of distance and proximity, however, were common from the very beginning,

whether with critical and deconstructive intent or as a twist, a gag and an additional way of engaging the spectators in the takes and double-takes of performative self-display. But, by the 1960s, a new urgency or uncertainty attached itself
to this kind of reflexivity: it was no longer enough simply to tell a story; a narrative had to reassure itself of its right to be, by recounting its own coming into
being, along with the story (and sometime in place of the story) which prompted
the act of storytelling in the first place. As the language of a cinema of crisis, this
modernist aesthetic nonetheless showed itself to be enormously inventive in
artfully transposing the doubling and mirroring – as hesitation, deferral, subter-
fuge or critical self-examination – into different narrative-pictorial forms,
whether through nested narration (a film within a film), through pictorial
framing which highlighted the constructedness of the *mise-en-scène*, or through
an accentuated paraphrasing of traditional plot stereotypes, genre patterns and
pastiche citations. The spectator no longer enters a film either through the
fiction of the transparent window or by crossing distinctly marked thresholds
one after the other. Whether one thinks of it in terms of the visual metaphor of
the mirror, moving forward while keeping one eye fixed on its own rear-view
reflection, or prefers the more Deleuzian image of "the fold" – indicating "the
inside of the outside", in which doubling is folded in upon itself, in such a way
that the recto cannot be separated from the verso[43] – it is clear that during the
1960s the altered terms of the relationship between spectator and film spoke to
anxieties and new possibilities as vividly as had the similarly "baroque" moment
when the cinema was first "invented". In retrospect, the extreme reflexivity in
the cinema of the 1960s has been seen to mark both the creative climax and the
swan song of European auteur cinema, from which it did not recover other than
by an ever more esoteric, cynical or frantic admission of its own artistry and
artificiality.

With 1980s post-modernism, however, belief in the critical possibilities of
reflexivity largely receded. The subsequent forms of irony and parody no longer
feed a dissenting impetus, but have become the emblem of a cynical and thus
ultimately affirmative stance. Nevertheless, one should not principally doubt
the critical possibility of reflexivity: better to distinguish between different
forms of self-reference in order to maintain a sense of the divergence of its uses
and contexts.

In "classical" cinema we are usually spared (or deprived of) the feeling that
we are sinking into an abyss or disintegrating into nothingness of self-multiplying,
endless reflections. Yet it is precisely this feeling of having the ground pulled
from under one that turns the mirror into a privileged place of ontological
uncertainty by virtue of the fact that the mirror absorbs the lack of groundedness of the cinematographic image and turns it into a double reflection. Lewis
Carroll's *Alice in Wonderland* was not the first text to explore the magical qualities

of the mirror, which can even turn the world (order) upside down and derail it. In cinema, however, – and there are few films without a mirror-shot drawing our attention to a pivotal moment in the plot or in the development of the protagonist – the function of the mirror oscillates between an ontological and a psychological one: often it points to the psychic instability of the hero or heroine.[44] Quite a number of famous film sequences focus certain key narrative moments as a look into the mirror: in Fritz Lang's M (GE, 1931) the child-murderer Beckert (Peter Lorre) grimaces in front of the mirror as if to mock the psychological profiling done by the police; in Jean Cocteau's ORPHÉE (FR, 1950) a mirror enables the mourning Orpheus to return to the land of the dead; and in Michelangelo Antonioni's L'ECLISSE (IT/FR, 1962, THE ECLIPSE) Vittoria (Monica Vitti) cannot and does not want to look at herself in the mirror. Similarly, in Roman Polanski's REPULSION (UK, 1964) Carol (Catherine Deneuve) has her first hallucinations in front of the mirror. Perhaps the most famous of all mirror scenes in this respect is the sequence from Martin Scorsese's TAXI DRIVER (US, 1975) in which Travis Bickle (Robert De Niro) addresses himself as the inimical Other ("You talkin' to me?!"), opening up new dimensions of abnormality in the hero's personality disorder.

Figure 3.6 M: the child murderer recognizes himself as being marked from the outside.

Figure 3.7 TAXI DRIVER (US, 1976, Martin Scorsese): the protagonist facing his hostile other/self in the famous mirror scene.

In numerous melodramas, women's pictures and noirs – from Lois Weber's SUSPENSE (US, 1913) to Cecil B. De Mille's THE CHEAT (US, 1915), from Orson Welles' THE LADY FROM SHANGHAI (US, 1947) to Robert Siodmak's PHANTOM LADY (US, 1943), from Douglas Sirk's ALL THAT HEAVEN ALLOWS (US, 1955) to R.W. Fassbinder's ALI: FEAR EATS THE SOUL (GE, 1973, ANGST ESSEN SEELE AUF), from Max Ophuls' LETTER FROM AN UNKNOWN WOMAN (US, 1948) to Todd Haynes' SAFE (US, 1995), from Nicholas Ray's BIGGER THAN LIFE (US, 1956) to David Lynch's MULHOLLAND DRIVE (US, 2001) – the mirror-shot marks a moment of rupture and doubling that simultaneously makes the spectator aware of how fragile the cinematic illusion is and immerses him/her deeper into the (often split) personality of the protagonist. We can contrast these "psycho-pathological" instances with the ontological – but also comic – use of the mirror in the Marx Brothers' DUCK SOUP (US, 1933) mirror routine, which had already been prefigured by Charlie Chaplin in THE FLOORWALKER (US, 1916) and by Max Linder in SEVEN YEARS BAD LUCK (US, 1921). It is restaged in an uncanny way with Arnold Schwarzenegger in Paul Verhoeven's TOTAL RECALL (US, 1990), as well as shifted into the register of hearing – rather than seeing – in David Lynch's LOST HIGHWAY (US, 1996), with the Mystery Man's (Robert Blake) invitation to Fred Madison (Bill Pullman) at a party to "call him" at his own home.

Mirror and face, perception, consciousness and action can be brought together in yet another way – and this is the third and final aspect of the mirror paradigm we want to turn to. It takes us outside traditional Film Studies into the area of cognitivism and neuroscience. The study of the mind has not only made remarkable advances in its own respective fields, but has increasingly also inspired scholars working in the humanities, not least in Film Studies. What has attracted special attention was the discovery in the mid-1990s of so-called

Figure 3.8 Duck Soup: the mirror as ontological groundlessness.

"mirror neurons" in the frontal lobes of monkeys, claimed by some as nothing short of a neuro-scientific revolution.[45] These neurons, whose presence in humans is beginning to be demonstrated as well, could help explain a series of psychological phenomena which until now have remained puzzling (e.g. human learning through imitative behavior, the possibility of empathy with others).[46] Mirror neurons are nerve cells activated in the brain when we observe others perform certain goal-oriented movements and actions: the exact same brain activity can be measured when we ourselves perform the operation (e.g. when we reach out for something with our hands) and when this same movement is observed by us being performed by another. Mirror neurons, therefore, seem to collapse, bridge or fuse the difference between active and passive, between inside and outside, between Self and Other. Some scientists are hypothesizing the existence of an entire system of mirror neurons, whose precise functioning and orchestration in the human brain, however, is yet to be clarified. From the point of view of these mirror neurons, there appears no difference between seeing and doing – and herein lies, of course, the potential that this new research field offers for film theory. Mirror neurons control not only motor mimicry, the key to human learning, but also empathy and compassion with other human beings. It should therefore be obvious why a scientifically verifiable theory of sympathy and empathy might well have far-reaching consequences for film theory – picking up where apparatus theory left off, or was deemed to be a failure, due to too many unproven assumptions.[47]

For the body of the spectator this theory implies a total wiring between the senses and the processing of information by the brain: body–brain correlation, motor-sensory control, seeing and doing (when considered from the perspective of brain activity) become one and the same. Apart from a few tentative essays (one of which is devoted to Bergman's PERSONA, the film we opened this chapter with),[48] we have yet to see what kind of overall theory of the cinema and the film experience these new theories will deliver around mirror and face. Perhaps the old polarity between phenomenological–realist and discursive–constructivist theories can be overcome and replaced with a more comprehensive one. Alternately, film theory could continue to reflect the dominant paradigms in the humanities, currently much pre-occupied with the uncertain status of the body in mediatized and technological environments, hence the interest in the senses and in mediated experience, in different modes of storage (memory, trauma, archive) and in contact (skin and touch), as well as in the transposition of dominant metaphors from the life sciences such as the computer as a model for the brain.

By way of summary and conclusion, it may help to survey the semantic field of the mirror once more, now concentrating upon its hidden paradoxes, antinomies and contradictions in order to render them productive. The first one is the *paradox of exteriorization and interiorization*. The passage from early to classical cinema can be described as a transformation in the status of screen space and auditorium space – from collective reception in "physical space" (supplemented by musical accompaniment, lecturers, performative interaction) to the individually absorbed spectator in imaginary space (that of the film's diegesis "centering" the viewer). The close-up concludes and seals this change from an actual to a virtual space, trading some gains (coherent diegetic space, immersion of the spectator in the narrative universe, linear time) against some losses (physical space, collective reception, cyclical time, direct address). Our discussion of the close-up's relation to intimacy and monumentality has shown how this transformation is based on an inherent tension: does the close-up exhibit an intimate monumentality or a monumental intimacy?

If we recall the first two modalities of the cinema (Chapters 1 and 2), a further *paradox of the mirror* emerges from the fact that window and frame, door and screen, once they lose their transparency and permeability, become this reflective surface: the mirror is thus, so to speak, merely the crisis form or limit-manifestation of the other two paradigms. Their respective transformation, it was suggested, has to do with the changing nature of the "contract" between film and spectator. At another, more philosophical and psychological level, the loss of transparency in the image is both increased and resolved by the appearance of the face: because something looks back, we no longer look through a transparent medium. We look at the face on the screen, and with it, at our own looking, now with transitive force. At the same time, the film spectator is accustomed to identifying with the look of others, and used to fusing with the look on the screen in order to avoid the look directed at the self. Within this constellation, the close-up oscillates between an increased self-reflexivity in which one's own spectatorial position is accentuated, and an increased identification in which one gives oneself over to another character. The face thus becomes a rather unstable representational object, even signaling the collapse of perspectival representation, if we want to put it in pictorial-representational, art-historical terms. The close-up would seem to simultaneously reaffirm and challenge the foundational calibration of classical cinema around the human body and "the camera at eye-level".

The face considered as an affection-image and close-up engenders another paradox, the *paradox of motility and inexpressiveness*. Even though we might say with Balázs that cinema rediscovers the face as an expressive medium, it does so by drastically reducing motility and mobility. When watching early films today, many spectators are amused by the theatrical style of acting and the ostentatious presentations of emotion: eyes wide open in horror, brows furrowed or the whole face wrinkled in a frown. The contemporary preference for minimalism in acting is evidenced for example in that today Buster Keaton, nicknamed "the great stone face", is often valued higher than Charlie Chaplin as a performer. Male actors are said to be great when they possess big eyes and largely expressionless faces: Henry Fonda, Paul Newman and the young Clint Eastwood. In ONCE UPON A TIME IN THE WEST (US/IT, 1968) Sergio Leone highlights the "desert landscape" of the classic face through alternations of panorama shots (Monument Valley) and close-up (Fonda's face). The smallest, almost imperceptible expressive movements of the face in close-up affect us most as spectators.

The *paradox of pure presence and decodable sign* brings once more to the fore the tensions between the mimetic–realistic and symbolic–semiotic theories, which constitute two main traditions in film theory. This tension becomes palpable in the "reaction shot" on a face as the standardized closing device of a soap-opera episode: on the one hand the over-dramatic expressivity produces an emotional surplus intended to generate affects strong enough to last until the following episode, which delivers the withheld "reverse shot". On the other hand, this affectively loaded image is not only wholly conventionalized within this particular genre, but also invested with narrative significance through its integration within a story, a significance that calls for a sign-oriented way of understanding, rather than "arresting" the narrative, as the close-up did in Dreyer, or as an insert shot does, in the "cinema of attractions".

Finally, the *paradox of scale and size* indicates once again how decisive space and the relation between spectator and screen are for the cinema. As we have already noted in the dynamic between monument and detail, the close-up oscillates between feeling intimately connected and overwhelmed by size. The close-up of a face is too close and too large, it produces a certain kind of emptiness because the proximity of the close-up allows (as the term already indicates) no stepping back. In this sense, the spectator is swallowed by space (as in THE BIG SWALLOW, and the opening of CONTEMPT) in that s/he loses all sense of proportion and cannot gain or retain a distance. The next chapter will detail the mechanisms that classical cinema has developed to control or overcome the instability that we have described through these paradoxes and which are a characteristic trait of cinema. And sure enough, a price will have to be paid for this anchoring.

Chapter 4

Cinema as eye
Look and gaze

Two men face each other sitting at a table on which devices are arranged that register eye movement as well as record and measure pupil dilation. The purpose of this set-up is to establish whether the test subject is human or a so-called "replicant", i.e. an artificial being with the external appearance of a biological organism. The interview proceeds in orderly fashion until the interviewee feels provoked by a question about his mother, upon which he pulls out a gun and shoots the interviewer with the words, "I'll tell you about my mother." This "Voight–Kampff test" can, by measuring empathy, supposedly distinguish between impassible replicants and empathetic people. Already the opening sequence of BLADE RUNNER (US, 1982, Ridley Scott) foregrounds the eye as its central motif. Initially, the eye functions as the organ of truth (and the soul) in a Cartesian sense, given that the boundary between a real human being and an artificial one is regulated by an eye test. On the other hand, it is not the active – searching, penetrating or investigating – eye that serves as a source of knowledge or defines this boundary. Rather, it is through the passive, receptive or reactive eye turned into an object of investigation that the distinction emerges in this science-fiction film. What complicates matters further is the fact that Deckard, the protagonist (Harrison Ford), who in contrast to the artificial beings seems to have neither a first name (normally a strong marker of individuality) nor strong feelings, in the end turns out to be a replicant,[1] while the emotionally more sensitive beings are the artificial ones, whose possession of memories makes the division of human and non-human even more fragile and porous, if not altogether untenable. Already the very first shot of the film reflects a series of distant gas explosions in a giant pupil, thus firmly establishing the central role of the eye while also alluding, through the motif of reflection, to the precarious status of the eye between subject and object, between being an agent or instrument of control and subject to overwhelming and disempowering sense-impressions.

In the present chapter we want to follow some of these leads: on the one hand we examine the role of the eye in cinema as an organ of world-disclosure

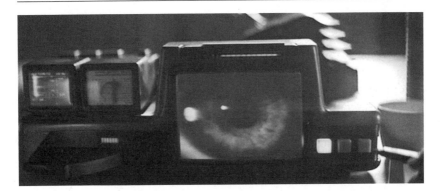

Figure 4.1 BLADE RUNNER: Voight–Kampff machines police the blurry line between humans and non-humans.

(because films make us discover the world primarily through sight) and, on the other hand, we discuss the unsettling and provisional nature of such disclosure as evidenced in those cases where the look seems to emanate from an a-personal or subject-less source. The look into the mirror, on which the previous chapter focused, presupposed a certain spatial arrangement within which the effects of doubling and splitting functioned as signs of reflection and reflexivity. The mirror also marked the point at which a character's action and its exteriority in relation to the body and the self gave way to an inescapable interiorization and subjectification. Unlike our first two "ontologies" of cinema, the window and the door, the mirror directly implicated the self in what it sees. With its focus on the eye and the look, the present chapter sets out to revisit these positions, to expand their inherent interaction and reciprocity, and thereby complicate them.

In the 1970s and 1980s, film theory saw the emergence of several positions which, on the one hand, were strongly influenced by Jacques Lacan's post-structuralist reworking of Freudian psychoanalysis and, on the other hand, built on Michel Foucault's theory of the panopticon as a model for both social control and subjectivity. In this perspective, the eye is the privileged point of convergence for various structures of visibility and looks which in film find their articulation in shot, framing and montage. Feminist film theory in particular has identified specific patterns of control and captivation (within the intra-diegetic space, between camera and characters, or between spectators and film) inherent in the look. Similar to the approaches discussed under mirror and face, such thinking presupposes that a certain distance, proper to "seeing" as a pure act of ocular perception, is maintained throughout. Unlike the frame or the window, however, this distance does not facilitate or regulate access to the diegetic world, but highlights the power potential of this arrangement and its promise or threat of mastery or possession.

If we regard the eye as an interface between spectator and film, we can distinguish among several configurations that shape the look and the activity of seeing in different ways. Even before they were adopted and further developed by the cinema, some of these configurations have long been culturally predetermined and deeply rooted in popular imagination. For instance, the eye is central to several myths of agency that range from the creative (or inner) eye of the Romantic imagination to the evil eye of the ethnic and cultural Other. The benevolent eye of an all-seeing Christian God (as depicted on the US dollar bill) translates into the democratic ideal of an eye that stands for transparency and visibility: the look of enlightenment and reason, characterized by light (*le siècle des lumières*) equates eye and sun as sources of knowledge. But the eye and the look can also be the occasion for an unrelenting demand for self-examination to the point of self-incrimination, as demonstrated by the witch-hunts of the Inquisition, by the Stalinist show-trials or any other type of extorted confession. In each case the guilt that one assigns to oneself is activated by the (imagined) gaze of the Other, which need not be transmitted through looking at all. Opaque and obscure, it can be invisible, while drawing its power in direct proportion to its capacity to remain outside the field of vision. The subsequent organization of the chapter will follow these two fundamental instances of the look and the gaze – on the one hand transparent and inoffensive, connoting knowledge and enlightenment, and, on the other hand, dark and malicious, associated with power and subjugation. Many of these configurations can also be found in the cinema, where they translate into the somewhat different dynamics of active and passive look on the one hand (with a clear division of subject and object, of power and subjugation), and the all-pervasive, surveillant and punitive eye on the other hand.

Before turning to these configurations in detail, a brief survey of the history of the eye in early cinema and classical avant-garde film is in order. The cinematic lens, from its beginnings, has often functioned as a prosthetic eye, serving as a mechanical extension of human perception. The world of a century ago, largely without aviation and private motorcars, knew only the railway as a readily available mechanized means of transportation.[2] Into this world, the cinema burst as an infinitely pliable, unfettered mobile eye: what a sense of elation it must have been to finally possess an organ that was no longer tied to the body and which, thanks to a mechanical invention, could roam and travel freely, could practically become invisible, was barred from almost no place (be it private, social or physical)[3] and not only seemed ever-present, but also made time travel possible – back into history and forward into the future, as for instance in Georges Méliès' LE VOYAGE DANS LA LUNE (FR, 1902, A TRIP TO THE MOON). No wonder, therefore, that films shot from the front or rear of railway trains (so-called "phantom rides"[4]) were immensely popular during the early days of the cinema, or that the arriving train has become such a powerful symbol for a force that overcomes all obstacles and reaches even the remotest reaches. The disembodied eye was celebrated as a strong illusion of power and omnipotence. One tends to forget that the voyeurism which was to become such an abiding preoccupation for film theory depends on forms of disembodiment, especially the idea of not having to take responsibility for one's bodily presence in a given space or at a given time.

Dziga Vertov's famous avant-garde film MAN WITH A MOVIE CAMERA (SU, 1929, CELOVEK S KINOAPPARATOM) can be read – in addition to influential recent readings by Lev Manovich, Yuri Tsivian or Jonathan Beller[5] – as giving expression to this jubilant eye, a sense-organ that discovers the world as if for the first time. When window shutters open in the beginning of the film as eyes onto a new day, and when the daredevil cameraman confronts an oncoming train in another scene to capture it on film without incurring bodily harm, Vertov's "cinema eye" appears disembodied and all-seeing. Indeed, he and his group of collaborators called themselves *kino-glaz* ("cinema eye"), evoking the mechanized seeing that challenges "the visual perception of the world by the human eye and offers its own 'I see!' "[6] In his writings and films, Vertov celebrated the technological dissociation of filmic seeing from the insufficiencies of human perception, i.e. the absolute, triumphal (optical) victory of film over the limitations of the human senses and the world they perceive. Walter Benjamin also enthusiastically welcomed the penetration of the human environment by the camera; for him, film facilitated access to the "optical unconscious", i.e. all those phenomena that for the first time become observable through enlargement, slow-motion, freeze-frame, eccentric angles and camera positioning, and time-lapse photography. In this respect, Benjamin sees film not as a realistic medium of representation, but endows it with the possibility of breaking open the urban space as well as regimented time:

> Our taverns and our metropolitan streets, our offices and furnished rooms, our railroad stations and our factories appeared to have us locked up hopelessly. Then came the film and burst this prison-world asunder by the dynamite of the tenth of a second, so that now, in the midst of its far-flung ruins and debris, we calmly and adventurously go traveling.[7]

This passionate and poetic enthusiasm for the capabilities of the camera to overcome the limitations of human perception is typical for the avant-garde of the 1920s and 1930s.[8]

In early cinema, the metaphorical role of seeing and of the eye is emphasized by the many prostheses with which they are related. In the previous chapter we discussed GRANDMA'S READING GLASS (GB, 1900, G.A. Smith), in which a

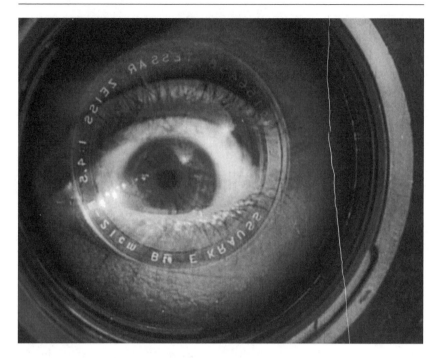

Figure 4.2 MAN WITH A MOVIE CAMERA: The "kino-eye" conquering time and space.

magnifying glass is used to explore not only the limited and enlarged world of the room of the sewing table but also grandma's piercing eye, making the spectator uncertain whether it is his/her own look that discovers grandma's eye or whether, on the contrary, grandma's angry look is directed at the spectator. Films like AS SEEN THROUGH A TELESCOPE (GB, 1900, G.A. Smith), THE GAY SHOE CLERK (US, 1903) and the French peephole films leave no doubt about the phallic nature of the probing, inquisitive eye: it is through the male gaze, aided by prosthetic devices, that the female body is being explored. These films seem to be giving away a secret that classical cinema would be more careful to camouflage – the (male) gaze of power on the (female) body is directly displayed in its voyeuristic nature instead of being narratively integrated.[9]

Similarly, the films of German Expressionism are often very explicit in their depiction of the pleasures and terrors of the eye: the heroes of films such as THE CABINET OF DR. CALIGARI (DAS KABINET DES DR CALIGARI, GE, 1919, Robert Wiene), THE STREET (DIE STRASSE, GE, 1923, Karl Grune) and NOSFERATU (GE, 1922, F.W. Murnau) are all "Peeping Toms" whereas Fritz Lang preferred to stage punitive looks: in the catacombs of METROPOLIS Rotwang virtually pierces Maria with the pointed beam of his flashlight before letting it glide over her, sadistically exposing and "undressing" her. DR. MABUSE has a hypnotizing look to which people (must) subject themselves, while Lang's early sound films M (GE, 1931) and THE TESTAMENT OF DR. MABUSE (GE, 1933) turn the complicated relation of seeing and hearing into a major resource of the films' disturbing power (see Chapter six). However, Lang's visual sadism (or that of his protagonists) is much surpassed by the opening scene of another film from the same period, Luis Buñuel's and Salvador Dalí's UN CHIEN ANDALOU (FR, 1928), in which the spectator is confronted in an almost unbearably direct manner with the simultaneous desire and vulnerability of the eye. In a parallel montage we see a (pointed) cloud (optically) pierce the moon while a man slices a woman's eye with a razor. Not only do we encounter here the "passive" eye familiar from the previous chapter as a window onto the soul (as in JEANNE D'ARC, FR,1928, Carl Theodor Dreyer) or as a blending of the "Self" with the "Other" (as in PERSONA, SE, 1965, Ingmar Bergman): we also experience in a brutally literal way the "gaze" of power. In UN CHIEN ANDALOU this gaze is represented by the man with the razor (played by Buñuel himself), whereas in REAR WINDOW it coincides at least briefly with the gaze of Mr. Thorwald (Raymond Burr) when he "returns" Jefferies' voyeuristic look of surveillance by storming violently and with murderous intent into the latter's apartment. In much of classical cinema, by contrast, such punishing gazes appear disembodied, displaced into

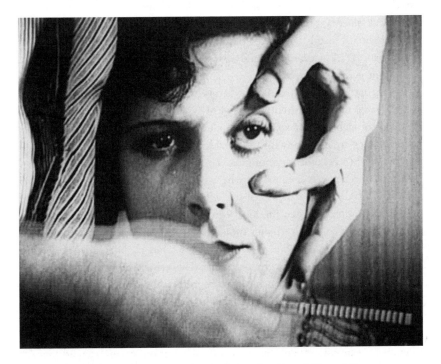

Figure 4.3 UN CHIEN ANDALOU: the desire and vulnerability of the eye.

an imaginary sphere, where neither origin nor direction and addressee are clearly determined. We will focus on this issue in the second part of this chapter; first, however, let us turn our attention to what we have called – using an extremely condensed formulation for a very complex issue – the "active" eye, and the corresponding look of power and desire.

To understand this mode of seeing in the cinema (as spectator) and mode of being of the cinema (as film), it is worth recalling Jean-Louis Baudry's "apparatus theory" (see Chapter 3). The paradigms discussed in the present chapter follow on from Baudry and Commolli, in that they emerged in opposition to, but also by building on, apparatus theory. This theory, it will be remembered, is based first of all on an analysis of the fixed and unchangeable arrangement of (disembodied, captive, and impressionable) spectators, (fixed) screen and (hidden) projector, all of which entertain a specific spatial relationship to one another. This arrangement creates an architecture of looks, linking camera, audience and protagonist(s) that turns the silver screen into an imaginary mirror of spectatorial desire. But several steps complicate this notion: Baudry initially premised his theory on an understanding of cinema as dream, but grounded this rather banal, and as we saw, misleading physiological analogy in key issues of Western epistemology and ontology: hence his return to Plato, particularly the latter's parable of the cave. Baudry's film theory – which should really be called a theory of cinema, given its emphasis on the specific situation of the audience in the cinema – readily supported both a Marxist critique of ideology and false consciousness (J.L. Commolli), and a psychoanalytic critique of ego-psychology and of bourgeois individualism.

It is the latter critique that Baudry's turn to Jacques Lacan brings to the fore, involving as it does a quasi-anthropological explanation for the predominance of the sense of sight and of vision in (modern) identity-formation. When born, human beings are not ready for the world, so to speak, depending on a nurturing "outside" to become autonomous. This evolutionary fact Lacan developed into a comprehensive account of why we are caught up in our self-images. Harking back to Freud's theory of the self (id/ego/superego), he also insisted on the distinction between the ideal ego and the ego ideal. When identifying with our ideal ego we are being subjected to the gaze of the Other, not by having internalized an Other (as our superego), but by imagining the Other looking, at the same time as we look at us. This critical look from outside we habitually adopt when we check ourselves in the mirror for posture, hair and attire – the steady restaging of the mirror-phase in any reflecting surface – and it demonstrates the everyday ordinariness of this drama of self-monitoring as self-consumption. The ego ideal, by contrast, is our idea of the person we aspire to emulate, our role model, our object of idealization, reverence and love. A conflict arises because the (imagined) look of the Other is never congruent with our own (narcissistic) look. If one takes these two sides of the ego together, it becomes clear why we can never "be" ourselves, always oscillating between ideal ego and ego ideal. It is this negative, forever divided view of human subjectivity and identity that Baudry imported into film theory. It suggests that the cinematic apparatus not only mimics Platonic idealism about the unknowability of the world other than through its reflection, but also re-enacts the inherently premature or incomplete nature of the human animal at birth, its lack of motor coordination, as well as its inability to provide for its own survival. The cinema thus offers the prosthetic experience of human ontogenesis, staging the drama of becoming "subject" in the form of compulsive repetition. Baudry's film theory is imbued with such deep pessimism that it qualifies as a genuinely "tragic view of cinema". A provocation to lovers of cinema, who did not relish seeing their "good object" tarnished, but also not welcome to all of those who, especially in the 1970s, wanted to believe in the liberating and progressive potential of film.

Given the radical implications of Baudry's theory, it is not surprising that certain aspects of it, if not the entire construction, were soon regarded as problematic. Here we want to focus on three areas of critique that proved to be particularly influential for subsequent developments: the function of narrative and narration, the role of gender and sexual difference, and the issue of the historical/empirical as well as the embodied/disembodied spectator. As to the role of the eye and the look in the filmic system of narration, we remember that Christian Metz distinguished between primary and secondary identification (Chapter 3), whereby primary identification – i.e. identification with the look of the camera, and thus with the act of filmic narration (or enunciation) – was so determining that it rendered secondary identification – i.e. identification with (the look of) individual characters – almost irrelevant from a theoretical point of view. The question that the emphasis on primary identification raises is therefore how to accommodate cuts and the shifts in camera perspective, i.e. how is it that the discontinuities and ruptures introduced through editing do not seem to break this "primary" bond with the spectator? Jean-Pierre Oudart, Daniel Dayan and Stephen Heath – still staying within Baudry's theoretical framework – devised an ingenious "solution" to this problem, which came to be known as "suture theory". The term "suture", borrowed from surgery, initially designated the stitching up of a wound after an operation, and came into film theory via Lacan and, in particular, through an essay by his follower Jacques-Alain Miller, when explaining the processes of binding or enfolding that pertain to subject formation.[10]

Without entering into its psychoanalytic ramifications, one can briefly summarize the meaning of "suture" for film theory as follows: given that it is based on the conflation of two looks, that of the camera and that of the spectator, different in time (that of recording and that of viewing), as well as a-symmetrical in agency (the active look of the camera, the passive look of the spectator), primary identification amounts to an ideological effect. It disguises how this fusion and reversal are brought about, and at what cost, making it inherently unstable. Or, as Stephen Heath puts it ironically: "[T]he eye in cinema is the *perfect* eye, the steady and ubiquitous control of the scene passed from director to spectator by virtue of the cinematic apparatus."[11] The moment of rupture introduced by editing potentially brings the otherwise hidden machinery of vision (the "apparatus") to the viewer's attention, and thus produces a moment of anxiety and loss, which the subsequent shot has to retrieve, bind up or stitch together, in short: has to *suture*. The shot does so – at least in so-called "continuity-editing" (see below, pp. 90–2) – by a match-cut, i.e. aligning the framing, angle, point of view of both shots, according to a set of rules that ensure that the second shot (cor-)responds to the first shot, either at the ocular level (for instance, by establishing a logic of "seeing–seen" between them, also known as "shot–reverse shot") or by answering an (implicit) question, like: "Where?" – "Here".) What may seem like a fragile bridge actually turns out to be an especially tight bond: the anxiety on the part of the spectators of losing coherence and the threat of being either abandoned or exposed become the very glue that makes her/him stick the more fervently to the filmic flow, which is to say, "identify" with its dominant look. Hence the appositeness of the term "suture" to mark the force or strength of continuity editing as the technique that not only ensures continuity and the sequential logic of actions, but also as the effect that "stitches" the viewing subject into the film thanks to rupture, rather than in spite of rupture.[12] As will be evident, a certain familiarity with the continuity system (which is often equated with classical cinema) is necessary to understand suture theory, so that a brief review of the key rules of continuity editing is in order.

Traditionally, "continuity editing" names the technique or the set of rules that allow for an inconspicuous compression of space and time at the same time as it creates and maintains a spatial and temporal coherence. How is this achieved? Cuts, i.e. interruptions of the spatio-temporal structure of a continuous shot, are usually "motivated" by the movement, action and interaction of characters, which also make the spectator overlook the cuts or perceive them as undisturbing. Decisive in this respect is the primacy of narration, to which all other filmic techniques of composition – including montage – are subordinated. Film is therefore understood primarily as a narrative medium, not as a medium of pure visuality of pictorial representation (as in the case of the avant-garde),[13] or as a medium of movement and time on an immanent level.[14] Historically, the system of continuity editing has been the dominant style of commercial cinema since the 1920s, so that even where a film does not conform to this system (for instance, Russian montage style, or many Japanese films from the 1940s and 1950s), it implicitly refers to this system by breaking or transgressing its norms, firmly established as these are in the minds of the world's spectators since the late 1910s. Films as different as BATTLESHIP POTEMKIN (see Chapter 1), UN CHIEN ANDALOU (FR, 1928, Luis Buñuel/Salvador Dalí) and THE IDIOTS (DK, 1998, Lars von Trier, IDIOTERNE) play with (and imply) continuity rules by strategically undermining them.

Thus, opponents of suture theory will argue that the logic of narration (or "narrative comprehension") provides a much simpler account for the efficacy and persistence of continuity editing (as well as its deviations), without the "ballast" of psychoanalysis.[15] On the other hand, it is significant that the continuity system bases itself primarily (if not exclusively) on looks: partly the looks of the characters within the diegetic world, partly imaginary ones, and that the spatial configuration of a film is defined by its lines of sight. One central element of spatial coherence, for instance, is the 180-degree rule: within one scene the camera remains on one side of the action. This side is formed by an imaginary line between major characters, and any crossing of the line is perceived as disruptive or at least as highly problematic. As the camera remains on one side of the action, consistent screen direction is maintained: a movement across a cut continues the (rough, i.e. left or right) direction of the movement because otherwise the axial line would be crossed. That is why soldiers rushing forward in a war film or characters fleeing in a slapstick comedy always move in the same direction from one cut to the next. At the same time, however, a cut must not be too close to the previous position of the camera: a shot should therefore deviate from the preceding one by at least 30–35° because otherwise the transition could be perceived as a disturbing "jump cut" (and, of course, the overall variation within one and the same sequence may not exceed 180° without crossing the axial line).

Additional techniques ensure that spatial continuity is maintained and that cuts are motivated by action. A case in point is the so-called "eyeline match" or "point-of-view shot" ("pov"), when we as spectators assume that the shot following the shot of a person looking (intensely) at something presents the object that the character looks at. Spectators interpret this sequence normally as being put in the character's perspective.[16] Generally speaking, any change in the relationships among characters and objects in a film is usually answered by a corresponding change in the type of shot, the passage motivated by movement. A cut in the middle of a movement is less obtrusive and disturbing because the spectator can follow the continuity of the action across the cut. The continuity of movement, therefore, has a stronger impact than the interruption caused by the cut. And, finally, parallel montage, the alternating presentation of two different plot strands – a discovery with which D.W. Griffith is usually credited

Figure 4.4 CASABLANCA: over-the-shoulder shot ensures continuity.

– gives spectators the impression of two simultaneous events. In Griffith's films, for instance BIRTH OF A NATION (US, 1915), various action strands converge and find their resolution in a common climax.

The question that arises from the above is whether these elaborate and quite specific rules of continuity are binding because of some "hard-wired" aspect of the psychology of human perception, or whether they are indeed ideologically or psychoanalytically determined, corresponding to some "geometry" of subject-formation or subjectification which the "rules" have merely codified and "naturalized". While scholars such as David Bordwell and Edward Branigan have offered detailed rebuttals of suture theory along the lines of cognitive psychology and the spatial logic of ordinary human perception, Slavoj Žižek has mounted a spirited defense of suture theory as more relevant than ever, when trying to understand a number of "post-classical" or art-cinema films, notably those of David Lynch and Krzysztof Kieslowski.[17] In other words, while for its advocates, suture theory explains some of the most powerful features of classical as well as post-classical cinema, namely the ability to weave the spectator not only into the external action, but also into the inner world of the protagonists through a sophisticated manipulation of look, gaze, framing and off-screen space, its opponents tend to see merely a metaphysical theory – proven neither experimentally nor empirically – because based on tenuous or tautologous assertions about the relation of perception to bodily integrity in the human infant.

The second main engagement with apparatus theory came from the ranks of emerging feminism and focused on the inscription and role of gender in Baudry's geometrical scheme. As much a refinement as a critique, this modification of apparatus theory also focused on the eye and the look: it posed the question of spectatorship not descriptively but in explicitly polemical terms. The center-piece of what came to be known as feminist film theory, "the look" dominated countless debates at least from the mid-1970s through the mid-1990s. If not its first, then by far its most succinct and successful, articulation can be found in Laura Mulvey's short but pithy essay, "Visual Pleasure and Narrative Cinema".[18] Historically, and for the discipline of Film Studies, Mulvey's theses represent a decisive moment. A manifesto of the second wave of feminism, its influence was not only foundational in film theory, but extended well beyond into art history, Cultural Studies and even literary theory. Most provocative – and finally, perhaps also most problematic – was its "anti-aesthetics", its radical iconoclasm and its stance against beauty and pleasure: "It is said that analysing pleasure, or beauty, destroys it. That is the intention of this article" (748). Mulvey, who builds both on Lacan's theory of the mirror stage and on suture theory, implicitly addresses various problems in Baudry's approach, while in a sense she shares his "tragic" view of cinema. Her main point of departure, however, is the idea that (narrative) cinema is structured primarily by a mobile, dynamic and wholly a-symmetrical configuration of looks. Following Christian Metz, Mulvey distinguishes among three types of looks that become important in conjunction with any cinematic experience: the look of the camera at the action, the spectator's look at the screen and, finally, the characters' intra-diegetic looks at one another.

These looks, which do not correlate with the looks of early film and avant-garde cinema but, instead, represent their "domesticated", narratively and spatially embedded form, are organized hierarchically in the Hollywood system and follow a logic according to which the first two (i.e. the look of the camera and the look of the spectator) are subordinated to, if not negated and replaced by, the third one (i.e. the looks of the characters). A classical film acknowledges neither the presence of the camera during the shooting nor the presence of the audience in the auditorium; instead, both are overridden by the above-mentioned rules of continuity. If the spectators are no longer folded and stitched into the diegetic fiction through looks, for instance when a character looks directly into the camera or when a character looking is not followed with his/her optical point-of-view, the seamless synchronization of spatial coherence and temporal succession starts to crack at the seams, as does spectator identification and narrative understanding. The result is a "cinema of displeasure" in which the usual subject-effects of plenitude or the ideological effects of illusionism deriving from smooth transitions and involvement in the filmic plot are foreclosed or denied.[19]

It is not only the classical *découpage* that fosters both the voyeuristic process whereby especially women are objectified and the narcissistic process of identification with an "ideal ego" that one sees up on the screen, but various other characteristics of the situation in the cinema add to these phenomena:

> Although the film is really being shown, is there to be seen, conditions of screening and narrative give the spectator an illusion of looking in on a private world. Among other things, the position of the spectators in the cinema is blatantly one of repression of their exhibitionism and projection of the suppressed desire on to the performer.
>
> (749)

Thus Mulvey formulates a psychoanalytically inflected theory of spectatorship: she locates film's power and fascination in two independent drives. The first is the pleasure of looking (what Freud called "scopophilia"), a pleasure which treats "other people as objects, subjecting them to a controlling and curious gaze" (748). This is apparent in the architectonic set-up of the cinema (darkness of the auditorium and brightness of the screen), as well as in the voyeuristic style of classical cinema, according to which the presence of the camera and of the cinematic apparatus, as well as the constructedness of the filmic discourse cannot be acknowledged openly (see above, p. 93). The other source of pleasure in cinema is located in a regression to an earlier stage of development, namely the mirror stage. As we saw in the previous chapter, in the mirror stage an infant of six to eighteen months identifies with its mirror image, which appears to possess more developed motor abilities. This originary moment of self-recognition is always already a moment of self-miscognition, and this is a decisive characteristic of subsequent processes of identification.

This shift of emphasis onto intra-diegetic looks and the disavowal of the spectatorial position gives, in patriarchal society, rise to yet another effect, which is central to Mulvey's text: "In a world ordered by sexual imbalance, pleasure in looking has been split between active/male and passive/female" (750). Mulvey's main argument contends that *in Hollywood cinema the normatively functioning hierarchy of looks is coded in terms of gender: the man looks, the woman is being looked at*. The decisive innovation of her approach is her turn from content to form, as she no longer criticizes the representation but the mode of representation. While preceding feminist texts had concerned themselves primarily with women's roles in films, focusing therefore on representation understood as mimetic realism, resulting for example in an influential study on the depiction

Figure 4.5 THE BLUE ANGEL: Dietrich as scopophilic object.

of women ranging from repression to rape,[20] Mulvey radicalized this critique by accusing *all* films of classical cinema – be they exponents of positive role models for women or not – of supporting the dominant phallocentric patriarchy and of perpetuating its structures.

Classical Hollywood cinema typically focuses not only on a male protagonist in the filmic narration but also assumes a male spectator (or a spectator coded as male):

> As the spectator identifies with the main male protagonist, he projects his look on to that of his like, his screen surrogate, so that the power of the male protagonist as he controls events coincides with the active power of the erotic look, both giving a satisfying sense of omnipotence.
>
> (751)

Only few genres such as the melodrama tend to have a female protagonist, and it is not by accident that these genres were often looked down upon as "women's films" or "weepies". An additional problem in these films is that they offer only a masochistic position of identification with the female protagonist (see below, p. 98). Furthermore, according to Mulvey, the presence of the woman in film

Figure 4.6 VERTIGO: woman banished from the symbolic order.

always denotes a lack because on a symbolic level a woman brings into play the threat of castration. In such a constellation the film has only two options to avert this "danger" of castration: fetishism or sadism. The woman is either elevated to the position of fetish (or part-object), and thus into the realm of the imaginary, as demonstrated according to Mulvey by Josef von Sternberg's films with Marlene Dietrich, or she is punished within the plot for her desire to see, and banished from the symbolic order, by "regressing" into dependency (for instance, in Alfred Hitchcock's films such as MARNIE, THE BIRDS or VERTIGO).

Mulvey's theses have been copied countless times and been reduced in this process to a checklist of psychoanalytic concepts such as fetishism, voyeurism, castration anxiety, phallus and disavowal. Generations of student essays have translated her complex if compressed argument into simple assertions such as "the look is male" or "woman as image, man as bearer of the look" (750), "[s]adism demands a story" (753) or "desire is lack". On the other hand, at least two generations of film theorists (whom we can only cast a passing glance at) have since the 1980s produced sophisticated commentaries on the narratological, gender-related and ideological implications of Mulvey's arguments about the cinema and the status of "sexual difference".

Among the most influential contributions to this ongoing dialog were – to cite only the book-length studies – Mary Ann Doane's transposition of Mulvey's model to the "woman's film", Teresa de Lauretis' complication of the identification model according to which the woman is always split between an identification with the passive (female) object and the active (male) subject, Kaja Silverman's inclusion of the acoustic dimension of cinema, Tania Modleski's study of women in Hitchcock, Sandy Flitterman-Lewis' analyses of the works of three French female directors (Germaine Dulac, Marie Epstein, Agnès Varda), and Barbara Klinger's historical contextualization of Douglas Sirk's melodramas.[21] The last two titles already suggest how film theory in general opened up toward historical investigations after the highly politicized but somewhat ahistorical studies published in the 1970s and early 1980s. What all of the above-named investigations share is the centrality of (male versus female) spectatorship, marked by the paradoxical loss of self (the voyeuristic and scopophilic pleasure of looking at other people, seemingly in secret) and the simultaneous empowerment of self (identification as a double moment of recognition, miscognition and the disavowal of this miscognition).

Mulvey's essay was also a major contribution to a virulent discussion in the 1970s and 1980s on the topic of women's representation in classical Hollywood cinema. The model that prevailed in the early 1970s can be called the role model thesis and had to do primarily with negative or positive stereotypes. These sociologically oriented content analyses were not particularly interested in the filmic mode of representation derived largely from formal parameters; instead, they aimed at a transformation of society through positive role models.[22] More radical voices from Great Britain – such as Pam Cook or Claire Johnston – accused these analyses of political and social naivety:

> If women's cinema is going to emerge, it should not only concern itself with substituting positive female protagonists, focusing on women's problems, etc.; it has to go much further than this if it is to impinge on consciousness. It requires a revolutionary strategy which can only be based on an analysis of how film operates as a medium within a specific cultural system.[23]

Related approaches that also drew their energy from the emerging theory of filmic narration were the "repression thesis" according to which women constitute an inconsistency and fragility in the textual system that film wants to hide and conceal under the surface.[24] The "disruption thesis" puts forward that the woman means "trouble" or "friction" for the system which generates in turn the core dynamic of a narrative progression concentrated on men. The woman, therefore, is necessary as a trigger (or catalyst) but she does not contribute at all to the resolution of the conflict or problem. The related "containment thesis" relies on the trope of woman-as-turbulence in order to set a narration in motion in the first place. Eventually, however, the woman must once again be "contained" so that the film may reach an ideologically acceptable ending.[25]

In the course of these debates, Mulvey's project was not only advanced but also criticized on a number of accounts, e.g. for constructing a heterosexist argument by implicitly or inadvertently setting heterosexual identification as the norm.[26] Her model leaves no room, so the argument went, for lesbian (or homosexual) identification, to which Mulvey replied in an essay that stressed "perverse" identification with the male look as a possible subject position for women.[27] Gaylyn Studlar has suggested that Mulvey overestimates sadism as a central source of pleasure, reminding us of masochism as the "originary" subject position in cinema.[28] Finally, Mulvey was criticized for portraying the ideological construction of a gender-specific identity as a successful hegemonic activity, although the patriarchal process of identity construction through cinema might be only partially successful, if not completely failing. From this perspective, Mulvey has been accused of not participating in the deconstruction of precisely the patriarchal structures that she criticizes and, instead, of supporting the ideology in its efforts to construct gender-specific identities through popular culture. By ascribing such great power to the patriarchal system, Mulvey indirectly risked consolidating this power by showing it as overly hegemonic.

It was precisely through analyses of individual films, cycles or genres that Mulvey's model of absolute dominance was softened and differentiated: in melodrama, critics working with different theoretical parameters, such as Linda Williams and Joan Copjec, have identified alternative socio-sexual and psychodynamic structures, whereas Mary Ann Doane has given the debate a Foucauldian twist in expanding melodrama to include the subgenre of "medical" women's films.[29] In horror film the gender-specific architecture of looks (to see/to be seen, intra- and extra-diegetic) shifts once again: Carol Clover has shown how the so-called "final girl", i.e. the girl who eventually hunts the monster down, extends an invitation to identify even to male teenage spectators, so that in cinema an alternative gender position can be tried out and exchanged in a playful manner, with no direct risks involved.[30] Even in relation to film noir and the femme fatale, some dissenting voices made themselves heard.[31]

A good case in point for the deconstruction of the male look as implicit norm and reference point is THE SILENCE OF THE LAMBS (US, 1990, Jonathan Demme), in which the female protagonist Clarice Starling (Jodie Foster) knows that she is being watched (by FBI agents, by Hannibal Lecter and by her superior), but she uses these looks as the source of a performative empowerment. This explains why the opinions of feminist critics about this film were split: on one side were those who saw the woman's role in this film similar to that in Hitchcock: exposed to the sadistic pleasure of men. On the other side were critics who took Starling to symbolize the new, post-feminist strong woman. This latter interpretation puts forward not only a positive (female) role model designed to demonstrate courage and determination but also a woman who must prove herself as a "professional" in a man's world. In the final showdown, Clarice knows that she is being watched without herself being able to see (the scene is set in the dark cellar of Buffalo Bill, who wears a device for night vision), but she retains control and keeps her finger on the trigger.

That THE SILENCE OF THE LAMBS caused an intense public debate demonstrates how, in the concrete context of cinema, the social force field can influence the reception of a film and therefore the "subject position" of the spectator(s).[32] The controversy played itself out among feminist theorists, as well as between feminist and gay activists. It was sparked by the film's "sexual politics", i.e. by the significance of Clarice's (and Jodie Foster's) sexuality and gender position. Gay activists, on the other hand, perceived Demme's film as homophobic because it pathologized homosexuality through the figure of James Gumb (or "Buffalo Bill"), the serial killer, transvestite and transsexual psychopath. From the perspective of empirical reception research (audience studies), the power structures in the public space of debate seemed much more important than the power structure inside the closed filmic (or textual) space between camera position (point of view) and subject position (suture).[33]

It is remarkable that the film could elicit such contradictory reception positions without becoming incoherent or losing its popular-cultural and mythological resonances. On the one hand, this demonstrates once again Hollywood's proficiency: how calculated and market-driven but also consciously ambivalent and ambiguous (post-)classical narration must be in order to offer and circulate such diverging reception positions in the first place. But, on the other hand, it also shows how problematic the relationship between the cinematic apparatus as a technology of seeing and making visible – which is cited and allegorized in a self-referential and knowing way in THE SILENCE OF THE LAMBS – and the resulting subject theory can be, especially when these two are mutually dependent on each other, as postulated by Baudry and feminist film theory.

Figure 4.7 THE SILENCE OF THE LAMBS: post-feminist empowerment or woman as object of the look?

Critics of the psychoanalytic and psycho-semiotic approaches in Film Studies have thus argued that "apparatus theory" bases itself on a similarly problematic assumption as Descartes: by separating the eye as a part of the brain from the eye as a part of the body, one gives precedence to the eye over all other organs of embodied sense perception, de-corporealizing it in the process. In short, such critics lament the focus in classical as well as Lacanian film theory on specular and visual perception because it systematically ignores the significance of the spectator's body as a continuous perceptive surface and as an organizing principle for spatial and temporal orientation even in the cinema. Apparatus theory, but also feminist film theory, thus strengthen, however inadvertently, the (bourgeois) ideology of looking at films in a disembodied, de-contextualized and dematerialized way, even while accusing mainstream cinema of producing alienated forms of human experience. Furthermore, in their efforts to theorize the cinematic experience, psychoanalytic film theories tend to treat the relationship between spectator and the screen as if it were based on a perceptual "illusion" (i.e. as if spectators believed that the objects seen on the screen were really present), when it is equally plausible to argue that what one sees are representations, i.e. symbolic constructions or culturally determined images. This has been the line of reasoning among many theorists inspired by cognitive theories of perception and comprehension, when discussing "identification" and spectatorship.[34]

In the following chapters (on skin and ear) we will come back to the question of embodied perception. For the moment, however, we want to address the question of the historicity of modes of seeing and forms of perception. As already mentioned several times, throughout the 1980s and 1990s film historiography had contributed to a transformation of the theoretical field. It may have been precisely because the (global) historical changes expected as inevitable in the late 1960s turned out to be illusionary in their anticipated form from the mid-1970s onwards that a new interest in history – partly archival, partly educational and sometimes even deconstructive – grew out of this disappointment and resignation. In Film Studies attention turned, among other things, to the "origins" of cinema,[35] and produced with the "new film history" a theoretically founded version of the previously unreflected positivist historiography.[36] In this process early cinema emerged as an independent field of study where new questions could be asked in a different form and backed up with empirical data. Feminist theory discovered early cinema as a public sphere in which women, unlike in classical cinema, were not marginalized or stereotyped, but were allowed both as producers and consumers a modicum of freedom and active participation.[37] Last but not least, in the larger context of the humanities and social sciences, post-structuralist investigations of historicity and the constructedness of history gave rise to a regenerative impulse toward historically oriented studies also about film and the media's relation to private and public memory.[38]

It is in this larger context that the third major critique of Baudry's theory can be located. It focused on the historicity of theory itself, and in particular on the historical imaginary underpinning Baudry's own, seemingly ahistorical, because universalizing theory. If one follows apparatus theory to the letter, then any engagement with individual films becomes mere illustration or decoration, since the immutability of the system would seem to crush any variation at the level of the individual work. However, it is quite striking that Baudry developed his influential theory at a time when the spatial arrangement, audience set-up and projection technology, with which his cinematic apparatus and its "metaphysics" are so intrinsically bound up, had already lost much of its supremacy and certainly its claim to "normativity". In the 1970s and 1980s it even appeared likely that the cinema in which this apparatus had first been used would not only hand over to television and its "channels", but that cinema as a public place was inevitably condemned to extinction. One can therefore assume that the insistence on the insurmountability and omnipotence of the apparatus in his theory was embedded in an ideologically symptomatic, contradictory relation to the dwindling influence that same apparatus began to have in practice. In other words: apparatus theory reacted to the crisis of cinema – which had been caused historically by the development of different audio-visual technologies and by changes in audience behavior – with a certain kind of mourning work vis-à-vis the cinema in which the loving, nostalgic look of the cinephiles gave way to a special kind of love–hate relationship in the face of cinema's looming demise.[39]

Given the focus of the present chapter, the look and gaze, too, cannot be exempted from this historicization of its own material, i.e. its technological, ideological and political conditions. This is why in the 1980s attempts were made to modify and refine Baudry's theses with the aim of understanding the subjectivities and subject positions shaped by the cinema as historically, socially and politically variable. Is it possible to treat the cinematic apparatus as an institution not only whose technologies but also whose psychic dimension can vary depending on the social context to which historical spectators are exposed? In their search for an answer to this question, film scholars have for instance turned to psychoanalyst Alexander Mitscherlich, who in his books about National Socialism and the "fatherless society" had diagnosed a type of look characteristic of modern societies. According to him, National Socialism is, among other things, a response to a "narcissistic offence" that modernity afflicted upon men by exposing them to a world of images and looks that do not reciprocate his own. Building on Walter Benjamin and Siegfried Kracauer who understood the conservative reaction to Weimar modernity in terms of an "aestheticization", Mitscherlich interpreted the public propaganda of images and media orchestrated by the National Socialists as a cultural revolution which tried to organize collectively the eye that returns the gaze, the eye of the benevolent father, and the look of the significant other.[40] These reflections proved useful insofar as they tried to uncover the historically determined conditions of a "political" history of the look and its ambivalences. The hypothesis of a form of exhibitionism that responds to an invisible look refers implicitly to various strategies of eluding the power of an authority (or of an apparatus of state surveillance) by perversely but productively exposing oneself to it. Popular culture – from the ostentatious carrying of garbage bags in the "punk" and "trash" scene all the way to Madonna's hyper-sexualized femme-fatale image – has often resorted to this strategy of performing (negative) stereotypes, in order to make them empowering, whether known as "pastiche", "parody", "signifying" or "hiding in plain sight".

Within film theory rather than Cultural Studies, the more influential models once again came from France: on the one hand, Jacques Lacan's conceptualization of "the big Other" to analyze the potential for power that we have previously called the opaque or dark look, and on the other hand, Michel Foucault's theorization of the "dispositif" of surveillance which he laid out most clearly in his commentary on the "panopticon", Jeremy Bentham's idea of a more "humane" prison. With this we have moved to the final part of this chapter, namely the look as "gaze" – the staring of power that appears to have no clear origin and is all the more powerful because of it, as the all-pervasive look of totalitarian states, certain types of prison architecture, but also our everyday security and control systems demonstrates.

The origin of the "gaze", i.e. of the look as a fixed stare or as a scopic regime of control and domination, cannot be located in any specific place or associated with any specific person. The term "gaze" encompasses both the historical (Foucault) and the structural (Lacan) dimensions of visual (power) relations. The gaze comprises, envelopes and dominates all individual looks due to its im- and trans-personal character. The gaze controls the visual field from "another scene" and enters the domain of the visible at best as a phantasm because, in a psychoanalytic sense, it belongs to the realm of the Real, which is to say, it functions as a force that is consistently outside any form of embodiment or representation. For (the later) Lacan and his followers (among whom Slavoj Žižek is perhaps the best known in the field of film), the Real is a domain paradoxically characterized by the fact that it cannot be defined other than in relation to what it is not: the Imaginary and the Symbolic, for which the Real marks both the boundary and the unbounded excess.

With specific reference to the gaze, the Real in Lacan's understanding signifies the uncanny fact that under certain circumstances the object of our look looks back at us. For him, the gaze belongs to the object, while look is of the order of the subject. Even though we may think that we can control our look and thereby an object as well, any feeling of voyeuristic and scopophilic power is always undercut by the fact that the materiality of existence, i.e. the Real, always transcends and breaks the meaning and significance that emerge in the symbolic order. One of Lacan's favorite examples, Hans Holbein's painting *The Ambassadors*, can help us to clarify the relationship between the look and the gaze. At first we recognize in the sixteenth-century painting two affluent gentlemen displaying emblems of wisdom, belief and wealth. As spectators, we get a feeling of mastering and controlling the scene visually until we discover a strange shape on the lower rim of the painting, a stain which on closer inspection reveals itself to be an anamorphic image: viewed from an acute angle the stain becomes a skull, which gazes at the onlooker. The fact that the object of the look (in this case the painting) returns our look serves as a powerful reminder that the symbolic order is separated from the materiality of the Real only by a thin layer of varnish. Normally, the Real lies at the outer limits of our perceptual horizon, still somehow within our field of vision, but not immediately recognizable, constantly present, yet not consciously so. It is only by putting oneself in a special position at an oblique angle that we can focus on the primordial force of the Real outside the pleasurable recognition afforded by the Imaginary and the social control of the Symbolic. The gaze therefore is external to the human subject, a force not controllable and assimilable, that can only be approached in the strangely twisted figure of watching oneself being watched.[41]

Figure 4.8 Hans Holbein: *The Ambassadors* (1533) – the Real as a stain on the symbolic order.

Slavoj Žižek, the most productive and original of Lacan's followers, but also a thinker who often deliberately polarizes, provokes and seems to leave no one indifferent,[42] has acted as an important intermediary in bringing Lacanian ideas to bear on contemporary as well as classical cinema. Practicing a kind of Socratic Hegelianism, his strength lies in the unexpected aptness of his examples, invariably drawn from popular culture, politics, news broadcasts, personal anecdotes and risqué jokes, as well as from opera, classical music, literature or philosophy. In the case of film theory, instead of using Lacan's highly complex conceptual edifice to explain contemporary cinema, Žižek chooses the opposite paths: he explains Lacan with the aid of examples borrowed from sometimes well-known, sometimes obscure, films, though Hitchcock and Lynch are clearly among his preferred directors.[43] Given Žižek's productivity – he has over 50 books to his name – it is impossible to do justice to his work in only a few pages.[44] What we shall do instead is to focus on a few motifs that are particularly relevant for our discussion of the gaze and the scopic regime.

VERTIGO, one of Hitchcock's best-known films, and also a Žižek favorite, can serve as an example. A key sequence in the film takes place in Ernie's restaurant. Scottie (James Stewart), a former policeman who is suffering from vertigo, but now works as a private detective, is sitting at the bar and sees Madeleine Elster (Kim Novak) for the first time, a woman he is supposed to tail, while she is having dinner with her husband in the back of the restaurant. Scottie is clearly enthralled by Madeleine's beauty, and he just cannot take his eyes off her. Yet twice in this scene we see shots of Madeleine that cannot be taken from Scottie's subjective position, although this is precisely what seems most logical and is also what Hitchcock interpreters tend to assume. Each of these shots is followed by actual shots from Scottie's point of view:

> We thus get, twice, the same movement from the excess of "subjectivity without subject-agent" to the standard procedure known as "suture" [. . .]. The excess is thus "domesticated," captivated in being caught within the subject–object mirror relationship [. . .]. What we encounter in this excess is the look as object, free from the strings that attach it to a particular subject. . .[45]

Žižek's re-reading of suture, as already indicated, is here not interpreted as a method designed to draw the spectator into the filmic fiction, but on the contrary, is given another turn of the screw (by Hitchcock reading Lacan, as it were, and keeping the shots un-sutured). Transgressing the norms of the classical style, Hitchcock makes visible, for just a second, the always gaping chasm between camera perspectives coded as "subjective" and the look of the camera when not attached to a human point of view. While, in terms of the story, the unsutured shots convey some of the hallucinatory power that "Madeleine" (as image) now has over Scottie, even though she is the "object" of his look, in terms of our theory, Hitchcock has given us an example of the gaze (the "object" looking at us) as it enfolds and overpowers the look (of Scottie). The gaze, in this sense, is the look "of an impossible subjectivity that cannot be located within the diegetic space".[46]

Similar, and yet opposed to Lacan in several respects, is Michel Foucault's famous theorization of the panopticon as a model of society and subjectivity: according to him, we have internalized the gaze of the Other and integrated it into our own subjectivity to such a degree that there is no longer a need for any (surveilling) person to uphold this system. The fact that we might be observed at any time holds us captive in this system even if no-one is fulfilling the function of overseer or inspector. The panoptical look emphasizes the fact of "being seen", and is little concerned with the active look that we discussed earlier. The flow of power is mainly one way, and when applied to the cinema, such an all-seeing eye tends to be associated with discipline or self-monitoring rather than with voyeurism or the inscription of sexual difference. Foucault once remarked, in a famous quote as if in response to the distinction made by feminist film theory between narration and spectacle:

> Our society is not one of spectacle but of surveillance [. . .]. We are neither in the amphitheatre, nor on the stage, but in the panoptic machine, invested by its effects of power, which we bring to ourselves, since we are part of its mechanism.[47]

Paranoia thrillers, such as they were popular in the 1970s (THREE DAYS OF THE CONDOR, US, 1975, Sydney Pollack; THE PARALLAX VIEW, US, 1971, Alan J. Pakula; KLUTE, US, 1971, Alan J. Pakula) and have had a come-back with the TV series 24 (US, 2001–, Fox); FLIGHTPLAN (US, 2005, Robert Schwentke) or EAGLE EYE (US, 2008, D.J. Caruso) in the atmosphere of post-9/11 concerns with the state security apparatus and its reaches into all spheres of life, readily lend themselves to a *mise-en-scène* of the panoptic gaze, now no longer central-ized, but dispersed over a myriad surveillances devices, of which, once again, not all have to be optical or concerned with vision. MINORITY REPORT is a state-of-the-art showcase for all kinds of surveillance and monitoring devices, even including an actual panopticon, as if to provide its own "archive" of obsolete technologies.

If one were to use Foucault's notions of discipline and control in order to deconstruct the acts of seeing and looking in a film, one would have to search not only for gender-specific imbalances and asymmetries but also for the way that vision and knowledge are a-symmetric in relation to each other: to see is no longer to know, i.e. ocular verification is no guarantee of truth. Likewise, the structures of political or economic power are rarely visible, and often too complex or volatile, for human beings to claim "knowledge" in the sense of mastery. Gilles Deleuze once described Foucault's concept of the gaze as his "folds of vision", in order to distinguish it from the ocular pyramid one associates with perspectival vision: "an ontological visibility, forever twisting itself into a self-seeing entity, on to a different dimension from that of the gaze and its objects."[48] The panoptical gaze of surveillance, despite the clear geometrical hierarchies that enable its functioning, is thus less tied to an eye than it signals a continuum from inner eye to external monitoring, implicating the gaze of someone who is looking but also the gaze emanating from an empty space, modeled both on power enforced by vision and power relayed by human conscience into "self surveillance".

Finally, Foucault and Lacan are not the only thinkers according to whom the (imagined) gaze of the Other upon the Self is constitutive of the development of subjectivity. In systems theory, Niklas Luhmann has also elaborated on the role of observation of first and second degree in the construction of identity:

> Individuals are self-observers. They distinguish themselves through the fact that they observe their own act of observation. In today's society they are no longer defined by their (more or less good) birth, nor by origin or traits that set them apart from all other individuals. Whether baptized or not, they are no longer "souls" – in the sense of indivisible substances – that guarantee them eternal life. It is often said of Simmel, Mead, or Sartre that they gain an identity only through the looks of the others; but this happens only if they watch themselves being watched.[49]

If we see in Luhmann's concept of modern self-observation a new societal model, then it coincides with what Deleuze has termed the control society, which he predicted was in the process of replacing the disciplinary society, analyzed by Foucault in his books on the history of prisons, of clinics and of human sexuality: not only does power become modular and flexible, developing ever new forms of binding libidinal energies to work and the body, but vision and visuality are no longer the guiding principles regulating subjectivity: the cinematic apparatus, regardless how we define it, is less in need of a theory capable of deconstructing it than it is threatened by obsolescence: overtaken by mechanisms of power and pleasure directly engaged with the body.[50]

But this already takes us into a realm that has more to do with the body and embodied perception than with the paradigm of the eye that we have explored across two interrelated aspects: on the one hand the active and passive eye of seeing and being seen in feminist film theory, and on the other hand the impersonal gaze that, subjectless from an unspecified position, exerts all the more control. The shift of focus in the following two chapters to the body and its perceptive surfaces, through the concepts of skin and ear, parallels the developments just sketched and marks a movement toward a stronger anchoring of filmic experience in the spectator as an embodied being.

Chapter 5

Cinema as skin and touch

Already with its title, CRASH (US, 2004, Paul Haggis), the 2005 surprise Oscar winner, announces a physical collision of bodies. The first dialog in the film confirms and develops this theme when images from an accident are accompanied by a voice-over lamenting the fact that the inhabitants of L.A. barricade themselves in their cars and compensate for this lack of contact through occasional violent collisions. One of the main characters, Detective Graham Waters (Don Cheadle) can be heard saying:

> It's the sense of touch. In any real city, you walk, you know? You brush past people, people bump into you. In L.A., nobody touches you. We're always behind this metal and glass. I think we miss that touch so much that we crash into each other, just so we can feel something.

The interwoven episodes of the film revolve around the idea of inter-personal contact and the impossibility of communication and understanding. But this is not the only reason why we have chosen this film as an emblematic entry into this chapter. There is another way in which CRASH highlights the paradigm of cinema as skin: it draws a picture of Los Angeles that is characterized by mis-communications, but also over-determined by racism and ethnic prejudice. The skin colors and bodily exteriors of African-Americans and Asian-Americans, of Hispanics and Iranian exiles, create a thematic resonance through which the film counterbalances its episodic structure. Even on a metaphorically and semantically more slippery level, the film remains committed to the skin-and-contact-paradigm: characters are stereotyped by virtue of their "prison-tattoos"; a magic cape protects the body of a five-year-old miraculously from a bullet, whereas St. Christopher, the patron saint of travellers, does not grant this kind of salvation to a young hitchhiker; and a racist policeman humiliates an affluent African-American woman by sexually molesting and assaulting her under the pretext of a strip-search. Time and again characters try to establish real contact, get under

Figure 5.1 Crash: interpersonal, interracial contact.

each other's skin and beyond the façade of the other – and time and again these attempts at somatic, affective, and haptic understanding shatter on the soft, but for all that, seemingly impenetrable surface of the skin. They fail because the skin is more than a "neutral wrapping" for the body; it is a culturally and seman-tically charged surface of interaction and communication.

For a long time an ocularcentric paradigm prevailed in film theory that gave precedence to approaches focusing on vision. This dominance began in the 1920s when Rudolf Arnheim imported so-called "Gestalt" theory into film theory and Béla Balázs emphasized the significance of close-ups. Eisenstein's constructivist montage theories and Bazin's conceptualization of reality as an ambiguous yet indivisible appearance of being whose basic ontological form is cinema also center on the eye as the organ of visual perception (see Chapter 1). Finally, the dominant theories of the 1960s and 1970s privileged the act of seeing even more than earlier theories: apparatus theory transported the seeing humans into Plato's cave, whereas feminist film theory was governed for a long time by key words and phrases such as voyeurism, fetishism, exhibitionism and the male gaze.

It would, of course, be absurd to deny the centrality of the visual sense to cinema, but, as we have tried to show in the previous chapter, the eye/gaze constellation contains its own aporia: the modern subject, these theories contend, is constituted by the gaze, a specular regime that does not "return the gaze", and in the final analysis, has no single location or viewing instance attached, but in its panoptic, all-seeing reach, is the more powerful for it. This self-constitution of the subject, turned to the outside, is supported by the domi-nance of public (media) spectacles which also do not "return the look", but require participating onlookers, voluntarily enforced exhibitionism and perfor-mative masquerade. The spectator is thus exposed to countless looks or orches-trations of seeing, behind which one easily assumes pervasive and perverse f surveillance, control, deception and manipulation. Another, rather irmative or acquiescent reaction to this public spectacle of visibility is to use exhibitionism and display as technologies of the self: no matter if we look at *Big Brother*-type reality soaps, make-over shows, or narcissistic performances of self online (YouTube, MySpace, Flickr, the blogosphere) – individuals seek to catch or capture the look of the Other for the construction of Self. Whether this need is being produced by the media that feeds on it, whether this happens to be an anthropological constant, or whether this is the *condition humaine* of (post-)modernity, is a question we cannot answer here. Either way, the media produces (and the cinema mediates) the deadlocks of our (post-)modern regimes of vision, always on the verge of "pathologizing" the spectator, who is at the same time participant and observer of the spectacle.

No doubt this emphasis on surface display is one of the reasons why there has been a resurgence of theories, often filed under headings such as phenomenology, synesthesia and intermodality, which include forms of sense perception other than those concentrating on the visual and its internal contradictions. The approaches presented in this (and the following) chapter are therefore not predicated on a negation of the visual, but rather attempt to understand the senses in their interplay and perception as embodied, as well as to theorize this embodiment in its own complexity. Vivian Sobchack, possibly the key thinker of the approaches in this chapter, summarizes the critique of ocularcentrism as follows:

> Until quite recently [...] contemporary film theory has generally ignored or elided both cinema's sensual address and the viewer's "corporeal-material being". [...] [M]ost film theorists seem either embarrassed or bemused by bodies that often act wantonly and crudely at the movies, involuntarily countering the fine-grained sensibilities, intellectual discriminations, and vocabulary of critical reflection.[1]

This is why this chapter will focus on the "return" to the body as a complex yet indivisible surface of communication and perception. On the one hand, it examines positions that conceptualize cinema as a specific kind of contact, as an encounter with the (racially or culturally coded) Other – for instance in postcolonial approaches and those that focus on inter-cultural cinema. On the other hand (often these two positions converge or overlap to a certain degree), it introduces approaches predicated upon the idea of skin as an organ of continuous perception that understands cinema also as a haptic experience. The intercultural and the phenomenological schools correspond to a fascination with the human body, its surface and vulnerability – all of which are important themes in the cinema of the past 20 years.

This change of paradigm is not only discernible in film theory, but it reso-
nates with broader cultural trends, once again showing that film theory cannot
be conceptualized in isolation. In popular and high culture alike, skin has become
a field of rich semantic references, as documented, among others, by Steven
Connor, for whom "skin has never been more visible".[2] Claudia Benthien's
literary study *Skin: on the Cultural Border Between Self and the World*, for
example, demonstrates that skin as a symbolic interface between Self and the
outside world can be seen as a privileged locus for many discourses, images,
fantasies and desires. Benthien argues that skin has become a central metaphor
of division and of boundary situations in the twentieth century, by which the
possibilities and impossibilities of encounters and limit experiences of all kinds
are depicted and mapped. In the eighteenth and nineteenth centuries, by contrast, skin was also associated with abstract notions, body images and figures of
thought that "covered" a wide spectrum of themes – such as penetration or
exposure, armoring or stigmatization, sheltering or peeling off. This way, the
body surface was transformed into the site of negotiation for differentiated and
oftentimes politically explosive identity questions.[3] It would almost seem that
contemporary cinema is re-claiming the cultural–historical terrain that modern
literature renounced and abandoned, this time in terms of its own medium.

A brief excursus can help explain why in many respects skin still provides an
important semantic and metaphorical field even for contemporary identity politics – beyond the political question of skin color. The skin is an organ, our
largest, and yet we are incapable of observing it from an external position. Skin
thus negotiates and re-distributes the relation between inside and outside; it
designates a transitional and uncertain liminality with respect to where the self
becomes the world and vice versa. Skin also leads back to the close-up in its
dramatization of scale and size (see Chapter 3): on the one hand, skin is every-
where around us, exceeds us as an individual, and on the other hand, its particular grain and structure is not visible to the "naked eye". In this respect, skin
touches on a central hypothesis of the present study, namely that, in the cinema,
the confusion, transformation and transgression between "inside" and "outside",
between Self and Other, is of a foundational nature, inherent and ingrained, and
thus justifies cinema's ongoing relation and proximity to the body.

Skin has a life of its own. When we blush or go pale it is outside our control,
yet again it is part of ourselves and bound up with our affective responses. Skin
is mutable: it can peel off, blister, grow callused and shed itself. It is alive but
also dies all the time, existing in an accelerated cycle of death and renewal,
without us being aware of it. Not coincidentally, the term "skinning" implies
the shedding of an old identity. Skin is an envelope and thus endless and seamless, but skin also evokes the cut, the incision and the mark, the scar and the
gash. Skin is also gender-determined in culture: soft for women, taut for men,

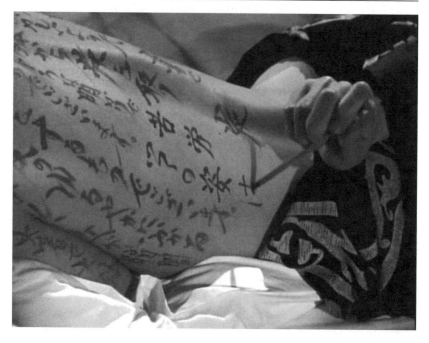

Figure 5.2 THE PILLOW BOOK: skin as writable surface.

light for women, dark for men. Acne scars can be seen as masculine, because male skin is seen as a carapace or armor, while women's skin must be yielding and smooth. Male skin is an envelope or container, while women's skin is more of a surface that can be used as a movable aperture or window to be regarded: the site of display for jewelry and necklaces, female skin is the canvas on which endless dramas of hiding and revealing, of self-exposure and modesty, of presentation and shame, or veiled allure and absolute vulnerability are played out and staged. The depiction of the skinless woman is culturally taboo because, historically and artistically, the female is represented by her skin. By contrast, the skinless – or flayed – man has sometimes presented a positive image of (self-)liberation: the artist as hero from the Marsyas myth through Michelangelo's self-portrait in the Sistine Chapel all the way to Robbie Williams who first strips then skins himself in the video *Rock-DJ* (2000) in order to attract the attention of attractive women.

Yet approaches linked by their interest in skin and contact are not only a reaction to the neglect of the body and embodied perception in film theory. The fact that the eye/gaze paradigm may have reached an impasse becomes apparent also when we think of films that present the privileging of sight in such an ostentatious and excessive way that one may speak of them as a pastiche or even parody of ocularcentrism.[4] In the beginning of the previous chapter we already

mentioned that BLADE RUNNER (US, 1982, Ridley Scott) openly exhibits the eye
as a key motif (one only has to think of Roy Batty's [Rutger Hauer] quip to the
genetic designer of his eyes: "If only you had seen what I have seen with your
eyes"). Also, Stanley Kubrick's A CLOCKWORK ORANGE (UK, 1971), which
begins with the close-up of an eye and Steven Spielberg's MINORITY REPORT (US
2002), which features portable eyes and eye-like spidery creations providing
information about imminent crimes and eyes as grotesquely disembodied identity indicators that float in a plastic bag like ornamental fish, whereas an eye-
scanning technique is used to recognize and personally greet clients in a
department store, display the ocularcentric paradigm to such a degree that one
can at least make out a tipping point. Whenever films knowingly stage and
flaunt a theoretical model, whenever theory looks back from the film as if it
were making fun of itself, we realize that possession of a theory does not necessarily give us an advantage over the film.

Another film we have discussed in the last chapter, THE SILENCE OF THE LAMBS
(US, 1990, Jonathan Demme), illustrates this ambivalent status of knowledge
(outside or inside the film/spectator) very clearly. The film stages the ocularcentric paradigm so "openly" that it, too, can be read as pastiche. In classic feminist theory, the male occupies the central position as agent and subject of the gaze
– man looks, the active subject, while woman is being looked at, passive object
(see Chapter 4). Now, the protagonist Clarice Starling (Jodie Foster) becomes
repeatedly the object of gazing scrutiny by men, but she is well aware of her
"to-be-looked-at-ness" which is ostentatiously demonstrated when she is surrounded by several tall FBI agents, all dressed identically, stressing the gender
divide. Yet again, as an FBI agent, she also possesses the phallic power of the
weapon which was traditionally reserved for men. In the final sequence of the
film, when the serial killer Buffalo Bill follows the heroine with the help of a
phallus-like night vision device, he becomes a parody of the voyeur who ends up
helplessly on his back kicking his legs in the air: more insect than human, more
Kafka's Gregor Samsa than Hitchcock's L.B. Jefferies. Clarice Sterling's second
antagonist is Hannibal Lecter, who holds absolute power but has no "view" (he
yearns for the Florentine "Belvedere" or a room "with a view"), which is why he
exercises his power not so much through the gaze as through his body and mind
– cannibalism and psychoanalysis are his weapons. When shifting the theoretical
focus from gaze to skin, the film could be said to signal a change of paradigm:
Buffalo Bill is driven by the pathological desire to vest himself in someone else's
skin. In this respect, the motif of "the skin", of skinning and sewing together, of
enfolding and pupating oneself, of transforming and re-styling oneself, is just as
central as the motif of the eye and the gaze. THE SILENCE OF THE LAMBS could
therefore be understood as a transition film in which the paradigm of the skin is
explicitly contrasted with and played off against that of the eye.[5]

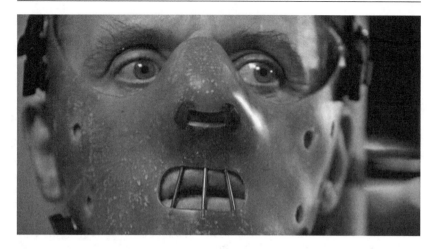

Figure 5.3 THE SILENCE OF THE LAMBS: mouth as threat.

A glance at Terrence Malick's THE NEW WORLD (US, 2005) underlines the
fact that not only film theory has undergone a transformation, but many contemporary films also revolve around the same theoretical preoccupations.
When approached with the tenets of narratology (see Chapter 2), THE NEW
WORLD slides away time and again since its plot links are extremely loose. Also,
the structures of looking (see Chapter 4) is undermined when the film evokes
the classical logic of continuity, but then withholds the reverse shot or the
eyeline match. A weightlessly floating camera glides over land and water, not
bound to any anthropomorphic point of observation, while the alternating
voice-overs make it impossible to discern a consistent and unitary focalization.
The film forcefully stages the failed communication and collapsing understanding between the early British settlers of what is today the US-state of Virginia
and the indigenous population as a series of contacts and bodily encounters that
unfold across haptically charged surfaces. Fabrics and materials, animals and
weapons, human skin and clothing, construction materials and bodily fluids,
grass and trees – the tactile properties of living and non-living things structure
the world just as much as communication, which relies on touch because of the
incompatibility between linguistic and cultural systems. In classic Hollywood
cinema, encounters with native Americans are conveyed primarily through the
landscapes of Westerns, with their prairies, ridges and canyons (Monument
Valley, Rocky Mountains and the Great Plains) in which Indians were always
depicted through the colonial eye both as an impending danger and as an impos-
ing apparition, as a colorful spectacle or as something camouflaged by the landscape until the moment of sudden attack. Malick's post-colonial gaze, however,
not only reveals the aforementioned change of paradigm from eye to skin as an

Figure 5.4 THE NEW WORLD: tactile encounter.

interface of contact and communication, but it also comes closer to the historical truth that so many native Americans perished not in battle, but from cough-
ing, typhus, venereal diseases, alcohol and other forms of contamination
resulting from their contact with the colonialist Other.

From this perspective, the shift to touch/skin becomes also a (possibly perverse) answer to the deadlock at the level of eye/gaze, an alternative set of
agendas rather than merely complementing the visual with the haptic in the
concert of the senses as synaesthetic *Gesamtkunstwerk*. In any case, there is no
emphatic notion of progress involved in the transition to contact, as the relationship remains deeply ambivalent. For, as we have seen in the example of CRASH,
or in the case of Buffalo Bill's pathological need to dress himself in someone
else's skin, the call to "reach out and touch someone" is itself fraught with its own
inner contradictions: this alternative, idealized as more equal or "level" form of
intersubjectivity, when compared to the hierarchical pyramids inscribed into the
scopic regime, will have its unintended consequences too. The value of touch/
skin as a cognitive model may thus not be carnal comprehension, but rather point
to violent collisions, murderous over-identification and ingestion, ethnic mis-
understanding and racist prejudice. CRASH illustrated this accurately, when the
attempts at empathic understanding invariably revert to their opposite: in the
film, anger hides a desire for tenderness, aggression is a perverted form of love,
while sexual harassment and the horror of being touched by someone become
the most common reactions to the Other's proximate body. The shift from look
to touch therefore does not mean the shift from a surveilling, controlling and
punishing eye to a caressing hand, but the skin holds contradictions one should
not ignore if one does not want to overburden a new paradigm with the demand
of solving all the problems accumulated by previous theories.

How can we then reasonably think about skin? On the one hand, skin is only
a cover, the unexpressive surface of the body which reveals nothing about the

functioning of the organs and vessels, the mind and spirit that lie hidden beneath it. From this perspective – which one could call hermeneutic – the surface conceals a hidden structure which one wants to reach analytically or diagnostically. On the other hand, today's culture displays a deep fascination with skin as a means of expression and surface of inscription, especially if we think of the ubiquity of tattoos and piercings, suggesting that much that used to be kept "inside" now wants to be exposed and displayed. The skin is therefore always ambivalent: on the one hand, an endless surface without beginning or end, similar to the Möbius strip, and, on the other hand, more than a wrapping for the body, but a semantically productive expanse. With respect to cinema, the positions centered on skin and contact concur to the extent that they all accord more significance than previous theories to the body in the relation between screen and spectator: "[W]e do not experience any movie only through our eyes. We see and comprehend and feel films with our entire bodily being, informed by the full history and carnal knowledge of our accultured sensorium."[6] Even if the body is often forgotten or not consciously experienced by spectators while watching a film, it nevertheless represents the irreducible condition of the possibility of sensory and aesthetic experience.

Building on Maurice Merleau-Ponty's phenomenology, Vivian Sobchack has developed a film theory in which intellectual understanding and cognitive skills are complemented by a strong bodily component. The process is circular or self-reinforcing: film is the expression of an experience, and this expression is itself experienced in the act of watching a film, becoming as a consequence the experience of an expression: "an expression of experience by experience."[7] In a chiasmus, a rhetorical inverted parallelism of words, following Merleau-Ponty,

Figure 5.5 EASTERN PROMISES: skin as a marker of accomplishments.

Sobchack suggests that this double structure is not sublatable into a dialectical synthesis, but, rather, always persists in a re-convertible form:

> [C]lassical and contemporary film theory have not fully addressed the cinema as life expressing life, as experience expressing experience. Nor have they explored the mutual possession of the experience of perception and its expression by filmmaker, film, and spectator – all *viewers viewing*, engaged as participants in dynamically and directionally reversible acts that reflexively and reflectively constitute the *perception of expression* and the *expression of perception*. Indeed, it is this mutual capacity for and possession of experience through common structures of embodied existence, through similar modes of being-in-the-world, that provide the *intersubjective* basis of objective cinematic communication.[8]

The intersubjective communication in the cinema between spectator, film and film-maker is predicated upon and enabled by shared structures of embodied experience that permits the perception of experience and the experience of perception in the first place. We take in films somatically, with our whole body, and we are affected by images even before cognitive information processing or unconscious identification addresses and envelops us on another level. Sobchack emphasizes the irreducibility and intrinsic nature of somatic and intermodal perception because no single sense ever functions in isolation. In an analysis of the first few shots in THE PIANO, she posits that her fingers "knew" before her visual perception and conscious recognition what could be seen on the screen: namely the look through hands that one holds before one's eyes.

> As I watched *The Piano*'s opening moments [. . .] something seemingly extraordinary happened. Despite my "almost blindness," the "unrecognizable blur," and resistance of the image to my eyes, *my fingers knew what I was looking at* – and this *before* the objective reverse shot that followed to put those fingers in their proper place (that is, to put them where they could be seen objectively rather than subjectively "looked through"). What I was seeing was, in fact, from the beginning, *not* an unrecognizable image, however blurred and indeterminate in my vision, however much my eyes could not "make it out". From the first (although I didn't consciously know it until the second shot), my fingers *comprehended* that image, *grasped* it with a nearly imperceptible tingle of attention and anticipation and, offscreen, "felt themselves" as a potentiality in the subjective and fleshy situation figured onscreen. And this *before* I refigured my carnal comprehension into the conscious thought: "Ah, those are fingers I am looking at." Indeed, at first, prior to this conscious recognition, I did not understand those fingers

as "those" fingers – that is, at a distance from my own fingers and objective in their "thereness." Rather, those fingers were first known sensually and sensibly as "these" fingers and were located ambiguously both offscreen and on – subjectively "here" as well as objectively "there," "mine" as well as the image's. Thus, although it should have been a surprising revelation given my "almost blindness" to the first shot, the second and objective reverse shot of a woman peering at the world through her outspread fingers really came as no surprise at all. Instead, it seemed a pleasurable culmination and confirmation of what my fingers – and I, reflexively if not yet reflectively – already knew.[9]

Sobchack's eloquent description of this scene implies that a theory based upon embodied perception such as phenomenology has to develop a different understanding of identification. In the previous chapters we have summarised a number of models describing this specific relation between film and spectator: Christian Metz, for example, distinguished between primary and secondary identification in which the former indicates the identification with the perceptual act which produces the film in the first place, while the latter refers to identification with the fictional characters. Neoformalist approaches are searching for cues that suggest a certain (cognitive, emotional) alignment of character in the film and spectator in the cinema. Both theories, no matter if psychoanalytically or cognitively inflected, locate the relationship between film and spectator on an abstract mental plane. Sobchack and other phenomenologists by contrast posit a double and simultaneous appropriation of a position of sympathy vis-à-vis the other, in which the self-awareness of one's own embodiment

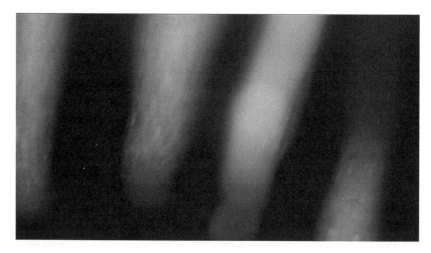

Figure 5.6 THE PIANO: fingers to be understood intuitively and somatically.

is the radically irreducible condition of empathy in the Other or another situation.

Film experience is therefore not principally different from other forms of experience, as perception presupposes subjectivity located in a living body.[10] By extension, the (film) image and the (spectator's) body cannot be contrasted according to the semiotic distinction between signifier and signified, as Steven Shaviro emphasizes:

> Cinema's greatest power may be its ability to evacuate meanings and identities, to proliferate resemblances without sense or origin. [. . .] There is no structuring lack, no primordial division, but a continuity between the physiological and affective responses of my own body and the appearances and disappearances, the mutations and perdurances, of the bodies and images on screen. The important distinction is not the hierarchical, binary one between bodies and images, or between the real and its representations. It is rather a question of discerning multiple and continually varying interactions among what can be defined indifferently as bodies and as images: degrees of stillness and motion, of action and passion, of clutter and emptiness, of light and dark.[11]

Shaviro both discards "structuring lack", a hallmark of psychoanalytical theories, as well as the primacy of narrative in which most neoformalists believe. His focus is squarely on the continuity (and reversibility) between the physiological and affective reactions of one's own body and what happens on the screen. In contrast to most theories discussed so far, which were predicated on the assumption of a distance or separation between film and spectator, a phenomenological approach highlights the interplay, continuity and transition between the two.

One should be aware of one problem: the continuous rhetorical invocation of the body as a central element of any given theory does not automatically undercut the distance between film and spectator in terms of phenomenology. Indeed, there are a number of approaches that constantly talk about the body but nevertheless cling to the representational paradigm familiar from Cultural Studies, whose ideology critique cannot be unproblematically reconciled with the phenomenological experience of the body. The body as a projection screen and as an object of the gaze was considered important even by the ocularcentric approaches (discussed in Chapters 3 and 4), not as perceiving, affective, sensual matter, but rather as a locus of erotic fetishization and of the reified, alienating commodity form.

The phenomenological paradigm has received a tremendous boost since the 1990s and it has generated its own differentiations. Besides the work of Laura Marks, to whom we shall return below (pp. 124–5), several contributions are noteworthy, because they share the same dissatisfaction with the ocularcentric paradigms, but which differ in the way they conceptualize the role of the other senses. The focus can be, still along the lines of the representational paradigm, on the depiction of touch and hands,[12] or, more innovatively, on avant-garde practices that overcome, deconstruct and question the (supposedly) disembodied perception of classical cinema. Three examples will suffice here: the Hungarian artist and avant-garde pioneer László Moholy-Nagy, who worked (among other things as a teacher at the Bauhaus) in Germany until he emigrated in 1933, developed an art practice and a film theory which was attempting to give equal weight to all senses. Moholy-Nagy believed that the function of art in a rapidly developing modern life-world was to address the (often fragmented) individual in a holistic manner in order to help him/her keep up with the consequences of technological, cultural and social modernization. Therefore, the schooling of the body and all its senses through film serves the purpose of adjusting the individual to the complex perceptual tasks and physiological aspects of modernity. Moholy-Nagy "acts on the assumption that it is only through the development of the subject's sensory perception that s/he can reach the highest, most complete level of all his/her sensualistic potentials capable of meeting the demands of his/her time."[13] This approach, as all positions concentrating on skin, contact and touch, focuses more strongly on the receiving subject than on the filmic material, the aesthetic experience becomes more important than the aesthetic object.

A second example of a transformed sensual address to the spectator in the avant-garde is VALIE EXPORT's *Tapp- und Tastkino* (1968, *Tap and Touch Cinema*), a situational "action cinema" bringing primarily feminist issues to the fore.[14] A curtained box covering the artist's naked torso (and emulating a cinema hall) permits passers-by to touch the female breasts in the tap-and-touch-cinema, even though these are not visible – pointing simultaneously to the reification and objectification of women's bodies in commercial cinema and to a possible reorientation of cinema from visual to haptic appropriation. A third example is Anthony McCall's equally simple and elegant installation *Line Describing a Cone*:

> In a dark room, a thirty-minute film showing a circle taking form is projected onto the wall. Artificial fog makes the beam of light from the projector clearly visible as it gradually develops from a line to a complete cone and the circle on the wall slowly closes.[15]

In this cinematic installation, light, the basic element in any type of projection, is no longer a transparent medium that allows coded information of the representational film to be visible and legible, but, rather, the projection beam makes

light itself visible and, in the fog-filled room, even haptically tangible as spectators traverse the cone of light, interact with the set-up and become a physical
part and participant in the work of art.

Another field in which the spectator and his/her (bodily) contact with film
have been used productively is genre research. Discussing three genres on the
lower end of the cultural value hierarchy – melodrama, horror and pornography
– Linda Williams reminds us forcefully of the role played by the corporeality of
spectators as affective and affecting creatures. Direct bodily reactions such as
crying in melodrama, the sweat of anxiety in the face of disfiguration, or the
bleeding bodies in the slasher-horror movies, and (male) spectator's response
to the sexual act in pornography underscore an excess compared to the classical
regime of regulated narration. But this is only one reason for the low esteem
these genres generally enjoy. Williams' so-called "body genres" display a (mostly
female) body in the grip of intense, uncontrollable emotions, a body that jerks
and twists uncontrollably while emitting inarticulate sounds. The low cultural
status derives from the sight of the body in its most inarticulate manifestations,
but also from the fact that such bodily reactions reach out to envelop and "touch"
the spectator: "In the body genres [. . .] it seems to be the case that the success
of these genres is often measured by the degree to which the audience sensation
mimics what is seen on the screen."[16] The directness with which these genres
deal with bodily fluids (tears, blood, sweat, sperm) makes them (culturally, but
also for the censors) suspect because they violate a basic rule of modern aesthetics, the (disinterested) distance between spectator and work: "What seems to
bracket these particular genres from others is an apparent lack of proper esthetic
distance, a sense of over-involvement in sensation and emotion."[17] According to
Williams, the excess and bodily mimicry is absorbed, displaced and mitigated
through the activation of several narrative fantasy scenarios known from psychoanalysis. In this process, fascination as well as fear aroused by these genres
are re-connected to fundamental tropes in psychoanalysis, such as castration
anxiety (horror films), the incestuous attachment to the mother (melodrama),
and the primordial scene involving the parents (pornography).

Also in respect to the horror film, Barbara Creed highlights the importance
of Julia Kristeva's notion of "the abject" which refers to that which acknowledges no boundaries, rules or fixed positions, and which upsets identity, system
and order. Kristeva includes here even bodily excretions such as saliva, urine,
feces and tears, which are neither part of the body nor completely separate from
it (in this they resemble the skin). The horror film is important here for three
reasons: first, because it displays images of the abject – mutilated or dead bodies,
bodily secretions, discharges and waste. Second, the horror film combines the
monstrous with the abject – the monster crosses boundaries between the human
and the non-human, while the abject challenges the very idea of a boundary.

And third, Creed postulates (based on a number of narrative analyses of horror films) that the horror film connects the abject with the maternal, i.e. the mother in the literal sense or such instances that adopt maternal functions. It is therefore the stable symbolic order (of society, the family and the subject) that is threatened by abject (deformed, boundless, disfigured) bodies in horror films. Hence the function of the genre according to Creed is to maintain boundaries and taboos (related to sexuality and physicality) in a post-religious, libertarian society precisely by displaying, thematizing and discussing them: "The horror film attempts to bring about a confrontation with the abject (the corpse, bodily wastes, the monstrous feminine) in order finally to eject the abject and redraw the boundaries between the human and the non-human."[18] A regulatory and disciplining function of cinema gains prominence in this approach, as boundaries are violated in order to re-draw them all the more decisively, once the "transgression" has been punished. Williams and Creed both stress the visceral immediacy and directness of the film's address that entails social devaluation, cultural exclusion and authoritarian prohibition. If one conceptualizes the body as a cultural medium of (self-)inscription, one invariably encounters the transgressive effects attributed to the media in general and the cinema specifically that have always been associated with popular entertainment, which is why such genres have an equally long history of regimentation and disciplinary action.

In a similar vein, research on early cinema – one of the most productive branches of Film Studies since the 1980s – has also tended to shift attention to the role of haptic perception. The so-called "rube films", depicting the naive responses of an ignorant country bumpkin to the modern city and, in particular, during a visit to the cinema, they foreground his confusion of the reality of events and characters with their on-screen representation. From these and similar films, some scholars of early cinema have concluded that movie-going provided a schooling of sorts for the urban masses, in which the real and imaginary distance (from the screen, from other persons, from objects, from events) had to be learned since the social mediation of life in the metropolis depended crucially upon such capabilities: mass transit, speed, anonymity, the assembly-line and the sheer spatial dimensions of the modern metropolis required a heightened attention to (one's own and the Other's) body in relation to distance and proximity. Because urban environments favor the senses in charge of distance, such as seeing and hearing, over senses that create physical proximity, such as smelling and touching, the cinema, as the medium most directly interdependent with the city, also took part in this disciplinary regime: the "rube", who reacted intuitively to films and – upon seeing a fistfight or a woman undressing – aspired to physical and tactile contact, was held up to ridicule in order to present to spectators the correct behavior consisting precisely in a fixation on the distancing act of seeing (and, to a lesser degree, of hearing).[19] One could

Figure 5.7 Poster of HOSTEL: PART II: getting under one's skin.

even argue that, in the course of film history, the movement we have outlined in this book – from a distanced exterior to a direct somatic bodily contact – made the birth of classical cinema possible in the first place, even if in the reverse order: spectators had to learn to manage distance, enjoy individualized reception and get used to silent contemplation in order for classical cinema to unfold its force. Not coincidentally, then, theoretical approaches which belong, in a broad sense, to the contact paradigm deal with films that exceed in different ways the classical paradigm (early cinema, avant-garde, post-classical film).

Consequently, Laura Marks, in her aptly titled *The Skin of Film*, discusses film and video productions originating from outside commercial Hollywood cinema.[20] Based on an analysis of ethnographic essay films from the 1980s and 1990s whose denominator is the connection between memory and embodied sense perception, she develops a theoretical edifice situated halfway between Deleuze's philosophy of time and Sobchack's phenomenology. For Marks, the skin of the film

> offers a metaphor to emphasize the way film signifies through its material-ity, through a contact between perceiver and object represented. It also suggests the way vision itself can be tactile, as though one were touching a film with one's eyes: I term this *haptic visuality*.[21]

The surface of film, often the depiction of a haptically charged surface such as the close-up of a body (e.g. an animal's skin or raised hairs, goose bumps), or any other conspicuous and interesting texture if not the film itself in its materiality, calls forth memories which were virtually present and needed the film to be actualised. In keeping with phenomenological premises, Marks does not under-stand memories as purely inner-psychic events, but as processes that involve the entire perceptual apparatus since it is the human capability of perceiving the outside world that allows such constructs as memories in the first place.

Yet, skin plays a part not only as a metaphor for the film's materiality and on the representational level of what is being shown, but also in the circulation of those films in which Marks is interested – so-called essay films. This type of film depends on a different form of spectator contact than the Hollywood block-buster, for it "moves in specific, traceable paths, from local broadcast to college lecture room, from community hall to art museum, from a screening for the maker's family and friends to an artist-run center" (20). The difficult accessibil-ity of these works, the visible traces of use on the (normally few) copies and the generally more active reception process (often screenings are framed by lec-tures, discussions and Q&As with the film-maker) facilitate for spectators to "get into the skin" of the film itself and to inscribe their act of reception more actively into the film. Such a cinema demonstrates the existence of another type of contact predicated on a reciprocal process of encounter and transfer between film and spectator. By contrast, the blockbuster offers a more standardized form of reception, from the projection spaces in multiplexes with its uniform refreshments on offer to the mass of identical copies that hit cinemas worldwide on the same day.

Marks derives from such differences the idea of haptic perception, according to which the eyes function as organs of touch, letting what she calls haptic images appeal to a more complex multi-sensory perception:

> In revaluing haptic visuality I am suggesting that a sensuous response may be elicited without abstraction, through the mimetic relationship between the perceiver and a sensuous object. This relationship does not require an initial separation between perceiver and object that is mediated by representation.
>
> (164)

Like so many others – and reminiscent of the revival of mimesis and the discovery of mirror-neurons discussed in Chapter 3 – Marks is interested in overcoming the representational paradigm in favor of a somatic, embodied and tactile reception. For this she often refers back to art history – especially Alois Riegl's concept of the haptic (originally developed in relation to late-Roman art and the symbolic language of the Egyptians) and its contrast with the optical, which are transferred to cinema.[22]

Authors such as Sobchack or Marks occasionally refer to Gilles Deleuze when discussing the surface of images or the specific temporality of the cinema, but their theories rely on the (un-Deleuzian and more directly phenomenological) notion of the subject that perceives these surfaces or temporalities. This is why they talk about "embodied perception" or "subjective memory" when discussing the relation of film and spectator, in contrast to Deleuze who sees images on an immanent plane without a perceiving subject. In this respect, Claire Perkins' cautious remarks are an important reminder of potential theoretical promiscuity:

> Deleuze [. . .] genuinely privileges the cinematic work beyond any conception of subject or object. [. . .] The image exists in itself as matter, not as a sign for matter which is hidden behind the image. For Deleuze, following Bergson, consciousness is on the outside or surface of things, rendering the image and the "thing" indistinguishable. Marks, despite her concern with the surface of the image, relies upon the phenomenological subject to perceive this surface and thereby bring into being the notion of embodied spectatorship. For Deleuze, the privileging of bodily perception subordinates movement itself by replacing it with either a subject to carry it out or an object to submit to it. For Marks the works examined are made for a viewer to feel out and constitute – they highlight the act of perception. For Deleuze, the set of movement-images which make up cinema are definitively not addressed to anyone – they are an Appearing in which there is "not even an eye".[23]

In other words: for Deleuze there might be consciousness, but the notion of intentionality, so central to phenomenology, is alien for Deleuze.

The motif of contact and touch also plays an important role in other schools of theory which have not been as influenced by phenomenology and which could more readily be associated with "post-colonial studies". Hamid Naficy, for instance, has developed the notion of an "accented" cinema, whose marks of otherness not only stem from the film-maker's own experience of migration or exile, but also display these marks as part of their (artisanal) mode of production. These films emerge not in open opposition to, but in what Naficy calls the "interstices" of, established institutions, and use the liminal spaces of transition in a productive way for a cinema that is meant to facilitate contact in various ways: with a lost homeland or a Utopian future, among people of different ethnic backgrounds or within a geographically dispersed diaspora. Typical of the cinema for transnational audiences often made by artists living in exile, or having a migration background, is the "tactile optics" that gives priority to images and memories of the non-visual, the haptic or the olfactory, to indicate their non-public, private and intimate provenance.[24] Unlike Marks, Naficy shares with Cultural Studies the paradigm of "representation", but many of the films he discusses emerge from cultural and religious contexts that have very different ideas about visuality and representation from those in the West, even if the film-makers live in the diaspora. The tension between the visual, the veiled, the indirect and the haptic serves to activate layers of memory or evokes feelings of loss attached to a past experience, more often than not shared in the form of perceptions of closeness and proximity such as smell or touch.

From here, a broad horizon of ethnographic and anthropological film practice as well as of post-colonial theories of film and its many uses and function opens up, which we can only glance at in passing here. Robert Stam's list of the countless research fields that have become prominent in the last two decades already demonstrates the productivity of these studies:

> the analysis of "minority" representation; the critique of imperialist and orientalist media; work on colonial and postcolonial discourse; theories of "Third World" and "Third Cinema" on the way to "World Cinema"; work on "indigenous" media; studies of "minority", "diasporic", and "exilic" cinemas; "whiteness" studies; and work on anti-racist and multicultural media pedagogy.[25]

While in a first wave, representational histories and strategies of minority groups had been the focus (gays and lesbians, blacks and native Americans in the US, labor immigrants in Europe etc.), more recently, critics have turned to the local anchoring and adaptation of global developments; in this perspective, they have also looked at the negotiation of dominant media content in subaltern groups, at the adoption of media in diasporic communities or at the cretive self-empowerment through the various uses of film, giving practical grounding to such concepts as "resistant reading" (Stuart Hall), "glocalisation" (Roland Robertson) or "textual poaching" (Henry Jenkins). What unites these diverse strands are an interest in the contact zones between film and spectator as figured around race, ethnicity, sexual orientation, gender and culture, an activist engagement with the (positive and negative) power of media, and the attempt to develop models for the direct exchange of affirmative, political and social energies.

Even Siegfried Kracauer's film theory, which is traditionally put alongside André Bazin as *the* classical theory of filmic realism, alludes at more than one point to a somatic–phenomenological understanding of the relation between spectator and film. Rather than advocating a realistic representation of an (unmediated) outside world or a naive mimetic realism, it can be argued that Kracauer is, in fact, more interested in material fragments of non-identical objects affecting a post-identity subject. The effect of this interrelation – and the vanishing point of Kracauer's thinking – is a theory of history that attempts to redeem the vanished material existence of history through the permanent ephemerality of the moving image.[26] In his introduction, Kracauer talks about the fact that we "assimilate the seemingly non essential" as spectators and that "the way [. . .] leads from, and through, the corporeal to the spiritual". In the chapter on the spectator, he concludes that "unlike the other types of pictures, film images affect primarily the spectator's senses, engaging him physiologically before he is in a position to respond intellectually." And in the Conclusion, a note is struck that appears to stress rather the mesh and entanglement of the body in the material world more than the disembodied eye and the objectified point of view attributed to realism: "What we want, then, is to touch reality not only with the fingertips but to seize it and shake hands with it."[27] The specific kind of modernity that finds its articulation in film and other kinds of mass entertainments, neither fully rationalized and abstracted nor a completely visceral experience, provides in Kracauer's perspective access to the contradictory and complex processes shaping the twentieth century.

In Kracauer's ambivalent attitude toward the body-based mass media of the modern world one can detect the positive and the negative sides of a phenomenologically inflected film theory: on the one hand it stands for the serious attempt to get close to the phenomena without having a ready-made verdict or a pre-established notion as to its meaning, which is often the critique leveled against ideological criticism, psychoanalytical theory or semiotics. If we really want to gain access to things, their intrinsic qualities and inherent attributes, we need to practice a genuinely open examination of what the camera reveals and discloses. On the other hand, the haptic turn and other body-based approaches to the cinematic experience are sometimes in danger of celebrating a big-tent, inclusive feel-good-theory of sensory empowerment. Negotiating these opposing poles, keeping a critically astute and aesthetically informed sensibility alive, as well as accounting for a spectator that is increasingly exchanging the immobility of the cinema seat for the dynamic movement of the hand-held audiovisual device, will therefore be one of the key challenges for this school of theory.

Chapter 6

Cinema as ear

Acoustics and space

online

Hollywood 1928: the actress Lina Lamont (Jean Hagen) is already a big star when the imminent introduction of sound film threatens her career because her shrill and piercing voice is inappropriate for talkies. In her first sound picture she is therefore dubbed by the young and talented Kathy Selden (Debbie Reynolds), but this substitution is being kept hidden from the public until Lamont is asked at a cinema theater to sing a song live on stage. Selden is standing in the wings, lip-synching the star with her beautiful voice until the curtain opens to reveal the deception and expose the discrepancy between image (Lamont) and sound (Selden). Body and voice no longer fit together, or rather: the scene restores their technical separation in the film-making process, usually hidden but now made palpable for the diegetic audience (the one watching the performance) as well as for the film audience (watching the film). SINGIN' IN THE RAIN (US, 1952) is not only the crowning achievement of a cycle of musicals made by Gene Kelly and Stanley Donen in the 1950s, but also an ironic, self-reflexive meditation on the transition from silent to sound film, as well as the "nature" of synchronized sound. In the film, the relation between body and voice is fundamentally called into question, as this problematic relation is staged time and again on several levels, primarily for comic effect. The ontological bond between a sound and its origin that appears so self-evident to us in every-day life is cancelled out and annihilated in the technological set-up of sound cinema.[1]

SINGIN' IN THE RAIN stages in various ways the collapse between body and voice, citing as well as contributing to a debate characteristic of the early days of sound film, when a number of critics and artists rejected the new techno-logy.[2] Typical of this transition was that, thanks to the radio, the growing popu-larity of the gramophone and of hit songs, in addition to an actor's face and body, his/her acoustic presence and performance became part of the film indus-try's marketing machine. But the aforementioned scene also illustrates how sound "embodies" the image – seeing is always directional, because we see only

Figure 6.1 Singin' in the Rain: the difficulties of converting to sound embodied by the actress and her (voice) double.

in one direction, whereas hearing is always a three-dimensional, spatial perception, i.e. it creates an acoustic space, because we hear in all directions. This holds true not only for the space of the cinema, where sound technologies like Dolby, THX and Surround systems have given blockbusters the kind of spatial presence that images alone cannot create, but applies also to diegetic film space, where sound – especially if one thinks of characters being surprised or terrified by something they hear, eavesdropping on others or reacting to noise in a variety of ways – contributes significantly to the creation of cinema's imaginary topography.

As we have argued at length in the previous chapter, Film Studies has increasingly taken cognizance of the fact that cinema always addresses the spectator in multisensory ways. As a consequence, research on the role of synaesthesia (the coupling of two separate domains of perception) and intermodality (the capability of linking sensations from different domains into a coherent schema) is once more on the rise.[3] However, the exact role of the different perceptual channels (visual, acoustic, tactile, etc.), as well as the way they relate to each other in the cinematic experience, is still in dispute. Transitions in critical methods, such as the one from the eye as an organ of the disembodied look to skin as a somatic contact-surface – the focus in the previous chapter – always depend on broader cultural developments as well. It is crucial to remember that in our cartography of film theory there is no progress in the emphatic sense, no linear advance toward an imaginary goal, even if the movement from outside and distanced observer (frame) to inside and immediate participant (brain) might invite such an interpretation. Over the past 80 years phenomenological–realist and constructivist–formalist models have constantly alternated in Film Studies (as they have done in Cultural Studies more generally). The approaches united in this chapter under the heading of ear and sound belong to the paradigm in which the phenomenological and sensory embodiment of cinematic experience is of central importance.

Before beginning our tour through the soundscapes of cinema, we should stress the fact that by using the word "ear" in the title of this chapter we do not think of acoustics in terms of an information carrier and communicative channel that complements the image, i.e. as a pure appendage and supplement to visual information. Rather, we believe that sound has a much more encompassing role of actually and metaphorically anchoring and stabilizing the spectator's body (and self-perception as a perceiving subject) in space:

> the main "anthropological" task of hearing [. . .] [is] to stabilize our body in space, hold it up, facilitate a three-dimensional orientation and, above all, ensure an all-round security that includes even those spaces, objects and events that we cannot see, especially what goes on behind our backs. Whereas the eye searches and plunders, the ear listens in on what is plundering us. The ear is the organ of fear.[4]

In the previous chapter about skin and contact we argued that the inclusion of the body in film theory is a way of overcoming the deadlocks of the representational model and of calling for a more diverse set of approaches to conceptualize the cinematic experience. In this respect the emphasis on skin is akin to approaches in which other parts of the body, in this case the ear, also represent a central element of perception, knowledge and experience. The main difference between these two consists in the fact that, whereas skin is still an outer surface, the ear allows cinematic experience to probe deeply into the spectator's (and listener's) inner self.[5] Furthermore, a focus on the ear and sound directly emphasizes the spatiality of the cinematic experience: we can hear around corners and through walls, in complete darkness and blinding brightness, even when we cannot see anything. While many traditional approaches treated the spectator in the cinema as someone solely concerned with looking in a rational-agent, goal-oriented way, and of processing information in objective fashion, the ear shifts the focus to factors such as the sense of balance and spatial sensibility. The spectator is no longer a passive recipient of images at the pointed end of the optical pyramid, but rather a bodily being enmeshed acoustically, spatially and affectively in the filmic texture. Technological developments such as the tremendous improvements of sound technology since the 1970s must also be part of the discussion, giving "voice" to theoreticians whose reflections focus primarily on cinematic sound.

This chapter is divided into three parts, each with its own theoretical and historical background. The first part deals with the so-called silent cinema and with one of the most crucial transitions in film history: the introduction of sound film. From its inception, the cinema attempted to synchronize visuals and acoustics, and to transpose sound into images. From a theoretical point of view, with the introduction of sound film, the unity and separation of body and voice were at stake, i.e. the integrity of the human body in the cinema. The second part of this chapter focuses on the role of sound in classical cinema and on the ability of (three-dimensional) sound to give body, extension and shape to the (two-dimensional) image. This again highlights the precarious (and ultimately brittle) connection between body and voice, in classical cinema mostly a hierarchical relationship between image and sound, whereby the latter is subordinated (and answers) to the former. The third and last part focuses from a film-historical perspective on the age of blockbusters, when technological sound improvements (Dolby, Surround Sound, THX, Sound Design) largely restructured the cinematic experience and upset many of the hierarchies of classical cinema, including those between sound and image. In the long run, this technological restructuring contributed to and prepared the ground for a completely transformed articulation of space in the age of mobile experiences which is characterized by variability and modularity, but also by a new materiality and plasticity of sound. This part leads into the era of iPods and cell-phones, an era where sound no longer implies an anchoring in a fixed spatial position, but becomes rather a mobile cloud or an invisible cloak that we can wrap ourselves into, in order to protect us from the (acoustic) demands of a noisy environment. Contemporary urban mobile experience finds its expression in a mobile soundscape that shakes up the connection between (surrounding) space, (confined) subject and (external) technology.

To begin with the historically most remote period: we have already on various occasions emphasized the importance of research on early cinema not only in bringing about historical revisions but also in generating theoretical impulses. Something similar happened when historians of early cinema discovered that the silent film was never really silent. Quite the contrary, films made before 1930 were characterized by a great variety of acoustic accompaniments and variations: from the film narrator in Japan (*benshi*) to the grand symphony orchestra in metropolitan film palaces, from the specifically built cinema organ to the Foley artist. As a textual unity, film was less stable until the introduction of sound in the late 1920s because the accompanying sound always threatened to attach another meaning to the images.[6] Up until the (necessary) standardization that came with the introduction of sound, each and every film screening was a unique performative event whose acoustic design and execution made each occasion different from any other screening of the same film.[7] In this perspective, it is the space of the cinema, the auditorium, and not only the space of the film where meaning is created. The spectator's location in the performative and variable space in which film achieved its unique status plays an important role in theories focused on the ear.

The purpose of these different and differently produced film sounds could be manifold: to synchronize sound and image and to relate one to the other, either by way of complement or in order to contrast the two; to create a sense of irony or to evoke some other affective state. The synchronization tendency dates back to the beginning of cinema: Thomas Alva Edison developed the Kinetoscope (a box-like apparatus that was placed in penny arcades where a single spectator could watch moving images through a peephole, now considered a forerunner of cinema), as a complement to his phonograph, i.e. the wax-cylinder predecessor of the record player. He famously stated that the Kinetoscope would do for the eye what the phonograph does for the ear. Already in the beginning of the media history of the cinema, we thus find the idea that the moving image is best thought of as a supplement to sound, in contrast to the notion that sound merely complements (or distracts from) the image.

It is important to realize that the "deficit", retrospectively often ascribed to cinema before the introduction of sound, was not always perceived as such by film directors at the time. Quite the opposite: there are numerous – and ingenious – examples of visualized sound in "silent" films: close-ups of ears that listen, feet that tiptoe on gravel, people who turn around in astonishment, shots of church bells and musical instruments, drums and artillery. We see people reacting to sound, in just the same way we see physical and psychic reactions to faces and bodies. Well-known examples of sound materializing on the screen as images are the steam whistles in Fritz Lang's METROPOLIS (GE, 1926), where discharging smoke transposes sound into the visual realm, but also the soaring trumpet sounds in F.W. Murnau's THE LAST LAUGH (DER LETZTE MANN, GE, 1924), in which the camera flies disembodiedly from the musical instrument to the backyard dweller's ear at the window, translating the diffusion of sound waves into dynamic camera movement, or the gunshots in Josef von Sternberg's THE LAST COMMAND (US, 1928), which are not directly visible on the screen but represented by the image of birds stirred up by the loud sound.

Theoreticians of the late silent film could not help but equate the imminent introduction of sound with the loss of purity and expressivity, arguing that sound betrays and corrupts an art form that was on the verge of maturity, reducing it

Figure 6.2 METROPOLIS: the sound of steam whistles visualized.

to the banalities of "ordinary talk". For a convinced proponent of silent film such
as Rudolf Arnheim, sound transformed the two-dimensional image, which
never pretended to be "realistic" in the first place but rather underlined the
figurative-formal qualities of representations (see Chapter 1), into an illusory
perspective projected onto three-dimensional reality:

> Acoustics completes the illusion to perfection. The edge of the screen is no
> longer a frame, but the margin of a whole, of a theatrical space: sound
> transforms the screen into a spatial stage. One of cinema's main and special
> appeals is the fact that every scene poses a competition: the fragmentation
> of images and motion on the surface versus plastic bodies and motion in
> space. Sound film suspends this aesthetically important double game almost
> completely.[8]

Arnheim had rightly realized that, unlike the reproduction of images which
entails a loss of dimensionality (from three to two dimensions), the reproduction of sound does not carry with it such a reduction in depth of information.
The mechanical reproduction of sound results, just like the original sound, in
the diffusion of acoustic waves through space, in fact bringing the mechanical
copy in a certain sense closer to a performed repetition of the original than a

reproduction or representation. From this fact, Arnheim drew the conclusion that sound transforms film from a formally abstract mode of (two-dimensional) representation into a medium of (three-dimensional) mimetic realism. Arnheim complemented this with another argument against the addition of (pre-recorded and synchronized) sound to film which highlighted issues of medium specificity and intermediality. Sound film, for Arnheim, was the marriage of two incompatible systems of artistic expression – the image track as silent film and the sound track as radio play. In fact, the mass diffusion of the radio in the 1920s had led to a number of experiments that the (then) young medium welcomed; famous among these attempts were Walter Ruttmann's sound film without images WEEKEND (1930), and Bertold Brecht's radio play on Charles Lindbergh's flight across the Atlantic (1929). In general, the emerging radio theory was interested in participation and interaction, i.e. the listener's possibility to talk back and reply to the messages s/he received, i.e. in social relations and in the technological set-up of a medium, not unlike the later theorization of video and more recently, the Internet as interactive medium.

For many critics in the late 1920s, then, sound film did not represent the perfection of film as an art form, but rather of film as merely adding a layer of (vulgar) illusion. Along with this disappointment came the feeling of loss of that special aura: had the cinema not managed to "silence" the already (too) loud and noisy world of modernity? More eloquent than anything else in capturing the "essence" of cinema were Asta Nielsen's gestures, Greta Garbo's face, or Louise Brooks' physiognomy. But even critics like Arnheim knew that the battle for/against sound film could not be fought and won by film theory, but that it was being waged at the box office and by big companies (because, besides sound films' unquestioned popularity, the financially strong and powerful electrical industry also helped expedite and implement the introduction of sound). Given the enormous expenditure in technology and equipment, it is surprising how quickly sound film established itself and stabilized its technical norms the world over. Aesthetically, the imposition of normativity took somewhat longer: after a brief (and, from today's vantage point, still exciting) transitional period in which aesthetic experiment and openness were common, the film industry arrived at a classically closed form that managed to integrate sound almost seamlessly into the stylistic system introduced and popularized in the 1920s. This brings us to the second part of our overview of sound film theory, which focuses on the relation of sound and image.

In classical cinema sound is usually analyzed strictly in relation to (and in dependence on) the image. One looks at whether the sound is *on-screen* or *off-screen* (i.e. if the source of the sound can be seen in the shot or not), whether the sound is *diegetic* or *non-diegetic* (i.e. if the source of the sound lies within the narrative world of the film or not), whether the sound is *synchronous* or *non-synchronous* (i.e. if a sound happens at the same time with its representation on-screen), and at the relationship between these parameters.[9] The analysis of sound is often framed in terms of a power struggle with the image over dominance and dependency, in which terms such as illustration and accompaniment or counterpoint and conflict prevail. In classical cinema, most scholars would conclude that narration, i.e. the filmic realization of the plot, is usually that to which all other parameters (editing, camera work and primarily sound) are subordinated.[10] An alternative to this view is offered by James Lastra, who emphasizes the historical interdependence of the different sound media, and Sarah Kozloff who, by shifting the ground to narration as a complex mediated act of transmission, analyzes the role of voice-over narration in classical cinema. Within a context that encompasses television, radio and other mass media, both stress the role of sound not as merely a reinforcement of what is visible in the image, but the fundamental and indispensable work that sound performs in creating a classical narrative.[11]

In keeping with our intent to focus on the spectator's body and its forms of perception, we will go beyond this hierarchy that gives prominence to the eye and approach sound from a different angle, that of the separation and connection between body and voice, which already preoccupied early theoreticians like Arnheim who rejected the combination of voice and body as unnatural. One should bear in mind here that images are recorded, stored, processed and displayed in a completely different way than sounds – the former is an optical–chemical process, the latter an acoustic–electronic one. But the popularity of musicals in the years following the introduction of sound suggests that audiences not only accepted this combination but also enjoyed the often ironically highlighted interaction or discrepancy between body and voice. Between 1930 and 1935, many films were made that staged, allegorized and dramatized, first of all, the separation between body and voice, and then the re-connection that followed it.[12] Returning to SINGIN' IN THE RAIN, it becomes clear that the film, apart from pointing to the epistemologically problematic connection between body and voice, also thematizes the marketability and commodification of the human voice in the age of radio, sheet music, hit songs and the gramophone, signaling the ever-increasing prominence of an audio-track in all walks of modern life, from public space to the private sphere and back again.[13]

This important transitional period of the "coming of sound" has been studied in recent years also as a possible blueprint for the current shift from analog to digital media technology. One of the most historically thorough and theoretically informed accounts is the one offered by Lastra. Reconstructing a discursive history of sound technology and film mainly through a close examination of the technical literature as manifest in the specialized journals of sound technicians and film artists, Lastra demonstrates that any relationship between sound and image is inherently fraught with difficulties, involving as it does the seemingly incompatible objectives of registration and representation, optimal storage and optimal "realism". Sound engineers, for example, always have to choose between intelligibility and fidelity when aiming at a "realistic" sound: in everyday life, dialog is often muffled or inaudible, something not easily accepted by film viewers.[14] Not only can one conclude that sound is as constructed and shaped by intersecting forces in the process of recording, post-production and reproduction as is the image. Moreover, the apparent stability of classical film style, in which all parameters are subordinated to realistic verisimilitude, is constantly threatened by internal tension.

On the one hand, sound gives film a "body", a third dimension, as already noted, since it is a spatial phenomenon unlike the flat image. But, on the other hand, film also threatens the integrity of the body, as shown by the example of SINGIN' IN THE RAIN, which dramatizes this very tension in its narrative intrigue. Sound also possesses tactile and haptic qualities, since it is a phenomenon related to waves, hence also to movement. In order to produce or emit a sound, an object must be touched (the strings of an instrument, the vocal chords, the wind in the trees), and sound in turn makes bodies vibrate. Sound covers and uncovers, touches and enfolds even the spectator's body (in this way, sound is closely related to the paradigm of skin and contact presented in Chapter 5). In many ways we are more susceptible to sound than to visual perceptions, a fact on which horror films capitalize when sound is used to evoke a threatening and yet unseen presence. When we cannot visually locate the origin of sounds in space, our directional grasp of aural information (identification, designation) is much weaker than with information perceived by the eye. Sound is also fleeting, transparent and diaphanous, it escapes our desire to capture, fixate and freeze it. While the film image can be stopped and reproduced through stills and frame enlargements, sound can be reproduced only in time, i.e. it cannot be reduced to a single moment. Sound, therefore, also reminds us of the irreversibility of time, it stands for loss and announces death – all the more reason, perhaps, why sound is so often associated with danger and fear.

If sound can carry meaning, enable communication and create reference – notably as language – it can also destroy or distort meaning as noise and interference, or it can hover on the border between meaning and non-sense, threatening to fall into the meaninglessness of babbling or muttering. The boundaries between these different states is blurred as a cry can become a scream, music might turn into noise or whispered words can drown in background sound. Sound is therefore more malleable than the image because it has always (long before digital technology enabled visual morphs) been endowed with the power of metamorphosis, i.e. it can alter its form at all times. And finally, sound is profoundly polysemic when it comes to its emotional effect: one need only think of how differently people react to sound intensity. Even its definition is highly ambivalent: sound is both material, in the sense that it owes its existence to matter, and immaterial, since it is a wave phenomenon that cannot be displayed and reproduced but can only be produced anew. Sound is both directional (it has a source and brings something about) and enveloping (it surrounds us constantly), both inside and outside, so that some of the paradoxes and tensions that we have formulated vis-à-vis the cinematic experience once again become relevant when sound is our focus.

Classical cinema dealt with the problems inherent in these polysemic qualities of sound, which always have the potential to destabilize the spectator, in such a way that the subordination of sound to image rendered the former "inaudible" to a certain extent. First of all, the images place and organize bodies and objects spatially, while sound plays a purely auxiliary role. The spatial impression of sound, highly disconcerting to a theoretician such as Arnheim, recedes and the visual markers of space take over. Moreover, sound and image are also rearranged across temporal markers: in classical cinema the principle dominates that sound asks "Where?" and the image replies "Here": the principle of a spatialized or delayed synchronization is bent toward intentionality and directionality. The image thus offers an orientation of what is "in the picture" and how this is to be understood. The relation between sound and image also creates a tension: sound and image dance around each other in a perpetual question-and-answer game. Sound moreover serves the image by attaching itself to it mimetically: this can either take the form of typical neo-romantic "scores", which have prevailed in Hollywood since the 1930s and where the emotions that music is meant to bring about in the spectator duplicate the affective states that the narrative is trying to evoke (suspense, fear, drama, sadness, humor),[15] or of the so-called "Mickey-mousing", in which sound imitates the visual action, for instance by translating an elephant's steps into timed and synchronized drum beats.

And finally, we usually think of sound as active, as something traveling or being sent: it emanates from an object, i.e. it has an origin, unlike color for instance, which appears to be inherent in an object, as belonging to its substance. When it comes to sound, we try to identify a point of origin, a source. In addition, we tend to regard sound as a force or special carrier of authority, a fact on which Michel Chion bases his theory of the "*acousmêtres*", i.e. of the bodiless voice in cinema that apparently has no origin, yet is powerful and ubiquitous. Chion coined this word by combining "acousmatic", an archaic term describing something that one hears but whose origin is invisible,[16] and *être*, the French verb "to be". With this compound word, Chion underlines the active force of sound which possesses the power to attack, invade or manipulate, rather than just being a transitory aural whiff carried by the wind. The place and origin of these "vocal characters" lie neither within film nor outside it: "The *acousmêtre* is this acousmatic character whose relationship to the screen involves a special kind of ambiguity and oscillation [. . .]. We may define it as neither inside nor outside the image."[17] The *acousmêtre* can see everything, know everything and have an impact on everything, and it is also ubiquitous. Examples of *acousmêtre* are the wizard in THE WIZARD OF OZ (US, 1939, Victor Fleming), the voice of the mother in PSYCHO (US, 1960, Alfred Hitchcock), Hal, the computer in 2001: A SPACE ODYSSEY (GB/US, 1968, Stanley Kubrick), or Mabuse in DAS TESTAMENT DES DR. MABUSE (GE, 1933, Fritz Lang). In all four films, the power of these uncanny voices must be exposed and broken within the diegetic worlds, "de-acousmatized" as Chion calls it, in order to neutralize the threat they pose to the (symbolic) order (of classical narration).

Chion's examples highlight the dark side of sound's ability to embody agency, a fact also present in another practice, namely ventriloquism. A voice originates not in the face or the mouth, but apparently in another part of the body, for instance in films like THE GREAT GABBO (US, 1929, James Cruze), DEAD OF NIGHT (GB, 1945, Alberto Cavalcanti and Charles Crichton) or THE EXORCIST (US, 1973, William Friedkin), in which the words that come out of the little girl's mouth are not her own but those of the Devil. The technological, socially

Figure 6.3 THE WIZARD OF OZ: Dorothy confronts the man behind the voice of the wizard – the "*acousmêtre*".

accepted form of ventriloquism is karaoke, the practice of miming along with a recording, made popular by the Japanese, frowned upon when musical performers lip-sync to their own playback, whereas the economically driven and culturally accepted form of ventriloquism is synchronization or "dubbing". We will return to this point later in connection with MULHOLLAND DRIVE (US, 2001, David Lynch). All these examples, Chion's *acousmêtre* as well as ventriloquism, playback and karaoke, base their appeal to spectators primarily on the tension between the two-dimensional image and the three-dimensional sound, i.e. between surface and space, as well as body and voice. Contrary to what Arnheim feared, the introduction of sound did not degrade cinema to the status of a spatial illusionism striving toward the three-dimensional image, but, rather, the antagonism between (image) surface and (sound) space was used in a variety of innovative ways. The oscillation between two and three dimensions also affects spectators (and listeners). When a film performance is no longer limited to the screen alone, by virtue of the spatial extension brought about by the envelope of sound, omnipresent in the room, then it becomes indeed difficult to decide whether the cinematic experience takes place "inside" or "outside" the body.

With this conclusion begins the third and final part of our tour through the soundscapes of film and cinema. The hierarchical arrangement of image and sound, where aural perception complements the visual one and both are in the service of narration, was not only challenged by theory and historical research. It was called into question by the very crisis that Hollywood found itself in, as the big studio-productions of the late 1960s failed to attract audiences, who nonetheless flocked to rock concerts and other spectacles driven by sound rather than image. The emergence during the 1970s of the blockbuster as the new key product of the American film industry was to a certain extent the answer to this crisis, by massively investing in new and emerging audio/sound technologies. Films such as NASHVILLE (US, 1975, Robert Altman), STAR WARS (US, 1977, George Lucas) or APOCALYPSE NOW (US, 1979, Francis Ford Coppola) represent landmarks of film history not least because they radically challenged the cinematic experience by their ways of recording and reproducing sound. Other films from the same period, such as THE CONVERSATION (US, 1974, Francis Ford Coppola) and BLOW-OUT (US, 1981, Brian de Palma) almost obsessively dramatize and foreground the capabilities provided by new sound technologies such as bugs, directional microphones, sound surveillance and post-production. We will return to the theoretical consequences of this important development, but want first of all to focus on its technological and cultural consequences, because in cinema any changes in the sound–image dynamics leave their impact on the construction of spectators' subjectivity and bodily self-presence.

Figure 6.4 APOCALYPSE NOW: helicopter attack using multi-channel sound to its fullest extent.

To take a step back in time: the development of sound recording and sound technologies and reproduction devices in the nineteenth century (starting with the gramophone) separated the (live) production of music from its (mechanical) reproduction and from the activity of listening to it. In the course of the second half of the twentieth century, the latter became mobile with the introduction of the transistor- and car-radio, a historical moment captured in films like AMERICAN GRAFFITI (US, 1973, George Lucas) and IM LAUF DER ZEIT (GE, 1976, Wim Wenders, KINGS OF THE ROAD). Both films nostalgically exhibit these technological *dispositifs* of music on the move as historically specific moments of (youth) culture, demonstrating an awareness of the dynamics inherent in media set-ups and their transformation (symbolized, for instance, in the aptly incongruous idea of a juke-box being transported in a removal truck in KINGS OF THE ROAD). New amplifying technologies began to transform the activity of listening to music from a private, individual act into a physical experience and a collective event. With its split screens and epic length, WOODSTOCK (US, 1970, Michael Wadleigh) attempted to turn this supposedly unique and epochal event into a cinematically reproducible one. Likewise, the electronic noise-suppression system known as Dolby enabled the separation of various tracks and accelerated the composition of overlapping soundtracks. It entered the cinemas in combination with different surround-systems and, together, altered the cinematic soundscape. Thanks to a bank of loudspeakers distributed throughout the auditorium (instead of being hidden behind the screen, as traditional cinema sound systems in the classical era), the new sound systems multiplied the possibility of layering sound as well as allowing the film to "transgress" the boundaries of the screen and "enter" into the spectator's space. Film no longer existed solely on the screen but extended into the auditorium as well:

> The complete dissolution of the screen's boundaries through the surround-technology had a suggestive effect. [...] The orientation in space, which had until then been transparent due to the coherence between screen and audio source, was now suspended. Sounds overcame the spectator simultaneously from all sides.[18]

Therefore, the ear became the conduit of radical changes affecting the spatial configuration of cinematic experience, which had previously, in the manner of a peep-show box or the projection beam, been focused on the film image "in front" of the spectator, with the ear straining in the forward direction to catch the sound source emanating from the same spot as the image.

The aesthetic effects of such technological advancements as Dolby and (subsequently) digitization (making multi-channel sound the default value) translate primarily into the emergence of a new kind of aural space. Film sound is henceforth multi-layered, multi-directional, and consists among other things of noises and sounds that are neither natural in origin nor produced by musical instruments (electronic noises, samples, digital sound). One side-effect of the changes that Dolby and related technologies brought about was to increase the budgets producers allocated to sound design, which in turn led to a professional (and artistic) upgrade of the staff in charge of sound: for the first time, in the 1970s "sound designer" replaced "sound engineer" as a job description. Walter Murch, who also worked as a film editor, is a key figure in this respect: his creative input on APOCALYPSE NOW earned him not only the first Oscar of his career, but also the title of "sound designer", a title used here for the first time, while his name was included in the opening credits instead of being hidden among the long list of (technical) staff at the end.[19]

If we recall our discussion of the look and the gaze (Chapter 4), we can now better understand why the gaze, in its psychoanalytic sense, need not be ocular, but is in fact often embodied in noises and hearing, as for instance in horror films. The fact that sound removes all barriers or frames from the image gives rise to various sounds that no longer have a recognizable origin but seem to come from a superior, because unlocalizable, position. These phenomena are of particular interest to Slavoj Žižek, who employs Michel Chion's already mentioned concept of the *acousmêtre* to open the notion of the gaze toward the acoustic dimension of the (psychoanalytically understood) scopic regime. In line with this logic of the acoustic gaze, sound not only helps us orient and stabilize ourselves in space, it also disorients and destabilizes. According to Žižek, hearing is more crucial than seeing for our bodily sense of orientation, even from a physiological standpoint: it is through sound that we first come into contact with the outside world. As a primordial medium of sorts, sound gathers all the undifferentiated emotions that are typical of the prenatal phase, such as fear, dependency and helplessness, as well as the pleasure of immersion and protection.[20] Walter Murch, for instance, pointed out that the acoustic envelopment in the womb (through the mother's voice, breathing and heartbeat) represents the environment in which we develop before birth:

> We begin to hear before we are born, four and a half months after conception. From then on, we develop in a continuous and luxurious bath of sounds [. . .]. Throughout the second four-and-a-half months, Sound rules as solitary Queen of our senses.[21]

The memory of the imaginary integrity of this protective but also invasive environment accompanies us for the rest of our lives.

While the psychoanalytical paradigm had initially concentrated on the look and the gaze, it has also shifted its attention to sound, especially to the voice. Mary Ann Doane has examined such liminal cases as *voice-off* (origin of voice is in the diegetic space, but not within the actual frame of the image) *voice-over* (origin of voice beyond the boundaries of the diegesis) and *interior monologue* (character is visible, but not the creation of sound as the sound is interiorized) under the aspect of sound as a "sonorous envelope". In this perspective, sound functions as the voice of the mother before birth that enfolds and encloses us. For Doane the cinema experience is characterized by the interaction of several spaces (auditorium, filmic space) generating as an effect the phantasmatic body "which offers a support as well as a point of identification for the subject addressed by the film".[22] Similarly, Kaja Silverman takes this psychoanalytic primordial experience of being immersed and enveloped by the mother's voice as her starting point, yet for her this immersive-acoustic Ur-experience is a retroactive fantasy. Silverman detects in the use of sound in classical cinema a similarly hierarchical gender logic as Mulvey had seen in the visual structures of look and gaze: "a textual model which holds the female voice and body insistently to the interior of the diegesis, while relegating the male subject to a position of apparent discursive exteriority by identifying him with mastering speech, vision, or hearing."[23] Silverman conceptualizes the maternal (i.e. female) voice in a state of tension between, on the one hand, a symbol of imaginary wholeness and happiness (from the perspective of the unconscious) and on the other hand a sign for powerlessness and captivity (from the perspective of consciousness).[24] This points to the ambiguous and polyvalent position of the female voice – a stance also underlined in Michel Chion's concept of the "screaming point". Certain films – Chion names KING KONG (US, 1933, Ernest B. Schoedsack and Merian C. Cooper), PSYCHO (US, 1960, Alfred Hitchcock) and BLOW-OUT (US, 1981, Brian de Palma) – systematically work toward producing a female scream which then exceeds and transcends this logic:

> the man is but the organizer of the spectacle, the producer of this extrava-
> ganza, but [. . .] the screaming point is beyond him, just as it is beyond the
> woman who issues it as the medium. [. . .] The screaming point is where
> speech is suddenly extinct, a black hole, the exit of being. [25]

This feature of sound, to slide without felt transition from meaning to non-sense, or to drop into a black hole beyond and prior to signification, was already on our minds when discussing the porous borderline between sound and noise above.

If sound is indeed so ambivalent in respect of gender, it makes sense that it should partake in a tendency prevalent in much of contemporary cinema, namely to unsettle the spectator "ontologically" with all kinds of "mind-games": a theme to which we will return in our chapter on mind and brain, as these games play with our sense of identity and memory. One of the features of the so-called "new sound picture" is that it puts the spectator into "free-fall", in time as well as in space, as many of the formal parameters that ensured the stabiliza-tion and orientation of the spectator in classical cinema are subverted, refigured or merely called into question. Hence the appropriateness of the tag-line from ALIEN (US, 1979, Ridley Scott): "In space, no-one can hear you scream", espe-cially when we recall how the film insists on the ambivalence of the maternal (the mother of the hostile aliens is the ultimate opponent, the humanoid bodies are themselves "hosts" to the aliens) and the traumatic associations of both pen-etration and the womb (in Ash giving "birth" to an alien, in the penetration into the space ship by the mother alien). These and related issues of inside/outside and mobile/fixed take on new pertinence at a time when sound is increasingly mobile, malleable, modular and invasive.

Figure 6.5 PSYCHO: the cinema as a machine for producing the female scream.

If, from this perspective, one focuses on sound as the "queen of the senses" even in the cinematic experience, one begins to understand why Chion seemingly inverts the traditional hierarchy of image and sound. Chion names three other reasons: first, cinema for him is an audio-event before it becomes a visual one. Second, he repeatedly stresses the ubiquity and materiality of sound in relation to the image, which crucially depends on the sound to give the image body and substance. Third, his concept of "rendering" points to a central characteristic of contemporary (digital) film sound, now regarded more as a substance, a filler that is being molded and shaped, before it is "laid down" and applied to the image track. In action films, where the noises and sounds produced by bodies and objects are often specially featured, much of an action's violence and brutality (the impact, the thud, the blow, the explosion, the crash) are conveyed acoustically. The post-apocalyptic landscape in the beginning of TERMINATOR 2: JUDGMENT DAY (US, 1991, James Cameron) takes shape over the crunch of a war robot's boots: what on first sight appears to be rubble turns out, not least through sound, to be recognizable as human skulls, or as Chion notes: "it is the ear that renders the image visible."

Both Chion and Žižek repeatedly turn to David Lynch, as one of the contemporary cinema's most important directors, not surprisingly in light of the fact that Lynch has upset the "power relations" between image and sound more than any other film-maker and inverted the characteristics of sound and image. In genres like the horror film or fantasy, it is the special effects applied to the image that generate the uncanny side of reality, as a ghostly or haunting presence; in Lynch's films, reminiscent of the cinema's nineteenth-century predecessors, it is often sound that creates phantasmagoric effects through acoustic ghosts and aural apparitions. At the same time, the image in Lynch is often on the verge of disappearing, of becoming blurred and losing any fixed form, whereas sound remains stable, referential, articulated, with clear borders and contours. Related as it is to the reversibility of active and passive, of subject and object, of living and inanimate, a spectacularly protracted play between sound and image is staged, for instance, in the Silencio Club sequence in MULHOLLAND DRIVE, where almost all the features we have been discussing in this chapter – separation of body and voice, of material support and aural apparition, ventriloquism and the supernatural – are demonstrated in exemplary, almost textbook fashion.[26]

The sequence can be understood as Lynch's way of commenting indirectly on the far-reaching developments in the musical and acoustic experience of the past few decades. Dolby systems exposed cinema spectators not just to the stereo experience that had prevailed in the domestic space since the 1960s but also to the specific "Walkman" experience, which entered cinemas via Dolby and digitization. It will be recalled how music and sound, traditionally listened to and enjoyed indoors, gained a new mobility when Sony in 1979 released the portable music player called Walkman, transporting the indoor experience outside, into public space.[27] Within this exterior space, headphones created an interior space that one did not have to share with anyone else. In other words, the Walkman tendentiously challenged, if not altogether rendered obsolete, customary boundaries such as the ones between interior and exterior, center and periphery, mobility and stasis, as well as further blurring the boundaries between private and public. Sound became something that one could imagine generating in one's own head or wear around one's body, since through the Walkman one became the (acoustic) epicenter of the world, irrespective of how peripherally one was physically positioned, in respect to other (social, spatial) markers of center or hierarchy.

A playful illustration of this can be found in a teen film from the early days of the Walkman, LA BOUM (FR, 1980, Claude Pinoteau). In one scene, in the midst of a party bustle, Matthieu (Alexandre Sterling) covers Vic's (Sophie Marceau) ears with headphones through which she listens to the ballad "Dreams Are My Reality" and cannot help but give in to a close dance with him. Here, then, the exterior space (of the Walkman) becomes the interior space (of its carrier), irrespective of what music happens to be playing "outside", for the others. A similar effect is being achieved with the Dolby surround-sound system in the cinema – irrespective of where one sits and at what angle to the screen, sound in combination with our acoustic sense gives us the impression that we are positioned centrally. Contributing to this feeling is the already mentioned materiality of the acoustic: sound acts upon the medium (air), needed in order to propagate itself, thereby lending sound a body and a presence, which our brains transmit to the image. When deep bass sounds are involved, we feel the air-pressure on our skin, just as we do in the case of hi-hats that keep the rhythm

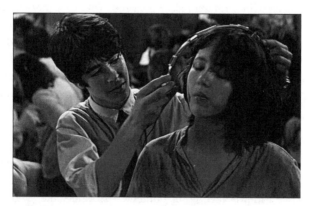

Figure 6.6 LA BOUM (FR, 1982, Claude Pinoteau): before the iPod – Walkman as mobile sound environment.

in percussion. A sense of centrality derives from the fact that we are surrounded by sound and wrongly believe ourselves in the middle of it, of which the image is also a beneficiary.

One conclusion to be drawn from this chapter is that the transfer between sound and image has created a new interdependence, which is nicely captured in a phrase not from David Lynch, but by his exact counterparts in the avant-garde, Jean-Marie Straub and Danièle Huillet. Straub and Huillet famously said that they wanted spectators to experience their films by "hearing with their eyes and seeing with their ears", a hope that Žižek, as we saw, would embrace as a "fact". Following from this, one could argue that the use of famous musical pieces by classical composers – e.g. Strauss in 2001: A SPACE ODYSSEY, Wagner in APOCALYPSE NOW, Schubert in MINORITY REPORT – act less as an accompaniment to reinforce the affects generated by the narrative (as they do in classical romantic scores), but rather exist as "images" in their own right. Film music increasingly creates its own aesthetic "reality" that stands side-by-side with the image, both spectacular and overwhelming, not necessarily supporting each other, but also destabilizing or trying to outdo the other. In the same way, the use of extra-diegetic pop music (as in the films of Quentin Tarantino) and of conspicuous scores that draw attention to themselves (by composers such as Ennio Morricone, John Williams or Hans Zimmer) fulfill the economic imperative of producing an album that can generate additional revenue as well as serving the aesthetic function of adding an extra layer to an already densely "rendered", "designed", "composed" and "produced" work.

In our Introduction we hinted at the possibility that one of the reasons we need a new theory of the cinema is that the malaise which the moving image has always engendered about a world become fluid, mobile and transient had, if anything, increased with the digital image, its malleability and perceived lack of referential stability. From what has been argued in the present chapter, one might conclude that the new prominence of sound helps to recover the so-called loss of the indexicality of the image, because it makes direct contact with the body and thus acts as a physical link to material reality. The new film sound, in this perspective, becomes a functional substitute or supplement in the cinematic experience, by providing a different kind of index and material trace, i.e. a set of "truth-conditions" for the digital image. Once invested in the photographic image, a sort of (phantasmatic) belief and (fetish-)reliance now requires the sound to "anchor" the image, adding another dimension to sound's technical prominence and cultural importance. But if one can no longer trust the image and one's eye, does this mean one can trust sound and one's ear? Better to assume that with the new sound picture, we can trust neither sound nor image, but at the same time we need both, so that they may verify and confirm each other. It is almost as if in this instance, two "lies" make (for) one "truth". In other words, if sound and image have become indispensable to each other, as well as equivalent, even to the point that each is as untrustworthy as the other, then their mutual untrustworthiness acts as the new "ground" of representation.

Yet what exactly is this "ground" in an environment that is becoming ever more mobile, fluid and unstable? The battle now is between, on the one hand, a sound-and-image combination stabilizing our balance, and "centering" our vision in the geometry of perspectival space, and on the other, sound-and-image having become "mobile" in our technical devices, as well as mobile in how they "transport" our senses and bodies. In the first case, we have the idea of "aural objects": thanks to Dolby and surround sound, the cinema's aural objects now have an architectural consistency in three dimensions. This technological sound lends movement and volume to the space thus made present. Because sound fills space with reverberation, its meaning is perceived to reside in the image, even though it may "come" from elsewhere. Thus, sound "stands for" the space implied by the image, since listening pulls one in, while seeing creates distance. In the second case, the increasing sound mobility in our everyday environment, thanks to MP3-enabled technology such as the iPod or a modern cell-phone, adds to this spatial extension a new uncertainty: how henceforth do we locate our bodies in this aural space? Rendered sound, as Chion demonstrates, is "liquid" and "transient", as well as "thick" and "plastic", which ensures that the image now has a new material feel of weight, density, detail and scale. With sound, the object world invades us in quite surprising ways. The new techno-logical "viscosity" or "velcro" quality of sound can cling to any material sub-stance, but also to any semantic substance: such sound is always poised on the brink of referentiality, but being transient, fleeting and multi-directional, it is also volatile and fickle in the way it attaches itself, or indeed detaches itself from, an image as well as from meaning. Thus, in modern film theory, despite the "turn" to the body and to "embodied perception", we need to be cautious not to presume that we have thus gained firmer ground than in the former days of disembodied sight: we might in fact be walking on crushed bones and skulls, to invoke the landscape of TERMINATOR 2. In the next and final chapter, we therefore want to consider whether the cinema, precisely because it is now so invested in the senses, does not also need to be re-investigated across that organ which processes all our sense-perceptions and motor-activities: the brain, and how the brain relates to the mind, when it comes to the cinematic experience as an embodied experience.

Chapter 7

Cinema as brain
Mind and body

A man wants to forget a woman so dear to him that he cannot bear to lose her. In classical cinema, such a state of mind, bordering on insanity, or simply due to a bout of heavy drinking, would have been cured by a good night's sleep, or a pep talk from his best friend, bringing him back to his senses (and the film to a happy end). Today, however, these methods no longer work, and instead, he decides to erase all memories of her (after learning that she had done the same to him) by means of a complicated operational procedure. During the actual process when all traces of his girlfriend are wiped from his mind, beginning in the "present" of the story and going back in time, the man rediscovers how much she means to him despite the mental anguish and suffering her capricious ways have caused him, so he tries to "hide" her in his childhood memories. But the plan fails, and all recollection is apparently gone. The next day, as if following a whim, he takes the train to the place where he had first met his great love and there he meets her ("once more", as it turns out), so that their story begins all over again. ETERNAL SUNSHINE OF THE SPOTLESS MIND (US, 2002, Michel Gondry) is emblematic for this chapter because it typifies the contemporary interest in identity, memory, trauma and twisted or looped temporal structures. The circular, Möbius-strip-like dynamics of the film calls into question the linear logic of classical cinema, according to which a problem can be recognized and solved, an obstacle can be tackled and overcome. The situation is quite different in ETERNAL SUNSHINE: a never-ending spiral is set in motion and we as spectators are no longer certain of our role in the game a film like this is into, tricked as we, like the characters, are into mistaking "replay" as play. Are we impartial witnesses, active participants or manipulated pawns? ETERNAL SUNSHINE and similar films revolve around questions that we have already pursued in previous chapters: does a film take place inside or outside the spectator's mind, is it objective or subjective? Is visual perception dis-embodied (i.e. purely visual) or embodied (i.e. does it require a body and consciousness)?

Figure 7.1 ETERNAL SUNSHINE: attempting to avoid memory erasure in "real" space.

After introductory remarks illustrating early understandings of the relation between mind and cinema, we will set up a classification of the ways in which one can relate film to mind and brain. A discussion of specific cinematic styles, both past and present, will follow, not from a historiographic perspective, but rather with the purpose of establishing a link between embodied/disembodied perception, cognition and particular types of films. The last part of this chapter then turns to a topic we consider to be one that any film theory must address: does the film we are watching exist independently from ourselves as spectators, and if not, does it take place on our retina, in our brain's synapses and our body's nerve system?

Films are often seen as pure entertainment, an innocuous pastime of make-believe, and sometimes as an art form or medium of artistic self-expression. The idea of film being detached from reality is voiced in the reassurance: "It's only a movie!" But whether uttered in order to bring credulous contemporaries to their senses or to ward off too much identification and emotional involve-ment, the phrase registers the fact that a film can leave a deep imprint, appeal-ing directly to one's consciousness and feelings. A film can change people's lives and their worldview, it can have very personal and private meanings, but it can also attach itself to various public discourses and ideologies in order to domi-nate, transform and distort their perception. Various types of films come under this category, such as propaganda films, characterized by their ability to manip-ulate people's convictions, but also cult films, which develop their momentum through a small but devoted reception before entering the popular imagination, i.e. are "known" even to people who have not seen them. Propaganda films and cult films do not "end" once a title proclaims "The End"; in fact, this is where their impact really starts as they attach themselves to spectators, taking hold of their minds and entering their fantasies. According to this view of cinema, certain films function like a virus or parasite that depends on a human host but also starts to lead a life independent from it. Famous film quotations are good examples as they detach themselves from their direct film context to virally propagate across the culture at large – "This is the beginning of a beautiful friendship" from CASABLANCA (US, 1942, Michael Curtiz), "Go ahead punk, make my day" from DIRTY HARRY (US, 1971, Don Siegel), "You talkin' to me?" from TAXI DRIVER (US, 1976, Martin Scorsese) or "I don't think we're in Kansas anymore" from THE WIZARD OF OZ (US, 1939, Victor Fleming). In the same way that quotations, fragments or clips are becoming a life form independent from the films themselves, one could also point to props or clothes that have been appropriated in popular culture as fashion accessories, such as the long coats from ONCE UPON A TIME IN THE WEST (IT/US, 1968, Sergio Leone), the knee-high boots from PRETTY WOMAN (US, 1990, Garry Marshall) or the sun-glasses from THE MATRIX (US, 1999, Andy and Larry Wachowski). Similarly, characters like Hannibal Lecter, Norman Bates, Maria, the robot in METROPOLIS or Dr. Mabuse have outgrown their respective films and earned their place in the hall of fame or infamy of popular culture. Film censorship works with a similar understanding of cinema's effectiveness, because it is only by acknowl-edging cinema's great impact, be it in the form of corrupting the young or of endangering the public order, that one can justify a ban, or limiting a film's circulation. Underlying this view of cinema is the idea that films are not simply exterior objects whose reception covers a limited time span and which "disap-pear", so to speak, after that, but rather that films, once seen, continue to live in us and can haunt and influence us in much the same manner as past memories or actual experiences. Neither fully external nor entirely "in the mind's eye", films are complexly woven into time, consciousness and self, which is why the role of memory in the construction of subjectivity and identity plays a decisive role in this chapter.

Speaking of cinema as brain or mind evokes a certain tradition in the history of philosophy, and one can distinguish among several notions of the cinema as an extension, analogy or substitute of the mind. Five concepts in particular will help us to clarify the relation. The first one refers to those moments in which an image becomes abstracted from its physical properties and generates a meta-phorical meaning. This happens when, through the clash of shots, a film sequence congeals into a concept. Sergej Eisenstein, whose classification of various montage types were discussed in the context of film as frame (see Chapter 1), used the term "conflict" to characterize such relations. In his idea of intellectual montage, something akin to conceptual or abstract thinking emerges in specific filmic compositions. Even though we have included Eisenstein in the paradigm of the frame, certain aspects of his overall thinking can also be brought to bear on the topic of the brain, especially given his emphasis on the processing of all sense perception in the brain: "The basic sign of the shot can be taken to be the final sum total of its effect on the cortex of the brain as a whole, irrespective of the ways in which the accumulating stimulants have come together."[1] Even if this exhibits a certain behaviorist determinism vis-à-vis the spectator's role as active participant, Eisenstein does not conceptualize the spectator's brain as a passive receiver and executor of signals, but as an active mind that oscillates between mechanical conditioning à la Pavlov and sensually activated memory à la Proust. The mental image, unlike a physical–perceptual image, is invisible, and the decisive qualitative leap contained therein leads from illustration, i.e. from graphic–visual factors, to a mental concept, and to (film) language.[2]

The second possible connection corresponds to Hugo Münsterberg's thesis that there exists a fundamental analogy between cinema and mind, since many techniques typical of cinema (associative montage of different spaces, isolation of details) resemble the way the mind works. Münsterberg, who studied psychology in Germany and taught at Harvard University where he directed the experimental psychology laboratory, had already in the early twentieth century compared film to mental processes, arguing that cinema was a "technical simulation of the unconscious". His book *The Photoplay*, published in 1916, is one of the first works to deal seriously with film and its psychological and cognitive possibilities, and ahead of its time in claiming and trying to systematically substantiate the analogy between cinematic and mental processes.[3] He argues that, with the help of typically cinematic means, such as the flashback or the close-up, motion pictures can render visible psychic phenomena such as attention, memory, fantasy and emotion. Münsterberg predicted that "the moving picture of the future would, more than any other art form, fall under the authority of psychologists who analyze the workings of the mind".[4] According to Friedrich Kittler, it is crucial that Münsterberg, besides being one of the first serious film theoreticians, was head of the psychology lab at Harvard and founder of "psychotechnology":

> Film theory . . . first became possible with psychotechnology, this coupling of physiological and technical experiments, of psychological and ergonomic data. For the first time in the history of the art [. . .] [Münsterberg] proved that film is capable of implementing the neurological data flow itself. [. . .] Film replays to its viewers their own processes of perception – and this with a precision achievable only via experiment, which is to say, it cannot be represented either by consciousness or language.[5]

This turn away from the philosophy of language and consciousness also preoccupies other thinkers subscribing to this paradigm, such as Gilles Deleuze.

Psychotechnology as an instrumentalized version of psychology and psychoa-nalysis tries to base the technological media on their material foundations, by giving priority to objectively measurable reactions to specific sensory stimuli. Or, to shift the metaphor, such a film theory pays less attention to the "soft-ware" (films, subject matter in the widest sense) and instead gives precedence to the "hardware" (interconnections, configurations, machine circuitry), as was already the case in early versions of "apparatus theory" (see Chapter 3). For Kittler, media and technology are not expressions of human subjectivity; instead, the writing machines and recording systems actually produce what we call human subjectivity. Accordingly, he has described his project as one that wants to "drive the human out of the humanities" ("den Geist aus den Geisteswis-senschaften"), according to the notorious title of one of his books.[6] In this sense, mechanically and technologically recorded data are not (visual, aural) represen-tations in the usual sense, but belong to the Lacanian Real (see Chapter 4). Only through the addition of culturally acquired cognitive "filters" (such as narrative, rhetorical tropes or various iconic codes) do they become representational, with the provision that there always remains a surplus or excess – the informa-tional "noise" and the "white noise" in the image (or sound) – that does not become completely absorbed in the "Symbolic" or the "Code".

Indirectly, this raises the question of the status of so-called subjective images in the cinema, especially those attributed to protagonists that the narrative signals as mentally disturbed. Can these images – often flagged by the use of expressive cinematic means, such as anamorphic distortions, surreal juxtaposi-tions, or an unrealistic use of color, as seen in the dream sequence that Salva-dor Dalí designed for Alfred Hitchcock's SPELLBOUND (US, 1945), or in Catherine Deneuve's fantasies in Roman Polanski's REPULSION (UK, 1965) – also be called mental? And what about the spiritualist images in the early cinema or the flashbacks in LE MYSTÈRE DES ROCHES DE KADOR (FR, 1912, Léonce Perret), in which the cinematographic apparatus is presented and employed therapeutically, as an apparatus for working through a trauma: is the basic technology of cinema more on the side of madness and trauma, rather than realism and documentation? Kittler's argument certainly suggests this conclusion, and it encourages one to think of the use of hypnosis and mind-reading in the films of Fritz Lang (e.g. the DR. MABUSE films) as also "experi-mental", in the sense of attempting to reproduce mental and psychic processes in Münsterberg's sense.[7]

A third way of conceptualizing the connection between cinema and mind is self-reflexive and meta-cinematographic: mind, cinema and consciousness relate to each other through the fact that a certain image makes the spectator aware of the act of perceiving images, growing conscious of the processes of consciousness itself; numerous European films of the 1960s emphasize this (see Chapter 3).

Figure 7.2 SPELLBOUND: dreaming as expressive and surrealistic imagery.

This goes beyond the spectator recognizing the implicit voyeurism of a film (as in REAR WINDOW, see Chapter 1) or realizing that the image on the screen "knows" that it is being perceived (as in LE MÈPRIS, see Chapter 3). What we are alluding to are those cases in which a specific scene draws attention to the fact that there might exist another level of reflexivity, less in the sense of the mirror or a *mise-en-abyme* construction and more as pure brain activity, as a "virtuality" in Deleuze's sense. Michael Haneke's CODE UNKNOWN (CODE INCONNU, FR/GR/RO, 2000) presents a film-within-a-film, but the film "within" the film is not marked, re-framed or otherwise "contained". Rather, it remains suspended, envelops and spills over into the film of which it is a part. This double layering is different from the de-framing in the opening of CACHÉ (FR/AT/GR/IT, 2005, Michael Haneke), where the spectator is profoundly unsettled in both time and space by the perspective the film is presenting: thinking we are looking at an event that "is just taking place", we eventually realize that it is pre-recorded, and is being replayed by spectators that we do not see, thus making us watchers being watched – in the tradition of similar scenes in Hitchcock and Lang, but now enhanced by the deceptive simulation of digital images, further camouflaged because the narrative refers to them as "videotapes".

   The so-called "mind-game films"[8] consist, at least in their key moments, of referential images that are not "framed" by point-of-view structures and by the

Figure 7.3 CACHÉ: unattributable view as a cognitive menace.

classical system of *decoupage*. These images bypass and exceed both the modernist paradigm of self-reference and reflexivity (see Chapter 3) and the "constructivist" paradigm of post-modernity. One could ascribe a "ghostly" or "spiritual"
character to these images, but not in the sense that they take on a subjective
perspective or suggest an otherworldly presence; rather, in the sense that the
cinema itself has a mind "outside" or in excess of (the narration or the characters, the auteur or the spectator) that eludes any fixed positionality (as in
Haneke's CACHÉ). Mind-game films implicate the spectator in ways that can no
longer be accounted for by classical theories of identification, alignment and
identification, because the "default value" or "degree zero" of normal human
interaction and perception are no longer in operation. In this way, any inner
framing (film-within-a-film, mental disturbance) or outer perspectivism
(auteurist reflexivity, distanciation) is lacking, or can be overturned and revised,
leaving the spectator in a state of irreducible uncertainty and ambiguity, as in
David Lynch's LOST HIGHWAY (1997), MULHOLLAND DRIVE (2001) or INLAND
EMPIRE (2006).

A similar kind of visuality can be found in films whose protagonists are in a
certain sense already dead or have barely survived their (symbolic) death, even
if they themselves are not aware of it yet: TIERRA (ES, 1996, Julio Medem), THE
SIXTH SENSE (US, 1999, M. Night Shyamalan), AMERICAN BEAUTY (US, 1999,
Sam Mendes), MEMENTO (US, 2000, Christopher Nolan), VANILLA SKY
(US, 2001, Cameron Crowe) and MINORITY REPORT (US, 2002, Steven Spielberg) are all examples of what has been called post-mortem cinema. The mental
and conceptual images in these films have to do with the limits of classical identity formation, where we assure ourselves of who we are through memory,

perception and bodily self-presence. When these indices of identity fail, or are temporarily disabled, as in conditions of trauma, amnesia or sensory overload, it challenges the idea of a unified, self-identical and rationally motivated individual, assumed and presupposed by humanist philosophy. Not only posthumanist philosophies, such as those of Deleuze and Foucault, but popular films and mainstream cinema, too, register this crisis in our ideas of identity. Protagonists suffer from amnesia (MEMENTO), schizophrenia (FIGHT CLUB, LOST HIGHWAY, DONNIE DARKO), have undergone traumatic experiences (MINORITY REPORT, MYSTIC RIVER) or might even have left the realm of the living altogether (THE SIXTH SENSE, THE OTHERS). The key issue in this respect is the fact that perceptual images are also mental images, and that the latter implicate the spectator in a kind of "schizo-logic" (Deleuze) which resolves itself only in a kind of loop, and therefore neither cancels out nor lays to rest the possibilities of the un-seen and in-visible within the visibly seen.[9]

A fourth type of mental image is a representation that does not attach itself to any point of view (i.e. it cannot be associated with any subject or onlooker whose perspective the scene or object shows), because there is no perceiving subject that we can discern, either intra-diegetically or extra-diegetically. We have already identified a pertinent example in VERTIGO (see Chapter 4), which can also be used to contrast Slavoj Žižek's notion of the mental image with Deleuze's notion of the crystal image.[10] Žižek associates suture and the ontogenesis of the subject with a Freudian slip or a parapraxis on the part of the spectator: in his analysis, several shots do not illustrate Scottie's desire for Madeleine but the paradoxical nature of desire itself. While Žižek sees such mental images arise in the play between disavowal and the fetish that constitutes (male) desire, Deleuze, on the other hand, dismisses desire as tied to a subjective consciousness, be it that of Scottie or of the spectator. For him, Madeleine's profile shot is a "crystal image" in which various temporal levels (past and present, real and virtual time, recollection and yearning) overlap and intersect like the different planes in a crystal.[11] Such mental images are quite rare in classical cinema, but in contemporary cinema they are more and more frequent, especially in postmortem and mind-game films (see above, pp. 154–6).

Finally, the fifth type of mental image is neither virtual nor imaginary, neither visual nor haptic: is it possible to extract a mental image from mimetic representation and realism itself? Examples would be Andrei Tarkovsky's STALKER (SU, 1979) and SOLARIS (SU, 1972), films which seem to take place in a coherent spatial continuum, but whose human interactions, temporal markers and camera movements designate a "world" that is not "realistic" either in terms of place or character psychology. Tarkovsky applies to the visual image (and to sound) that quality of the "rendered" which Michel Chion theorized in relation to sound (see Chapter 6), creating a mental universe of pervasive paranoia or

Figure 7.4 2001: mental image or psychedelic reality?

imminent catastrophe. It raises the question as to whether images that induce such strong affects of anxiety, threat and fear as do those of Tarkovsky's films, without resorting to narrative suspense or graphic violence, should be called embodied or dis-embodied. Perhaps what has been labeled "haptic" (see Chapter 5) is better described as "mental"? Similarly, the "psychedelic effects" in Stanley Kubrick's 2001: A SPACE ODYSSEY (UK/US, 1968) and other forms of abstraction in avant-garde cinema would qualify as mental images. We shall return to this particular film in our discussion of Annette Michelson's understanding of film as a cognitive experience.

In this and previous chapters, the name of Gilles Deleuze has been frequently mentioned, not least because his two books on the cinema have been widely read and discussed within the Film Studies community. In the process they have turned a difficult and in many ways dissident view of cinema into a modern classic, making his writings the single most important resource in film theory of the last two decades.[12] But what exactly is Deleuze's project? Based on Henri Bergson's philosophy of immanence and Charles Sanders Peirce's semiotics, Deleuze proposed a theory of moving images that can be interpreted both as a philosophy of film and as a history of cinema. From Bergson he takes the primacy of matter, movement and time in the constitution of being and consciousness, and from Pierce he takes an unusual taxonomy and nomenclature, to produce a map or assemblage of cinema as a life-form: Deleuze himself described his work as a "natural history of cinema" akin to a Linnéan classificatory scheme, while drawing nonetheless mostly on the canon of great auteurs as identified by the *Cahiers du Cinéma* school, and inspired by André Bazin (see Chapter 1). On account of his special interest in intensities, energies, connections, affective states and sensory perception, Deleuze has often been labeled a phenomenologist. This designation is problematic for at least two reasons: first of all, because phenomenology has since the time of Edmund Husserl differentiated itself into several sub-strands, being more a way of doing work in different disciplines (philosophy, psychology, cinema studies) than a discipline on its own, so that applied to an idiosyncratic thinker such as Deleuze, the label suggests too little and too much.

Second, and more critically, Deleuze does not refer himself to phenomenology's founding figures, Husserl or Maurice Merleau-Ponty, whose revived relevance for film theory we explored in connection with Vivian Sobchack, but instead turns to the vitalist life philosophy of Henri Bergson. In fact, Deleuze's interest in cinema is partly an attempt to overcome a split that is constitutive of phenomenology – the split between subject and object, between consciousness and its content. He also rejects any kind of transcendence that would lay claim to a position outside and beyond itself, a problem implicit in all attempts at systematic philosophy since Kant first drew attention to it. Deleuze's philosophy can be understood as a critique of the three Hs who, however indirectly, operate with a transcendental category – Hegel, Husserl and Heidegger – even where they leave it suspended, or formulate it as the condition of possibility. The cinema for Deleuze is a form of philosophy precisely to the degree that it overcomes both the Cartesian division between subject and object (*res cogitans* and *res extensa*) and the phenomenologist's assertion that consciousness is always the consciousness of something, and thus involves intentionality. For Deleuze, cinema is material and immaterial, a form of becoming rather than a mode of signification or meaning, and he posits for it an immanence of being in which matter, motion and consciousness are inseparably intertwined. The film image, therefore, exists as a special state of matter, neither an object of heightened perception and of enhanced sensations, nor a sign whose meaning is hidden in or behind the image, as in linguistic or psycho-semiotic theories. This explains why Deleuze shows no interest in concepts such as "representation", "subject position", or "self-reflexivity", i.e. in key concepts of ideological critique and radical practice. By rejecting a transcendental perspective, one must also abandon the idea of an Archimedean point which would allow one to critique the cinema as an ideology. Instead, the cinema is a reality and a way of thinking, which might be translated into saying that, as we speak about the cinema, we are already in the cinema and the cinema is always already in us.

According to Deleuze, cinema deals essentially with two major (philosophical) issues: movement and time. For him cinema is neither a medium for telling stories in which the universe presents itself as a world ordered by narrative, as narratologists believe (see Chapter 2), nor a medium of materialistic conflict montage in which the discrepancies of the world are superseded by the dialectic movement of immanent forces, as the Russian constructivists believed (see Chapter 1). Rather, cinema is a medium akin to modern philosophy because it philosophizes about movement and time with its own means (i.e. its own movement in time). It is crucial to note that Deleuze is not interested in films that may represent and narrate key question of philosophy as conflicts in their story,[13] but cinema is itself a form of philosophy making great film-makers also great thinkers, possibly the only philosophers of the twentieth century able to think technology, body and brain within a single life-world.

Deleuze distinguishes fundamentally two types of images, the movement-image and the time-image, each of which he further divides into sub-categories. The movement-image stands for a cinema of perceptions, affects and actions in which the sensory-motor schema of the human body is a functioning unit. A chain links perceptions to feelings, and feelings to sensations and sensations to actions, which in turn gives rise to perceptions, etc., and puts the human being as agent at the center of the motion that is a movie. This is how classical-realist cinema works for Deleuze, especially Hollywood cinema until the 1950s: "The cinema of action depicts sensory-motor situations: there are characters, in a certain situation, who act, perhaps very violently, according to how they perceive the situation. Actions are linked to perceptions and perceptions develop into actions."[14] According to the logic of the movement-image, time is subordinated to movement and thus can be expressed or depicted only indirectly. Even such mental and temporal inserts as flashbacks and dream sequences serve the logic of actions and support the sensory-motor chain.

Things are different when it comes to the time-image, which appears for the first time in the deep crisis of the European post-war order, when Italian Neorealism suspended the links between action and perception and transformed characters from agents into observers:

> If the major break comes at the end of the war, with neorealism, it's precisely because neorealism registers the collapse of sensory-motor schemes: characters no longer "know" how to react to situations that are beyond them, too awful, or too beautiful, or insoluble [. . .]. So [. . .] the possibility appears of temporalizing the cinematic image: pure time, a little bit of time in its pure form, rather than motion.[15]

Time thus emerges as a central element of modern cinema in the films of such auteurs as Yasujiro Ozu, Michelangelo Antonioni or Alain Resnais, to name just a few. In keeping with Bergson, Deleuze believes that time is not an abstract unit of measurement that can be subdivided into individual segments; instead, time is an indivisible continuum that splits in the present moment.

Whatever intellectual commitment one may have to Deleuze's overall project – besides a sizeable number of often unconditional adherents, there are also many who reject Deleuze, either dismissing his ideas on cinema as "a mere curiosity", or ignoring them altogether – the distinction between movement-image and time-image has provided film theory with a powerful if reductive model of historiography. Deleuze sees a distinct moment of rupture or epistemic break between classical and modern cinema, which he argues on both formal-aesthetic and historical-political grounds. This contrasts with another tendency in contemporary film theory, which has tried to break as decisively as did Deleuze with semiotic, psychoanalytic and feminist film theory, namely cognitivist film theory, but without putting forward a similar periodization of historical modes. Yet Deleuzians and the cognitivists have more in common than either side is willing to concede. While dismissing or ignoring Deleuze, Anglo-American cognitivism also arose out of a similarly profound dissatisfaction with conceptualizing cinema in terms of the mirror (Chapter 3), of language, signs and the look (Chapters 3 and 4). Like Deleuze, they opted instead for a more philosophical approach, but concentrated on an analysis of the mental schemata and cognitive processes that make it possible for us to understand moving images at all: as representations, as stories, or how it comes that we recognize in the characters on-screen emotions or motives that we, as spectators, will always have to infer, construct and to attribute, rather than see by way of direct evidence and proof.

But before examining more fully the manner in which cognitivist film theory is also focused on mind and brain, it is necessary to outline how a theory of avant-garde film conceives of the cinema as a mental event as well as a bodily experience, inserting itself into the classificatory schemes of classical and modern cinema just outlined (but also of art cinema, auteurism and issues of gender and representation) from a different historiographic as well as aesthetic vantage point.

Annette Michelson, a critic and writer from New York and a long-time professor at New York University, is one of the most influential theorists of avant-garde films. She sees continuity between the concerns raised by the moving image for the historical avant-gardes (Eisenstein, Vertov, Epstein, Dulac, Leger or Duchamp), and the way these problems have been taken up and transformed by directors such as Paul Sharits, Stan Brakhage, Ken Jacobs and Michael Snow, all of whom believe in cinema as an epistemological force. Their approach to film-making is philosophical, in that they are convinced that cinema can generate new knowledge about the world, a unique type of knowledge not to be acquired or transmitted in any other way. In this respect, Michelson is closer to Deleuze, who also used cinema as a philosophical tool, than to Lacan and Foucault, who were pessimistic vis-à-vis cinema's epistemological potential (as eye: see Chapter 4), but she is also sympathetic to cognitivism as a way to examine the underlying mental–perceptual capabilities (such as abstract or mathematical thinking) that a non-narrative or para-narrative cinema calls upon.

In one of her most influential articles, Michelson has shown that even a commercial film like 2001: A SPACE ODYSSEY (albeit one made by an eccentric American émigré in England) can have the unique epistemological effect of changing our ways of seeing that is more often attributed to avant-garde film or a modernist artwork. Under modernism, artists have broken with art's mimetic function, asking instead for the condition of possibility of knowledge through art:

> Art now takes the nature of reality, the nature of consciousness in and through perception, as its subject or domain. As exploration of the conditions and terms of perception, art henceforth converges with philosophy and science upon the problem of reality as known and knowable.[16]

Although this ambition was already at the heart of German Romanticism and its aesthetics, in the modernist period, it may be film and the cinema that most fully take up the challenge of how a work of art can embody a sensuous form of knowledge while possessing all the conceptual clarity of philosophical reasoning and scientific thought.

Michelson begins by claiming that cinema brings to us "a dream for waking minds" (59), a paradoxical kind of consciousness that includes the unconscious. But cinema can also give us bodily experiences that are at least as paradoxical.

Figure 7.5 CELESTIAL SUBWAY LINE (2004, Ken Jacobs): exploring the epistemological possibilities of the cinema.

For instance, 2001: A SPACE ODYSSEY might be said to reinvent cinema as "bodies in space" through the use it makes of its images of zero gravity. As the scenes of floating bodies demonstrate, the cinema can suspend the philosophical opposition between body and mind, by making us question our normal assumptions of (pictorial) space as geometric and anthropocentric, i.e. organized in terms of "in front" and "behind", "above" and "below", suggesting that we should re-think the relation between these coordinates. Kubrick successfully extends the physical sensation of weightlessness to spectators' bodies, not through some new technological device, as in IMAX-cinema, but by means of subtle yet substantial permutations in the spectator's consciousness, brought about by editing, the combination of music and image, or the variations of scale and size. This generates a new reflexivity about the specific nature of film experience as the articulation of space and time. The way Michelson describes the complex zero-gravity process and presents the potentially confusing character of these scenes for a mainstream audience touches upon an aspect that has been central also to our argument, namely that contemporary cinema is deeply involved in a re-orientation of the traditional picture plane as a two-dimensional surface giving access to a three-dimensional view:

> The difference between the two qualities [our own inner coordinates and what we see] and intensities of response is the difference between things seen and things felt, between situations visually observed and those sensed haptically, between a narrative emblem and a radically formal embodiment of spatial logic.
>
> (60)

This drama between things "seen" and things "felt", between the coordinates of embodied and disembodied perception, between sensation and cognition, translates in Kubrick into the difference between physical groundedness and a feeling of weightlessness, which for Michaelson becomes "the sub-plot of the film". It is as if we were perceiving the world through a completely different mental disposition, but one that has a physical dimension, so that the spectator partakes in the fundamental dynamics of motion. 2001 is therefore a film that teaches the spectator how it wants to be seen and understood, ideally acquiring the ability to orient oneself in space and time differently as body and consciousness. For Michelson, who refers to the developmental psychologist Jean Piaget when discussing how children learn to locate themselves in space, it is precisely this seminal connection between body and consciousness that represents the essence of cinema: "Seeing films, in general, one gains an intimation of the link between the development of sensory-motor knowledge to that of intelligence itself" (62). Losing and regaining balance in weightless space becomes a process

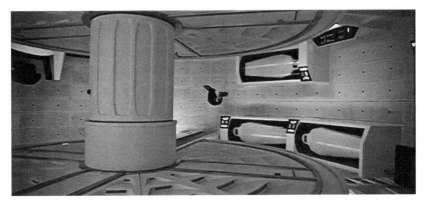

Figure 7.6 2001: weightlessness asking us to rethink the relation of body and
      mind.

of open learning that resembles our entrance into this world: "Acceptance of
imbalance is [. . .] the condition of receptivity to this film. [. . .] [We] rediscover
the space and dimension of the body as theatre of consciousness" (62f.). Following Michelson's analysis of 2001: A SPACE ODYSSEY, one could conclude that the
cinema promises to locate the mind on new ground and trains it to renounce all
orientation and direction: the body in (outer) space as a haptic, or rather
sensory-motor, experience that revokes or takes back evolutionary "progress".
In the film's most famous scene of the ape and his bone, the first murder (or
original sin) in human history coincides with the moment of upward and forward
bodily orientation.

Both Deleuze in the 1980s and Michelson in the 1960s would agree that,
when talking about the cinema as an epistemological "tool", it is no longer fea-
sible to deal with mind and body in separation; in the cinema, neither the body
(and sensation) dominates the mind nor the mind (cognition) negates physical
presence, but rather a body–brain or brain–body, a neuronal web unites consciousness and body into a single, indivisible whole. In Deleuze's modern
(European) cinema, and Michaelson's (North-American) avant-garde film, it
makes more sense to speak of a camera consciousness than to perpetuate the
body–mind dualism. If Italian Neorealism called Hollywood realism into question by emphasizing elliptical storylines, accidental encounters, arbitrary dis-
ruptions and fragmented connections, the cinema of Kubrick, Sharits or Snow
made us think of continuity, movement and surfaces in radically different
ways.

Cognitivist film theory, too, has begun to rethink how the fundamental categories of time and space, agency and emotion in the cinema are related to the
minds and bodies of spectators. For instance, another way of rethinking European art cinema of the 1960s has been proposed by the Danish cognitivist

Torben Grodal. Grodal has argued that our notions of high culture and mass art have their origin in how we think about sensations and perceptions, specifically how we relate our bodies to the very different experiences of European art films (disembodied, abstract and permanent meaning – soul) and to American action pictures (embodied, concrete and "fleeting" meaning – body).[17] Grodal borrows a three-level model of the Self from neuroscientist António Damásio which couples the activities of the mind with the functioning of the body: the first level is the comatose self, which controls the vegetative (bodily) functions; he refers to the second level as the embodied core consciousness which reacts to impulses from the environment and exists only in the present (not unlike the sensory-motor links in Deleuze's movement-image); and he refers to the third as the autobiographical (narrated) self in which an identity develops through projections into the past (memory, trauma, pleasant or painful experience) and into the future (plans, hopes, promises). Grodal posits that art cinema marks a break, rupture or blockage between core consciousness and autobiographical self: either the claims of the supra-temporal, disembodied identity cannot be reconciled with the present, embodied experiences (Grodal names Bess in Lars von Trier's BREAKING THE WAVES [DK, 1996] as a character who can no longer connect bodily consummated love and spiritual love) or the autobiographical self blocks, by way of ambivalences or traumas, any possibility of experience for the core consciousness (Alain Resnais' L'ANNÉE DERNIÈRE À MARIENBAD [FR/ IT, 1961] and Krzysztof Kieslowski's TROIS COULEURS: BLEU [FR, 1993]). The European art cinema resolves this tension by bringing an eternal and supra-personal authority into play (the "soul" independent from the body), which is articulated through auteurist intentionality and abstract moral concepts.

Grodal therefore returns to the "soul" of cinema, understood not so much as an unveiling of reality, as Bazin believed (see Chapter 1), or as an appearance of the human face in the form of a close-up, as Balázs believed (see Chapter 3), but rather as a blockage and severed connections between core consciousness and abstract Self. While the classical film stays in the present of the core consciousness, the art film revolves around the discrepancy between fleeting present and eternal values, between body and mind. For a cognitivist and constructivist, the power of cinema lies in its ability to deflect, block or repress affect and action, or to correlate them and terminate one in favor of the other. Cognitivism is not interested in "What is cinema?" (i.e. the very question that gave Bazin's collected writings its title) but in what (cinema/camera) consciousness is, whether it is embodied or dis-embodied. In this perspective, cinema serves as a test case for more general theories of the embodied Self and of consciousness. In this respect cognitivists share the view that cinema has become a sort of default value of human experience, even if they sometimes reverse the equation and claim that film perception is no different than normal perception.

If one were to apply Grodal's scheme to post-classical cinema (or "mind-game films"), one might say that here the "autobiographical brain" is what is blocked or absent (FIGHT CLUB, MEMENTO, THE SIXTH SENSE, etc.), ensuring that the body becomes the locus not only for a new kind of bodily investment, but also for new forms of spirituality. This would be the positive version. By contrast, from a Foucauldian perspective, the argument would be that such films, with their emphasis on the different bodily states, illustrate the dominant power structures of contemporary society: no longer based on interdiction, the law, or coercion, but controlling the individual through "body-politics", the "care of the self", and "discipline through fun".[18] The separation between body and mind is now overcome by casting the latter as psychopathic, pathological or dysfunctional, whereas the body is sensitized somatically. In post-classical American cinema the body *is* the mind, a neuronal network with high-speed circuits and hyper-sensitive physical reactions.[19]

If we look back once more at the various cinematic metaphors that we have analyzed and applied so far, this might be the point where we could usefully return to and re-interpret the foundations of our body-based system of distinctions and differentiations: tracing the various modalities we have identified back to the history of film theory from their current manifestations in contemporary cinema. It is in this sense that we designated films like TIERRA and MINORITY REPORT, AMERICAN BEAUTY and DONNIE DARKO, VOLVER and RUN, LOLA, RUN as post-mortem films: while the body is (un)dead, the brain goes on living and leads an afterlife of sorts or finds different – ghostly, but also banal, mundane – forms of embodiment.

Films that introduce us without mediation or "frame" into the world of an unfamiliar consciousness, making little perceivable distinction between subjective and objective, inside and outside, private or public, would therefore put us in the presence of such a "brain" as Damásio or Grodal locate between the

Figure 7.7 DONNIE DARKO: the film theatre as the site of post-mortem existence.

comatose self and the autobiographical brain. Given our symbiotic existence with machines, objects and various hybrid forms of intelligence under the guise of numerous automated systems, from the ATM to the coffee machine, and from the Internet to the car, it is not clear whether such a re-orientation of the body and of sense perception in contemporary cinema is "part of the problem" (a new form of dependency and control, as in the dystopian conception of Foucault and Deleuze) or already "part of the solution" (a new form of adaptation and evolution, as the cognitivists or various popular science writers argue).[20]

Grodal's position is already an attenuated version of the cognitivist stance. As we argued in earlier chapters, classical cinema projects an essentially disembodied spectator, as do most theories that emphasize vision, be they constructivist or realist (see Chapter 1), narratological (see Chapter 2) or critical of dominant ideology (see Chapters 3 and 4), after the motto: "I see, therefore I am (in the cinema)." This statement may take a more convoluted form in Lacan ("I see what I do not know, and I know what I do not see") and in Foucault's theory of the panoptic gaze ("I see, therefore I am perceived"). The cognitivist position would not consider cinema a special case of perception governed by its own rules; as a version of constructivism, it would hold that all sense perception and physical sensations are processed by the brain, in order to be "seen" or "felt", including in the cinema. Therefore it is neither "the body" nor "the senses" but the brain that decides whether something is pleasant or painful, hot or cold, wet or dry.

Cognitivists would further argue that, while the same processes that govern our interaction with the sensible world also apply in the cinema, it is nonetheless the case that, there, sense perceptions are reduced only to the eye and ear. This position is taken by Joseph D. Anderson, whose "ecological approach" (following Gregory Bateson) sets out to transform the evolutionary development of the brain in reaction to environmental conditions into the basis for a film theory:

> The viewer can be thought of as a standard biological audio/video processor. The central processing unit, the brain along with its sensory modules, is standard. The same model with only minor variations is issued to everyone. The basic operating system is also standard and universal, for both the brain and its functions were created over 150 million years of mammalian evolution.[21]

Within the parameters of this approach, film theory's task is to specify the distinctions between film perception and everyday perception, but to do so from the perspective of neuroscience, rather than within the hermeneutic and histor-

ical critique of the humanities.[22] Another version of cognitivism, following the
tenets of analytical philosophy, has engaged more directly with psychoanalytic
and linguistic film theory, questioning the assumption that in cinema we are
confronted with illusion/simulation or mis-cognition and disavowal. They
argue that there are fundamentally different forms of "seeing", involving the
perception, recognition and apprehension of (fictitious) objects or (imaginary)
people, not all of which are subject to either ocular deception or require the
suspension of disbelief.[23] Once again, there are contracts, frames and conventions that regulate our engagement with make-believe worlds and as-if situations, which rely on ordinary cognitive faculties, mental schemas and perceptive
activities, and so can explain the processes of "identification" in the cinema,
without recourse to more complex (and unproven) psychic processes or unconscious mechanisms.[24]

This returns us to the central question of our book: how do films work on
spectators and how do spectators work on films? Are they purely mental
structures that our brain processes, and then "relays back" to our senses and
the body, or are they first and foremost bodily experiences that one can classify,
make sense of and rationalize only *after the fact*? This leads us once again to
the Cartesian separation between body and soul: is film a matter of the mind,
disembodied, and abstracted, pure visibility that does not necessitate any
matter at all? Or are we in cinema primarily physical beings, i.e. are feeling,
perception and thinking activities that would not be possible in the first
place without the body and its embedded, tacit knowledge? Depending on
the answers we give, touch, skin, the body and the other body-based sensory
perceptions that we have analyzed in previous chapters are either nothing more
than metaphors for describing our manifold relation with the moving image,
or they can be understood as bringing us closer to what is historically so
unique and aesthetically so exciting about the cinema. In the latter event, film
theory would move closer to aesthetics and art history than to philosophy
and cognitivism. Art history around 1900 – at the very time the cinema emerged
– was developing theories to account for the kind of embodied perception
that manifests itself in metaphorical locutions like a "velvety" color, or that
expresses itself via synesthesia, the conflation of different sensory registers,
associating a particular letter with a color, or a sound with a tactile sensation.
For instance, the theory of "empathy" (or "Einfühlung") tried to cover responses
that ranged from an involuntary, instinctual, somatic form of mimicry (such as
we discussed in Chapter 3, under "mirror neurons") to more mediated forms of
affective contact with inanimate objects, including spaces, colors and sounds,
predicated on relationships of proximity and projection. However, the goal of
establishing some kind of physiological basis for aesthetic experience proved
elusive:

Nineteenth-century "empathy" theory [...] tried to account for the capacity of images to stimulate certain psycho-physical responses in beholders. Obviously images do such things, and there is little that is semiotic about it. The "content" of the visual stimulus is only partially governed by a conventional code. But knowledge about such somatic processes was completely inadequate, and still is. There is no physiology of aesthetics. Empathy theory did contribute to one very extraordinary art-historical model: Aby Warburg's "iconology." Influenced by the theories of Friedrich Vischer and Robert Vischer and by Darwin's writings on the expression of emotions, Warburg developed a concept of the symbol that would bridge the phenomenal world and the mind.[25]

In other words, many of the questions film theory asked throughout its 100-year history were also raised in art history, such as whether tactile sensations are conveyed verbally, visually or by some other physiological–somatic processes; whether language (or "inner speech") is involved in the translation of sense perception into conscious thought; how important is sight in "haptic" perception, and what does it mean to look, but not to touch, as a way to stimulate desire and to sharpen the senses? All this suggests that no clear line of separation can be drawn between vision, or sight and the other senses, while nevertheless

Figure 7.8 Adolph Menzel: *Procession in Hofgastein* (1880) – tactile sensations and somatic processes.

retaining a distinction between visual perception (seeing as scrutinizing, demonstrating, differentiating) and embodied perception (seeing as participatory, inclusive, empathetic). Yet how can one factor in, rather than merely dismiss, the Marxist critique that such embodied perception is typical of commodity fetishism? This is a point taken up by Walter Benjamin when he argues that a capitalist society of consumption is based on the commodity's visual appeal, and that this visual appeal corresponds to Marx's idea of fetishism as "the religion of sensuous appetite". This would make the turn to embodied perception something like the ideology of "late" capitalism, as it extends the sensory potential of visual experience, in order to "commodify" it. On the other hand, the "return" to theories of empathy and embodiment may well have its ideological corollary and materialist base in the particular qualities of the digital image, when compared to the photographic image, a possibility we shall explore and address in the Conclusion. One of the key questions will be the extent to which the digital image can be said to be optical–perceptual at all, or belongs into a different register of perception, one that is only inadequately described as either "embodied" or "haptic". Just as in Chion's theory of sound perception, the term he chose for describing the new digital sound was "rendered" rather than "heard", the metaphors relevant for the digital image may not be taken from sight and the eye, but instead derive from substances like putty and wax, or recall liquids of difference viscosity, like oil or water, setting up frames of reference within which the optical and the visual appear merely as "effects" of this new materiality that "touches" the eye but does not give it anything to "see". The digital image would then be cast as a kind of material challenge for representation, joining at the level of technology and practice the critique of visual representation that this study has been conducting at the theoretical level.

Conclusion

Digital cinema – the body and the senses refigured?

A classic movie situation: in a Western frontier town, the camera pans from the saloon to a wooden shack and suddenly the criminal One-eyed Bob appears in front of a Wanted poster featuring his face. The gun-slinging villain robs a bank frequented by farmers and the female teacher, but Sheriff Woody saves the day, putting the bank robber behind bars. And yet, at the edges of the frame, another presence makes its appearance: the protagonists are in fact toys manipulated by a little boy. Like a director, he stages the scene and creates the unfolding events, animating the figures and giving them voices from just beyond the frame; not until he leaves his room do we realize that the hapless and manipulated toys have in fact a life of their own quite distinct from the scene first acted out (be) for(e) our eyes. Consequently, a double reality unfolds in which the apparent master and manipulator (the boy) in fact is being played with, in a game of illusion acted out by the toys. This shift of agency from the human to the non-human is prepared stylistically with a series of subjective point-of-view shots from the perspective of the toy sheriff being tossed around. Emblematically, the opening of TOY STORY (US, 1996, John Lasseter) marks a crucial moment in film history, as this film is the first one exclusively made digitally without any traditional opto-chemical photographic process. Therefore, not only does the narrative of the film dramatize the transition from human to non-human agency (from acting body and drawing hand to generated pixel and computing processor); it also allegorically represents the shift from analog to digital, from photographic to graphic film, from representation to presentation. But as it opens with a familiar movie scene, it also seems to announce that, even though everything has changed (underneath), everything will stay the same (on the surface).

If this were to be our conclusion for the digital age, we would hardly need a final chapter to discuss possible futures and virtual scenarios for film theory, but it is not quite as straightforward. What this conclusion sets out to sketch is how the configurations developed in the seven preceding chapters can be extended into the theories of digital media, inasmuch as they in turn refer back to the

Figure C.1 TOY STORY: whose agency? Mastery and manipulation between humans and non-humans.

cinema. So far, we have dealt mainly with approaches predicated on the cinema in its classical form: photographically based, dependent on theatrical projection, dealing primarily with the live-action feature film. But the salient features selected from the history of film theory for our systematic–historical overview were chosen in the full awareness that we are at a point of transition. From the start we tried to keep our categories and conceptual metaphors open toward future developments – even as these future developments are set to modify and revise the past. Foregrounding window or mirror, for instance, was also a way of suggesting that these metaphors, while constitutive for realist, formalist and reflexive theories of the cinema, may not be so forever: indeed, it is their historicity, and thus variability, that allows one to see them as pertinent metaphors in the first place. However, it is our contention that in the era of digital cinema, the body and the senses are, if anything, even more central for a theoretical understanding of the film experience, whether it is the feeling of bodily presence created through digital sound, the sensory overload and profusion of detail achieved by high-definition digital images when projected in an IMAX theater, or the "freedom" to have "movies to go" on portable devices, and control their sequence and flow with our hands. However, the objective is not to develop our own theory of these phenomena, but once more to extrapolate from recent writings (and films) their degree or level of pertinence for the ongoing reconfiguration of the film experience, i.e. the cinematic body interacting with the spectatorial body. Put differently: what kinds of sensory envelopes and perceptual registers do contemporary theories of cinema and digital media practice propose, and how do these relate to or modify the classical formulations of the cinematic experience that we have discussed in previous chapters?

To return once more to TOY STORY, the emblematic film that allegorizes the shift from analog to digital in a number of ways: what we have sketched above is in fact only the first scene of the film that wants to lure us into believing that everything will stay the same. It is as if a film at this juncture had to reassure the audience about this transition into a different register, by clearly signaling that the same old stories are being told. As it is, the little boy gets a new toy for his birthday: the space warrior Buzz Lightyear. But even the ensuing battle between old frontier (West) and new frontier (space) turns out to be a red herring, a MacGuffin as Hitchcock would call it, as a new threat arises and the opposing mythical heroes have to put aside their differences and work together in order to master the transition to a new world because the family is moving into another house. As formulated by TOY STORY, the task of the sheriffs and space warriors of film theory is to make sure that no one and nothing is left behind in the radical move that the cinema undergoes stylistically as well as technologically, which is to say, aesthetically, as an affective and affecting experience. In order to clarify this apparently contradictory relation between the old and the new, we will be focusing on three locutions meant to characterize contemporary media culture.

The terms often used unquestioningly to hide or unite paradoxes and semantic contradictions are: digital cinema, virtual reality and media convergence. At first glance they seem merely descriptive, bringing together the old (cinema, realism, media specificity) with the new (digital, virtual, media convergence). But the fact that no neologism has yet been coined for post-photographic moving images (in the way the horseless carriage in due course became the automobile, and the wireless was renamed radio) could also indicate either that there is some special value in treating the cinema as a hybrid medium, or that the embedded contradictions (both "digital cinema" and "virtual reality" can be construed as oxymorons, i.e. as adjective–noun contradictions) point to a common denominator, toward which they gesture, but which they cannot (yet) name.

Figure C.2 TOY STORY: old and new frontier battling it out at the digital divide.

To address these issues we shall interrogate a number of digital media theorists, but as in previous chapters, we are also continuing to put to the test our claim that the cinema itself reflects on its changing (epistemological, ontological) status with its own means: we will therefore, in keeping with the overall design of the book, let some recent films speak to the transitions, tensions and recon-figurations, in short: to their own ongoing state-of-being as "cinema".

Although "digital cinema" has become such a commonplace term, broadly understood as the achievement of cinematic effects by digital means, it is worth unpacking some of the inherent assumptions. Lev Manovich, one of the key theorists of digital media with a (film-)historical background, has pointed out that the term "digital cinema" largely missed the point of what was new and dif-ferent. For him, a category shift had to be recognized, whereby every definition hitherto given of cinema (narrative, live action, realism, projection, indexical-ity), had to be relativized and historicized.[1] Expressed even more strongly: the digital, understood as the capacity of converting all analog inscriptions (of sounds and images) and symbolic notations (of written text and musical scores) into electric impulses which can be stored numerically and reproduced in any chosen medium, meant that the digital was indeed a new "ontology". Every-thing we hitherto associate with cinema had thereby become merely the local or specific manifestation of a higher organizing principle, which is to say: every-thing we might think of as "essential" about cinema had become one of the "special effects" of the digital. Arguing along similar lines, Sean Cubitt has tried to redefine what he calls "the cinema effect" across the categories of pixel, cut and vector (relating to firstness, secondness and thirdness in C.S. Peirce's tax-onomy), thus re-constructing from hindsight the (history of) cinema by way of (anachronistic–anticipatory) digital concepts.[2] We want to argue for a different scenario: rather than accepting a (paratactic) conjunction of old and new, con-noting hybridity and transition, or assuming that the cinema had always in some sense "wanted" to be digital, "digital cinema" gives notice of a new hierarchy and power-relation, whereby the adjective trumps the noun, and the tail wags the dog: cinema is henceforth an adjective or attribute of the digital, rather than the other way round: this tacit reversal, then, would be the common denominator, to which the embedded contradiction can only point.

What implications does this have for our contention that the cinema is inher-ently linked to the body and the senses? At first glance it seems to deal it a deadly blow, seeing how digitization is a technological parameter, implying a move from concrete to abstract, from matter-and-mind to mathematical mod-eling, from diversity and sensory plenitude to the tyranny of the single numeri-cal code. But this, of course, is merely to paint the reverse side of its strengths, obvious when one moves from recording and storage to presentation and display. Digital cinema's chameleon-like mutations, its morphing of shapes,

scaling of sizes and rendering of materials, in short: its re-embodied manifestations of everything visible, tactile and sensory allow the digital to become much
more closely aligned and attuned to the body and the senses. The fact that Toy
Story provides a puppet with a point-of-view, with feelings and affects, testi-
fies to the new malleability of the cinematic image when approached not from
the basis of the code, but rather from the perspective of the spectator's experience. A related position has been formulated by Vivian Sobchack, a phenomenologist who already figured prominently in the chapter on skin and contact.
For Sobchack the morph is not simply a new technique made possible by digital
technology. It relates to earlier practices of temporal change and dynamic development, such as the cut or the long take. In its reversibility of form and apparent ease of shape-shifting, the morph reminds us of the malleable and liquid
nature of identity and matter that is at the heart of our phenomenal being – and
that is also central for understanding moving images as part of human culture:

> As our physical double, the morph interrogates the dominant philosophies
> and fantasies that fix our embodied human being and constitute our identi-
> ties as discrete and thus reminds us of our true instability: our physical flux,
> our lack of self-coincidence, our subatomic as well as subcutaneous exist-
> ence that is always in motion and ever changing.[3]

But the digital not only affects film's material substance and textual properties;
a switch of vantage point to the spectator helps to re-focus and re-consider the
impact of the digital on the cinema in the public sphere. As popular spectacle
and public event, the "digital" does not appear to have fundamentally changed
the experience, but merely enhanced the cinema's attractions and attractive-

Figure C.3 Terminator 2 (US, 1991, James Cameron): morphing – physical flux, subatomic and subcutaneous existence.

ness, delivering "better" sound and image quality – without us needing to decide whether this "better" inscribes itself in the (teleo-)logic of "greater and greater realism" or, as already suggested, "merely" provides a more densely textured surface of visual information and acoustic stimuli. In order to achieve this layered density of sensory data, digital cinema has had to (and will continue to) affect the major areas of movie-making: production – how a movie is scripted, story-boarded and shot; post-production – how a movie is edited, synchronized and assembled; distribution – how a movie is shipped or electronically delivered from the production company to movie theaters; exhibition and projection – how a film theater presents, projects and exploits a movie. As a consequence, the entry points that the cinema as public institution provides for the spectator – the doors and openings sketched in Chapter 2 – are being transformed and "remediated", a term influentially introduced by Jay David Bolter and Richard Grusin to describe the changes media undergo when faced with a transformed media enviroment.[4] The result is a striking case of uneven development and non-synchronicity, with respect to the technological, economic and cultural factors involved. While the majority of cinemas in the US used digital (data) projectors by early 2009, the print is still delivered physically as a hard drive (and not streamed from a satellite or via cable) for fear of piracy; at the same time, European cinemas have not yet invested the capital required for a conversion that no one is supposed to notice (only the bookkeepers will register the lower cost). At the same time, major film archives are still routinely transferring digital information to celluloid prints for storage because these have proven to be stable and durable under controlled environmental conditions, while the digital raises a number of open questions (platform accessibility, stability of carrier, agreed standards). The so-called "transition to the digital" is therefore far from smooth and unidirectional, but instead hides a complex set of ongoing negotiations among different parties bringing to the debate their own agendas and concerns.

When going to the local multiplex to watch the latest Hollywood blockbuster, little seems to have changed – stars and genres are still the bait, concessions and merchandise provide additional or even core revenue for the exhibitor, and the audience is still offered a social experience along with a consumerist fantasy. At the same time, changes of size, scale and space are also at work: at one extreme, the modern multiplex with its stadium seating, digital surround-sound and spectacular effects (as in the IMAX or the increasingly popular digital 3-D) creates new spatial configurations, while eliciting affects and corporeal sensations that are closer to the immersivity of virtual reality (see below, pp. 176–9) than to the distanced, contemplative engagement with art cinema, or the tightly controlled focalizing strategies of involvement typical of classical narrative cinema. At the other end of the spectrum, buying a current release or a digitally re-mastered classic on DVD for the price of a theater ticket, and watching it on a laptop, a hand-held device or in high-definition on home-entertainment equipment, represents a new form of appropriation and ownership. It has altered many of the previously fixed parameters, even when compared to the television era and the pre-recorded videotape. The DVD allows one to scale down the experience, displace movie viewing by making it mobile, and manipulate the film in ways that engage our bodies not only as total sensory or perceptual surface, but enabling or empowering it with different kinds of agency: as owners, users and consumers, as prod-users and prosumers of the commodity "film", we can treat it as an experience to be shared, a text to be studied or a possession to be treasured.

Digital cinema thus lays out several paths into the future, where films will come in all lengths and genres, are shown on screens of all sizes, are available in all program formats and at a cost that is determined by the value we put on the occasion, not by the price of the product. Moving images will surround us in ever more diverse ways, becoming so common and ubiquitous that we will take them for granted: no longer a "window on the world", an "interface" to reality, but the very face of it. Yet besides opening up to the future, digital cinema also allows a new access to the cinema's own past: it shifts and re-arranges, for instance, the relation between public and private, collective distraction and individual contemplation, which played such a large role in the early years of cinema. The public nature of the event has once more come to the fore, not just because sociability is a major factor in people's choice of "going to the movies" or enjoying films at a film festival. At the same time, thanks to dedicated Internet sites, blogging and social networking, communal reception is becoming the norm, even when individuals stay at home and isolate themselves in front of their computer or home cinema. Comment and reviews have mobilized spectators in ways that tilt the balance not only in favor of fan communities, "word-of-mouth" and cult success, but also in favor of the amateur as arbiter of taste, at the expense of the professional reviewer, though not necessarily to the detriment of the star-critic-as-blogger.[5]

One of the key points in the discussion of the differences between the "cinematic" and the "digital" concerns the meaning of the term "virtual" in an ocular–specular system of representation, and in a symbolic/numerical system. "Virtual reality" is one of the terms people most readily associate with the idea of "digital cinema" or digital media, but there may be crucial differences as to what is meant by "virtual reality" as well as between the idea of virtual reality and the philosophical concept of "the virtual". Pragmatically, virtual reality can be defined along three complementary parameters: the representation of real environments for the purpose of simulation, often with the practical aim of training, education or therapy. Dangerous, inaccessible or remote situations offer themselves for

Figure C.4 Homepage: David Bordwell – the star critic as blogger.

such simulation. Second, VR can be employed in the context of "abstract systems", making visible and representational that which is either invisible to the human eye or does not in situ qualify for visualization, such as statistical, random or dynamic processes. Third, artistic works and entertainment objects might benefit from VR, but these are, as it were, afterthoughts to the much more directly "useful" applications in the military field, in architectural design, medicine or the modeling of systems, whose 3-D visualization facilitates the purpose of remote control or "tele-action". In an almost paradigmatic way, the framing "documentary" of James Cameron's TITANIC (US, 1999), which tells of the underwater expedition to locate and explore the sunken ocean-liner, fits this pragmatic definition of virtual reality in a double sense, since the "simulated" exploration of the shipwreck gives literally "rise" to the virtual reality of the romantic tale, the remoteness in deep underwater space of the sunken ship supplying the appropriate metaphor for the remoteness in time and memory of the love story. It moreover hints at the potential of "augmented reality" and the use of locative media, in which different "worlds", both actual and virtual, co-exist in the same physical space with the viewer or user, but where the virtual is defined not in terms of illusion or simulation, but rather as a mediated form of presence of something elsewhere in either time or space, or both.

This dilemma of the virtual not being definable in opposition to realism has given rise to two different responses: one school of thought has turned to a reassessment of "illusionism" as an aesthetic value in its own right,[6] while others have pointed to the enunciative dimension of the "index", and thus to make indexicality an aspect of enunciation and deixis.[7] Both these contexts break, at the conceptual level, with our traditional definitions of cinematic "realism", because "reality" in virtual reality is no longer understood as index, trace and reference of an elsewhere, but as a total environment: it thus is a function of a coherence theory (of truth), rather than a correspondence theory (of the sign). Second, while there seems a great deal of emphasis on the "immersive", tactile and "haptic" properties of virtual reality, i.e. the body-based nature of the experience, the bodily sensations are distinct from pictorial illusionism, just as visualization in this sense refers to the use of images or pictorial signs as a symbolic language, in order to render visible a set of abstract data or processes: what we "see" is information translated into a (conventionalized) language of vision, not something that is in any sense really "out there". It is as if several different perceptual and cognitive systems were deployed together, to render the "effect" of virtual reality. Instead of making up one continuous "field", these reality effects are a composite, which in its amalgamated and fused discontinuity either leaves one cold and distanced, or sucks one into a fascinated self-oblivion and immersive self-presence.

Thus "virtual reality" can also refer us back to familiar terrain for which a precedent can be found in the history of film theory. *Virtual reality*, made possible by particular technologies of simulation, involves the spectator's presence, and to this extent, it is comparable to the *imaginary reality* that a spectator attributes to any fiction or narrative, to whose representations (be they verbal, visual or acoustic) the mind grants reality status. We can usefully refer back to "diegesis" here: just as narratives establish their diegetic space by allowing the viewer to give a consistent reading to a film's markers of temporal continuity and spatial contiguity (despite "actual" discontinuity and non-contiguity), virtual realities – especially in their most frequent applications, i.e. in game environments – establish diegetic coherence by a set of rules and conventions, one of which is that the body of the participant or player is fully co-opted into the diegetic space, while nonetheless knowing that s/he also exists in extra-diegetic space, whether it is a bedroom or a video-arcade. Alexander Galloway has concluded that it is "difficult to demarcate the difference between diegetic and non-diegetic acts in a video game, for the process of good game continuity is to fuse these acts together as seamlessly as possible".[8] The body of the operator (as Galloway calls the player), the control of the game (via joystick, keyboard, console) and the action on-screen fuse to create an imaginary reality that connect the machine and the human. Virtual reality thus appeals even more directly to the body and the senses, but not in any simple or straightforwardly "physical" way:

Figure C.5 LAWNMOWER MAN (US, 1992, Brett Leonard): virtual reality as bodily presence and imaginary reality in a futuristic 1990s scenario.

contact (whether by eye or hand or both) is mediated, translated, relayed. Likewise, the game space is modeled as a 3-D environment in the computer, so that the actual view on the screen is being generated from this model, rather than drawn from a set of pre-existing objects or representations. This digital rendering of a virtual space, existing inside the computer as a computational model, happens at one remove and is thus different from the representational reality created by earlier techniques.

At the same time, one only has to think of "Microsoft Windows" to remind oneself of the powerful associations that the window also carries in the digital. Taking her cue from Leon Battista Alberti and the so-called invention of single-point-perspective, Anne Friedberg has argued that many ideological critiques of this set-up have misunderstood the window metaphor as Cartesian when it should rather be conceptualized in terms of Maurice Merleau-Ponty. When inflected phenomenologically, the window and the frame no longer stand in opposition as classical film theory argued for Bazin and Eisenstein and their respective conception of the parameters of depth and flatness, representation and figuration; now it is the lived body encountering the window/frame as "container" in which the dimensions of time and space are held, that allows one to distinguish a "here" and an "I" from a "there" and a "you".[9] Thus, the cinema in the new digital environment both modifies the scope and re-energizes with new meaning one of our key metaphors, window and frame, and paradoxically the one most commonly associated with the photographic image and with "realism". In light of the above, any conceptualization of "window and frame" now has to include their function as portal or segment, thus approximating some of the properties we previously ascribed to "door", but figured as an opening that provides access to an always possible "beyond", fracturing into "multiples" (as in the frames of Web pages) rather than marking off a clearly circumscribed composition, or delimiting a physically plausible space.

In this respect, the premise of MONSTERS INC. (US, 2001, Pete Docter), a film already alluded to in Chapter 2, in which an endless row of doors provides access to countless sleeping children and their dreams, offers a striking example for the door and the frame as a conceptual tool. The monsters enter the nightly bedrooms in order to scare the children and "collect" the children's scream of terror as a source of energy without which the city of the monsters, a parallel (virtual) reality, could not function. The instant and continuous access through a series of portals (the Internet) into the unconscious world of dreams and monsters (the mirror in our taxonomy) interacts with the affective labor of extracting emotions (from the body) and the operation of a society in general (the entertainment industry as economically dependent on the exploitation of affective states and dream-like experiences). Here, Hollywood cleverly and wittily demonstrates its awareness of the rapidly changing media culture, at the same time as it highlights the continuing importance of transitional or liminal spaces, even for the world of digital media with its potentially infinite, extendable and doubled spaces.

Our choice of the films produced by Pixar, the leading animation company in the digital age, is no accident. It points to the renewed attention given to animation, the stepchild of cinema for much of the history of analog photographic cinema, coming back to claim its birthrights and legitimacy. Animation has seen nothing less than a re-animation, a new lease of life, thanks to digitization and new technologies of rendering, morphing, line drawing and compositing. From this perspective, the narrative feature film should perhaps be seen as merely the current "default value" of the cinematic system, which in itself is not grounded on or constituted by this norm. As Lev Manovich has argued, the

Figure C.6 MONSTERS INC. (US, 2001, Pete Docter): emotional labor and extracting affect as the engine of popular culture.

photographic is only one manifestation of the graphic, which is much older than the photographic and is destined to outlive it.[10] Put differently: cinema's step-child, animation, has now become the (grand-)father of the feature film via the story-board. Therefore, it is not too far-fetched to claim that the films of Pixar – from TOY STORY (1996) to WALL-E (2008) – provide a meta-commentary on several of the transformations that the digital has brought about, without reducing these to "technical" issues or "special effects", not even to a matter of convergence. On the contrary, the Pixar films "think" cinema in its wider context at the same time as they are rethinking cinema's relation to the animate and the inanimate, to life and the life-like, to subjectivities and objects. In particular, they seem deeply involved in the question of what a thing is, an object, and what kind of object relations can a subject have with the (things of the) world. Many philosophers and psychologists have understood human social and psychic reality as being determined by object relations: after all, they establish and shape our access to the world, no matter if we discuss objects in terms of Marx's "commodity fetishism", Heideggers's "Ge-Stell", McLuhan's "extensions of man" or the psychoanalytic theories of Melanie Klein and D.W. Winnicott. As our environment becomes increasingly permeated with technology, our relationship to the world is being fashioned by objects that more often behave like subjects that actively shape their environment rather than as simple tools we control and bend to our will. In this way, Pixar unfolds a theory of object relations that addresses questions of agency, freedom, nature and technology across a series of animation films. In TOY STORY, humans are only present as partial objects, while the object world takes center stage, turning the initial premise of cinema, namely to show humans and their world, on its head. In fact, Pixar has almost exclusively dealt in its films with non-human protagonists; the focus instead is either on animals (fish, rats, insects) or on objects to which humans often cultivate a peculiar close and affective relation (toys, cars, robots). This comes full circle in WALL-E, which presents a planet whose only survivor of an apocalyptic ecological catastrophe is a pre-programmed cleaning robot that develops feelings out of its algorithmic routines (echoing Steven Spielberg's earlier AI [US, 2001]). The deceptive autonomy of the digital image, where an object world is generated by another object in which human interference is no longer directly visible, reaches its apotheosis in WALL-E. For the better part of the film, humanoids are conspicuously absent, even language is reduced to its absolute minimum in this machine world that does not feature a dystopian war of robots against humans as in the TERMINATOR series, but rather shows a utopian world free of human intervention (and therefore a better place). It is indeed the survival of the human race and the future of history in the face of environmental danger and massive pollution that this film negotiates, and thus prepares for a "return to things" (Edmund Husserl), as we see it in the theories of Bernard

Figure C.7 Wᴀʟʟ-E (US, 2008, Andrew Stanton): a world devoid of humans
— entertainment as utopia.

Stiegler, Giorgio Agamben, Bruno Latour and the renewed attention to Maurice
Merleau-Ponty and other thinkers of phenomenology.[11]

This insistence on the place and role of objects in everyday life is also meant
to underline the fact that the transformed media environment is not solely concerned with the digital code into which all images, sounds and texts are being
translated. In our thoroughly designed world of "gadgets", we tend to think of
the digital as referring to objects like iPods and mobile phones, laptops and
Blackberries, LED TVs and touch-screens – devices of communication and
interaction that seem to be increasingly "networked" thanks to their ability not
only to access or transmit digital information of whatever kind, but also to be
"on-line", i.e. permanently ready to both send and receive messages. The argument that often follows is that the common denominator of all modern media is
their convergence with each other, propelled by the shared digital code. This,
however, would be to reduce media to their technical specification or operating
system, disregarding their culturally diverse uses and discarding their respective
social histories. The separate and yet intertwined trajectories of cinema, photography, gramophone, radio and television – the analog sound-and-image media
of the twentieth century – suggest that these complex genealogies and multi-
faceted interactions are likely to continue, even if the Internet is increasingly
the environment (and default value) where these differences and complementa-
rities play themselves out.

With respect to the cinema, the case for convergence is especially complicated, and seems at first glance again quite paradoxical. On the one hand, there
is a tendency for moving image platforms to become more mobile, more mini-
aturized and multi-purpose (converging, if at all, around hand-held appliances,
rather than the domestic television set and the computer screen, as had been
predicted only a decade ago). On the other hand, the projection experience, so

typical – some would say, so essential and indispensible – for the cinema, has transferred to ever-larger screens, in multiplexes, IMAX theaters, town squares, open-air venues as well as in the home.[12] Here, the dynamics reconfigure themselves around the dramatic social changes that have re-drawn, blurred or all but abolished the traditional boundaries between private and public, with their quite different affective and perceptual "experience economies". These, to a remarkable degree, have revitalized the cinema as a public sphere, whether one approves of the event-driven popularity of mainstream movies, or regrets their single-minded investment in special effects and spectacular attraction. At the same time, however, while the new mobility of the cinema screen owes much to the portability of sound, which genealogically connects the iPod and the mobile phone to the Walkman and other portable music devices (well established even before the "digital revolution"), the new giant screens are not, strictly speaking, predicated on projection, but are rather based on light-emitting diodes (LEDs) or on liquid-crystal displays (LCDs), and thus utilize principles of illumination quite contrary to those of photographic transparency and luminosity – proving that technological convergence may not entail convergence as to a medium's personal use, social function or cultural status. More relevant in tracking the logic behind these divergent–convergent tendencies seems to be the varied needs, activities and desires of the human user, how his/her senses and bodies are engaged and addressed, enveloped and challenged. In this context, the cinema retains its value as a unique kind of social space and a fixed architectural site, with its own cultural values, mainly invested in the political significance of "public", or rather, in the contradictory, but increasingly pertinent, combination of intimate and public that now defines the "social". Maybe one could argue that the recent comeback of the documentary not only as a genre, but as a significant player in the public sphere, is less related to "digitization" in the technological sense as is so often argued (easy and cheap access to production equipment and online editing, small cameras that allow access and presence in different ways, new distribution channels via DVD and the Internet), but is equally owed to the changes in the public sphere that emerge as "collateral damage", as it were, of the (social, cultural) transformations brought about by the digital. In this respect, Michael Moore's FAHRENHEIT 9/11 (2004) and Al Gore's AN INCONVENIENT TRUTH (2006) would be examples for the return of a traditionally public sphere predicated on enlightened individuals whose decisions matter and make a difference. Yet, this Habermasian model of free discourse and rational individuality does not stand unchallenged when "abject (pseudo-)documentaries" such as JACKASS: THE MOVIE (2002, Jeff Tremaine), TROPIC THUNDER (2008, Ben Stiller) or BORAT: CULTURAL LEARNING OF AMERICA FOR MAKE BENEFIT GLORIOUS NATION OF KAZAKHSTAN (2006, Larry Charles) demonstrate the fragility and illusory nature of this seemingly

Figure C.8 Tropic Thunder (US, 2008, Ben Stiller): the abject (pseudo-) documentary meets the gross-out comedy.

rationally constructed public which vanishes into thin air when confronted with a wholly cynical and dark worldview. While the former group addresses the spectator as rational and enlightened individuals whose minds reign supreme over their bodies, the latter group wallows and indulges in the body's abject functions and in the capability of the cinema to communicate pain, shame and anguish to a spectator as much physically addressed as rationally involved.

So, while the digital is often defined technologically as the numerical 1/0, the on/off of the binary logic, a look at virtual reality and contemporary film-making proposes another possible genealogy for the digital image that leads us into the etymology of the term "digital", where it not only implies the most basic of differences in computing, but also reminds us of the hand (with its fingers, i.e. digits) as that most versatile of human tools, accessory, extension and implement. Whereas the eye appears to have been the most important body part and sensory channel for much of the twentieth-century history of film (theory), today the hand (of the video-game player, the camera operator, the designer and draftsperson) enters the media again, especially as in the eye–hand coordination so central to computer games and to any action conducted with the mouse, another technological extension of humans into the (in)animate realm of conceptual metaphor. The recently popular touch-screens of mobile phones and displays as well as the haptic interfaces for other mobile applications (iPod, palm tops, netbook PCs) testify to the renewed importance of doing things with the hand. It is as if the possibility of accomplishing certain tasks by means of tele-action (via keyboard, mouse, remote control or touch-screen) raises questions of active/passive, responsibility and even culpability which the "regime of the eye and gaze" posed differently. Tele-presence, action by proxy and other substitutive processes such as those discussed in relation to virtual reality require us to reconsider what it is we really do when we do things with a computer. This is one reason why so many films today are about "agency" – using new imaging techniques to show what you can "do" by merely dreaming, as in Richard Linklater's WAKING LIFE (2001), or by trying to remember, as in Ari Folman's WALTZ WITH BASHIR (2008); many recent Asian films such as those of Hirokazu Kore-Eda or Kim Ki-Duk exhibit a strangely dislocated form of passive–aggressive behavior, and the mind-game films already discussed revolve around a mysterious form of agency in which the relation between chance/ contingency and (pre-)determination appears to have taken the place of free will, individuality and rational decision-taking. This has at first glance nothing to do with the digital in the technical sense, but indirectly it does, because of the way the so-called "interactivity" of the digital both stresses and represses the knowledge that "we" are not doing the "doing". So the cinema becomes a meta-reflection on agency, which is, of course, all about the body and the senses and their coordination. So, the second life of the media – the imaginary spaces, stories and characters that we can wear, inhabit and live – spill over into the "real world", making the border between real and imaginary harder and harder to draw as the moving image along with recorded sound has become a pervasive and ever-present reality in our lives.

As the preceding chapters have tried to demonstrate, the cinema has always been preoccupied with the body and the senses, but also with matters of life (and death) that extend beyond individual films and movie theaters into the realms of identity, community and our "being-in-the-world". Today, many see the moving image as our most precious (and endangered) historical heritage, a unique "archive" of life and of things over the past 120 years. Some have argued that cinema is the key and template for our cultural understanding of the new (digital) media;[13] and, for yet others, the cinema constitutes a material–mental organism in its own right, a new and vibrant articulation of matter, energy and

Figure C.9 WALTZ WITH BASHIR (IS, 2008, Ari Folman): remembering (the Lebanon war) as dreaming and dreaming as remembering

information, and thus a "thing" that "thinks", which philosophy can help us understand.[14] This is why it makes sense to speak of both the cinema's "epistemologies" (ways of knowing, as well as ways of questioning how the cinema knows what it claims to know) and "ontologies" (ways of being, as well as ways of classifying what is and exists) as the proper domain of film theory.

If the previous chapters treated the body as a perceptual surface and disassembled the various senses in their relationship to images, narratives, affects and the public sphere, then the gradual but inescapable shift from photographic to digital images should not and need not be seen as the radical break it is often claimed to be. By deliberately choosing parameters such as the body and the senses, and criteria of pertinence such as window, mirror, eye, skin, ear, etc., which are neither based on technological properties of cinema, nor intended to be normative in their view of "what is cinema" (which would be the case, for instance, if we were to make "projection" or "photography" a necessary condition of "cinema"), our approach should make it possible to adjust, extend and re-assess "what is cinema". This allows us to include digital cinema in our overall scheme, without either submerging the differences between photographically based cinema and its post-photographic successor in a generalized notion of convergence as the new goal or telos, or having to argue that it is merely business as usual, on the basis that the cinema is still mostly used for telling stories, with – as we saw at the beginning of this chapter – many of them appearing deceptively familiar and even archly old-fashioned. Once we accept the shifting power-relations within our terminological oxymorons and the potential reversibility of the terms in our contradictory locutions, we may not have to decide to what extent the numerically generated image is simply a photographic image produced by other means, or a graphic image that incorporates the photographic image as one of its possibilities. Bearing in mind the long history of anthropomorphism applied to the technologies of cinema from the "camera eye" of Dziga Vertov via Béla Balázs' "visible man", to Laura Marks' "skin of film" and Gilles Deleuze's "the brain is the screen", to all of which our study pays tribute, does the digital image break with the ocular-centric paradigm, by merely mimicking its effects, and thus subsuming the perspectival system under more inclusive categories? Or does the digital image oppose the optical, by reinstating a different "regime"? We already hinted at the possibility that the turn to "haptical vision" is mainly due to the tactility, proximity and sense of texture intuitively associated with the digital image. Similar associations are manifest in the (somewhat metaphorical) analogies drawn between digital software and the paintbrush, between pixel and pigment, or the semantics of sculpting and stereoscopy ("rendering", "3-D"), to indicate the different relations of hand-to-eye-to-body in contemporary processes of image production and image manipulation.

The question that poses itself at such a juncture is: can film theory remain comfortable within such a broad brief that includes the whole of the digital media, or does it need to extricate itself from wanting to explain everything, and instead find its own re-definition – but if so, on what basis? It is clear that ever since the widespread reception of Gilles Deleuze's cinema books in the 1990s, the cinema, or rather "film" has entered an entirely different space of reflexivity and conceptualization. Deleuze's intervention and the subsequent "philosophical turn" of film theory coincided with digitization, but that does not necessarily imply a causal relation. On the one hand we have the possible exhaustion of the paradigms of "representation", "subjectivity" and gendered "identity" (all of which Deleuze pointedly avoids), and on the other we have the crisis into which the (definitions of) cinema has been plunged by digitization. But when Film Studies aligns itself with philosophy and when philosophy (across a spectrum that ranges from "continental" philosophy to cognitivism, while also including Stanley Cavell and Anglo-American pragmatism) takes an interest in the cinema, many other issues apart from digitization are equally at stake: questions of evidence and epistemology, of the cinema's relations to truth, trust and belief, as well as of ontology, of "becoming", "disclosure" and of "being in the world". One can thus be fairly optimistic that, in the decade to come, film theory will re-invent itself, even if (or perhaps because) the cinema as we have known it for its first 100 years is no more. Whether film theory revives and survives by putting the digital as universal code in the forefront and redefines itself around it (as most of those working in the digital media seem to think, or as writers like Sean Cubitt and Anne Friedberg propose), whether the graphic mode will prevail and re-articulate both photographic and post-photographic (as Manovich argued for a time), whether the image-anthropology of Hans Belting or George Didi-Huberman will "inherit" film theory and the cinema, or whether philosophy will be the master-discipline, as both the disciples of Deleuze and the analytical philosophers turned cognitivists believe – our contention remains that the complex and delicate relationships we have been trying to delineate and extract around the body, its senses and its cinematic interfaces will play their part in most, if not in all of these rescue missions.

Notes

Introduction: film theory, cinema, the body and the senses

1 It might be a sign of the further institutionalization of Film Studies that recently the history of the discipline itself has become an object of study; see e.g. Dana Polan: *Scenes of Instruction: the Beginnings of the US Study of Film*. Berkeley, CA: University of California Press 2007; Lee Grieveson and Haidee Wasson (eds.): *Inventing Film Studies*. Durham, NC: Duke University Press 2008.

2 We find this juxtaposition already in Siegfried Kracauer: *Theory of Film: the Redemption of Physical Reality*. New York: Oxford University Press 1960. Dudley Andrew popularized this distinction in *The Major Film Theories: an Introduction*. New York: Oxford University Press 1976.

3 See, for example, the chapters in John Hill and Pamela Church Gibson (eds.): *The Oxford Guide to Film Studies*. New York: Oxford University Press 1998, bearing titles such as "Film and Psychoanalysis" or "Marxism and Film".

4 See the two most comprehensive and complete overviews in English to date: Francesco Casetti: *Theories of Cinema, 1945–1995*. Austin, TX: University of Texas Press 1999 (originally: *Teorie del cinema 1945–1990*. Milano: Bompiani 1993) and Robert Stam: *Film Theory: an Introduction*. Malden, MA, Oxford: Blackwell 2000.

5 On the topic of diegesis, see Etienne Souriau: "La structure de l'univers filmique et le vocabulaire de la filmologie". In: *Revue internationale de la filmologie*, 2, 7–8, 1951: 231–40. David Bordwell's *Narration in the Fiction Film*. Methuen/Madison, WI: University of Wisconsin Press 1985 is an influential formulation of the distinction in English. For further considerations, see Gérard Genette: *Narrative Discourse Revisited* (trans. Jane E. Lewin). Ithaca, NY: Cornell University Press 1988.

6 See in recent years Garrett Stewart: *Between Film and Screen: Modernism's Photo Synthesis*. Chicago, IL: Chicago University Press 1999; Phil Rosen: *Change Mummified: Cinema, Historicity, Theory*. Minneapolis, MN: University of Minnesota Press 2001; Laura Mulvey: *Death 24× a Second: Stillness and the Moving Image*. London: Reaktion Books 2006. The question is also addressed by Warren Buckland: "Realism in the Photographic and Digital Image (JURASSIC PARK and THE LOST WORLD)". In: Thomas Elsaesser and Warren Buckland (eds.): *Studying Contemporary American Film: a Guide to Movie Analysis*. London: Arnold 2002: 195–219.

7 Gilles Deleuze: *Cinema 1: the Movement-Image* and *Cinema 2: the Time-Image* (both trans. Hugh Tomlinson). Minneapolis, MN: University of Minnesota Press 1986 and 1989.

8 A case can be made that Bazin, with his emphasis on Egyptian mummies and the Turin shroud, had a theory of photography that already included a critique of ocular-centric perception.

9 See Iurii Tynianov *et al.*: *Poetika Kino*. Berkeley, CA: Slavic Specialities 1984.

10 Writers who have similarly tried to address these film–philosophical continuities across the "digital divide" include Lev Manovich, Sean Cubitt, David Rodowick and Garrett Stewart. Some of their texts will be discussed in the concluding chapter.

I Cinema as window and frame

1 REAR WINDOW has, ever since its release, been interpreted as a metaphor for the scopic relationship between spectator and film. See, for instance, Jean Douchet: "Hitch et son public". In: *Cahiers du Cinéma*, Vol. XIX, No. 113, November 1960: 7–15, especially pp. 8–10 (published in English as "Hitch and his Audience". In: Jim Hillier (ed.): *Cahiers du Cinéma, 1960–1968: New Wave, New Cinema, Reevaluating Hollywood*. Cambridge, MA: Harvard University Press 1986: 150–7); as well as Robert Stam and Roberta Pearson: "Hitchcock's REAR WINDOW: Reflexivity and the Critique of Voyeurism". In: *Enclictic*, Vol. 7, No. 1, Spring 1983: 136–45. Republished in Marshall Deutelbaum and Leland Poague (eds.): *A Hitchcock Reader*. Ames, IO: Iowa State University Press 1986: 193–206.

2 Robert Stam and Roberta Pearson: "Hitchcock's REAR WINDOW: Reflexivity and the Critique of Voyeurism". In: *Enclictic*, Vol. 7, No. 1, Spring 1983: 136–45. Republished in Marshall Deutelbaum and Leland Poague (eds.): *A Hitchcock Reader*. Ames, IO: Iowa State University Press 1986: 195.

3 Siegfried Kracauer: *Theory of Film: the Redemption of Physical Reality*. New York: Oxford University Press 1960. Dudley Andrew: *The Major Film Theories: an Introduction*. New York: Oxford University Press 1976.

4 Bazin reserves the concept of frame for painting and sets it in opposition to the "cache", the black edge of the screen which sharply delineates the image from the surrounding darkness. Nevertheless, the idea persists here that there is a framed reality unfolding beyond the screen and strictly disconnected from the auditorium. See his essay "Painting and Film". In: André Bazin: *What Is Cinema? Volume 1*. Berkeley, CA: University of California Press 1967: 164–9.

5 Charles F. Altman: "Psychoanalysis and Cinema: the Imaginary Discourse". In: *Quarterly Review of Film Studies*, Vol. 2, No. 3, August 1977: 157–272, here 261.

6 The differentiation between open and closed works of art was introduced and theorized by Umberto Eco. See *The Open Work*. Cambridge, MA: Harvard University Press 1989 [orig. Italian 1962].

7 Leo Braudy: *The World in a Frame: What We See in Films*. Garden City, NY: Anchor Press/ Doubleday 1976: 44–51.

8 Leo Braudy: *The World in a Frame: What We See in Films*. Garden City, NY: Anchor Press/ Doubleday 1976: 49.

9 See, for the genesis of the classical style in US cinema, David Bordwell, Janet Staiger and Kristin Thompson: *The Classical Hollywood Cinema: Film Style and Mode of Production to 1960*. London: Routledge & Kegan Paul 1985; Eileen Bowser: *History of the American Cinema 2: the Transformation of Cinema 1907–1915*. New York: Charles Scribner's Sons 1990; Charlie Keil: *Early American Cinema in Transition: Story, Style, and Filmmaking, 1907–1913*. Madison, WI: University of Wisconsin Press 2001.

10 See, for a good overview of the central issues in documentary, Bill Nichols: *Introduction to Documentary*. Bloomington, IN: Indiana University Press 2001.

11 Stephen Heath: "Narrative Space" [orig. 1976]. In: *Questions of Cinema*. London: Macmillan/ Bloomington, IN: Indiana University Press 1981: 19–75, here 28ff (emphasis in the original).

12 See Erwin Panofsky: *Perspective as Symbolic Form* (trans. Christopher S. Wood). New York: Zone Books 1993 [orig. German 1927]; Erwin Panofsky: "Style and Medium in the Motion Picture" [orig. German 1936]. In: Leo Braudy and Marshall Cohen (eds.): *Film Theory and Criticism: Introductory Readings* (sixth edition). New York: Oxford University Press 2004: 289–302. See also John Berger: *Ways of Seeing*. London: Penguin 1972 for an ideological critique of Western perspective.

13 Helmut H. Diederichs maintains the most comprehensive homepage about Arnheim in English and German: www.soziales.fh-dortmund.de/diederichs/arnheim.htm (accessed 7 November 2008).

14 Rudolf Arnheim: *Film as Art*. London: Faber & Faber 1958 [orig. German 1932]. Further quotations in the text are from this edition.

15 Rudolf Arnheim: "Silent Beauty and Noisy Nonsense" [orig. German 1929]. In: *Film Essays and Criticism* (trans. Brenda Benthien). Madison, WI: University of Wisconsin Press 1997: 147–51.

16 Rudolf Arnheim: "The New Laocoon". In: *Film as Art*. London: Faber & Faber 1958.

17 For a (theoretical and practical) overview of Eisenstein's oeuvre, see Jacques Aumont: *Montage Eisenstein*. Bloomington, IN: Indiana University Press 1987 [orig. French 1979]; David Bordwell: *The Cinema of Eisenstein*. Cambridge, MA: Harvard University Press 1993. For biographical overviews of Eisenstein's labyrinthine trajectory through life, see Marie Seton: *Sergei M. Eisenstein: a Biography*. New York: Grove 1960; Yon Barna: *Eisenstein* (Foreword by Jay Leyda). London: Secker & Warburg 1973 [orig. Romanian 1966]; Ronald Bergan: *Sergei Eisenstein: a Life in Conflict*. London: Little, Brown and Company 1997.

18 Not coincidentally, Aumont's book announces this already in its title: *Montage Eisenstein* (Bloomington, IN: Indiana University Press 1987).

19 There are numerous compilations of Eisenstein's writings, the most comprehensive in Russian is a six-volume edition (*Izbrannye prozvedeniia v shesti tomakh*, Moscow 1960–9). We will be quoting from a four-volume edition in English – Sergej Eisenstein: *Selected Works* (edited by Richard Taylor). London: British Film Institute 1988, 1991, 1995, 1996.

20 Exemplary introductory texts that provide concise overviews of the development of Eisenstein's thinking are Dudley Andrew: "Sergei Eisenstein". In: *The Major Film Theories: an Introduction*. New York: Oxford University Press 1976: 42–75; Vance Kepley Jr.: "Eisenstein and Soviet Cinema". In: Peter Lehman (ed.): *Defining Cinema*. London: Athlone Press 1997: 37–55.

21 Sergej M. Eisenstein: "Beyond the Shot" (1929). In: *Selected Works, Vol. 1: Writings 1922–1934* (ed. and trans. Richard Taylor). London: British Film Institute: 138–50, here 146.

22 Sergej M. Eisenstein: "Beyond the Shot" (1929). In: *Selected Works, Vol. 1: Writings 1922–1934* (ed. and trans. Richard Taylor). London: British Film Institute: 148 [translation modified; original: Sergej Mikhailovich Eizenshtein [Eisenstein], Montazh, ed. Naum Kleman (Moscow: Muzei Kino 2000), 500].

23 See Sergej M. Eisenstein: "The Dynamic Square" (1931). In: *Selected Works, Vol. 1: Writings 1922–1935*. London: British Film Institute 1988: 206–18.

24 Sergej M. Eisenstein: "Beyond the Shot" (1929). In: *Selected Works, Vol. 1: Writings 1922–1934* (ed. and trans. Richard Taylor). London: British Film Institute/Bloomington and Indiana: Indiana University Press 1988: 138–50, here 144.

25 Sergej M. Eisenstein: "The Montage of Film Attractions" (1924). In: *Selected Works, Vol. 1: Writings 1922–1934* (ed. and trans. Richard Taylor). London: British Film Institute/Bloomington and Indiana: Indiana University Press 1988: 39–58, here 39.

26 Sergej M. Eisenstein: "The Montage of Film Attractions" (1924). In: *Selected Works, Vol. 1: Writings 1922–1934* (ed. and trans. Richard Taylor). London: British Film Institute/Bloomington and Indiana: Indiana University Press 1988: 40f.

27 See Sergej M. Eisenstein: "The Fourth Dimension in Cinema" (1929). In: *Selected Works, Vol. 1: Writings 1922–1934* (ed. and trans. Richard Taylor). London: British Film Institute/Bloomington and Indiana: Indiana University Press 1988: 181–94.

28 Sergej M. Eisenstein: "The Fourth Dimension in Cinema" (1929). In: *Selected Works, Vol. 1: Writings 1922–1934* (ed. and trans. Richard Taylor). London: British Film Institute/Bloomington and Indiana: Indiana University Press 1988: 188.

29 In English the essay is entitled "The Virtues and Limitations of Montage". In: *What is Cinema?, Volume 1* (with a foreword by Jean Renoir and an introduction by Hugh Gray). Berkeley and Los Angeles, CA: University of California Press 1967: 41–52.

30 See his essay "An Aesthetic of Reality: Cinematic Realism and the Italian School of the Liberation". In: *What is Cinema?, Volume 2* (with a foreword by Dudley Andrew and an introduction by François Truffaut). Berkeley and Los Angeles, CA: University of California Press 2005: 16–40.

31 Classic formulations of these positions can be found in Walter Benjamin: "The Work of Art

in the Age of Mechanical Reproduction"; Siegfried Kracauer: "The Mass Ornament". In: *The Mass Ornament: Weimar Essays*. Cambridge: Harvard University Press 1995: 74–86.

32 André Bazin: "An Aesthetic of Reality: Cinematic Realism and the Italian School of the Liberation". In: *What is Cinema?, Volume 2* (with a foreword by Dudley Andrew and an introduction by François Truffaut). Berkeley and Los Angeles, CA: University of California Press 2005: 20–1 (emphasis in the original).

33 Dudley Andrew: *Concepts in Film Theory*. Oxford: Oxford University Press 1984: 50. See also Bazin's text "In Defense of Rossellini". In: *What is Cinema?, Volume 2* (with a foreword by Dudley Andrew and an introduction by François Truffaut). Berkeley and Los Angeles, CA: University of California Press 2005: 93–101.

34 André Bazin: "In Defense of Rossellini". In: *What is Cinema?, Volume 2* (with a foreword by Dudley Andrew and an introduction by François Truffaut). Berkeley and Los Angeles, CA: University of California Press 2005: 97.

35 André Bazin: "Ladri di biciclette"/"Bicycle Thief". In: *What is Cinema?, Volume 2* (with a foreword by Dudley Andrew and an introduction by François Truffaut). Berkeley and Los Angeles, CA: University of California Press 2005: 47–60, here 60.

36 André Bazin: "De Sica: Metteur en Scène". In: *What is Cinema?, Volume 2* (with a foreword by Dudley Andrew and an introduction by François Truffaut). Berkeley and Los Angeles, CA: University of California Press 2005: 61–78. See also Marsha Kinder: "The Subversive Potential of the Pseudo-Iterative". In: *Film Quarterly*, Vol. 43, No. 2, Winter 1989–90: 2–16.

37 André Bazin: "In Defense of Rossellini". In: *What is Cinema?, Volume 2* (with a foreword by Dudley Andrew and an introduction by François Truffaut). Berkeley and Los Angeles, CA: University of California Press 2005: 99.

38 Two important books on Bazin's life and work are Dudley Andrew: *André Bazin*. New York: Oxford University Press 1978 and Jean Ungaro: *André Bazin: genealogies d'une théorie*. Paris: L'Harmattan 2000.

39 Even the history of the publication of Bazin's works attests to this fragmentary nature: the collection of essays entitled *Qu'est-ce que le cinéma?*, which Bazin started editing shortly before his death, appeared posthumously – with the exception of the first volume, which Bazin was able to hold in his hands – between 1958 and 1962. Most translations contain only a selection of the original edition, as does the so-called French *Édition définitive*, a misnomer as it contains only the central essays in one volume. In English, a two-volume selection is the most commonly used source: *What Is Cinema?* 2 Vols. (trans. Hugh Gray). Berkeley, CA: University of California Press 1967, 1971. A significant number of important essays not included in this collection can be found in Bert Cadullo (ed.): *Bazin at Work: Major Essays and Reviews from the Forties and Fifties* (trans. Alain Piette and Bert Cadullo). London, New York: Routledge 1997. Temporal delay and selectivity continue, therefore, to this day to mark the reception of Bazin's work, but this holds true for the transnational dimension of film theory in general.

40 David Bordwell, Janet Staiger and Kristin Thompson: *The Classical Hollywood Cinema: Film Style and Mode of Production to 1960*. London: Routledge & Kegan Paul 1985; David Bordwell: *The Cinema of Eisenstein*. Cambridge, MA: Harvard University Press 1993; David Bordwell: *Ozu and the Poetics of Cinema*. Princeton, NJ: Princeton University Press 1988.

41 David Bordwell: "Exceptionally Exact Perceptions: On Staging in Depth". In: *On the History of Film Style*. Cambridge, MA: Harvard University Press 1997: 158–74.

42 André Bazin: "William Wyler, or the Jansenist of Directing". In: Bert Cadullo (ed.): *Bazin at Work: Major Essays and Reviews from the Forties and Fifties* (trans. Alain Piette and Bert Cadullo). London, New York: Routledge 1997: 1–22.

43 Jacques Aumont: *The Image* (trans. Claire Pajackowska). London: British Film Institute 1997 [orig. French 1990].

44 Three classic texts which associate the birth of Hollywood with consumer society and advertising culture are Charles Eckert: "The Carole Lombard in Macy's Window". In: *Quarterly Review of Film Studies*, Vol. 3, No. 1, Winter 1978: 1–21; Jeanne Allen: "The Film Viewer as Consumer". In: *Quarterly Review of Film Studies*, Vol. 5, No. 4, Fall 1980: 481–99; Jane

Gaines: "The QUEEN CHRISTINA Tie-Ups. Convergence of Show Window and Screen". In: *Quarterly Review of Film and Video*, Vol. 11, No. 4, 1989: 35–60. See also the essays collected in David Desser and Garth S. Jowett (eds.): *Hollywood Goes Shopping*. Minneapolis, MN: University of Minnesota Press 2000.

45 One could cite here Jean Baudrillard's simulacrum theory, according to which the (electronic) media produce copies without originals. Similarly, this strand of film theory posits that what film reveals is not an authentic reality but an artificial and constructed world of illusions.

46 The *locus classicus* for the conception of cinema as *flanerie* through imaginary (commodified) worlds can be found in a book that dates back to the climax of the post-modernism debate: Anne Friedberg: *Window Shopping: Cinema and the Postmodern*. Berkeley, CA: University of California Press 1993. Connected with this is also Harun Farocki's brilliant cinematic meditation on the creation of artistic shopping worlds in his essay film DIE SCHÖPFER DER EINKAUF-SWELTEN/THE CREATORS OF SHOPPING WORLDS (GE, 2001).

47 See Anne Friedberg: *The Virtual Window: From Alberti to Microsoft*. Cambridge, MA: MIT Press 2006.

2 Cinema as door – screen and threshold

1 Through his notion of the "dynamic square" Sergej Eisenstein advocated a less limited and more flexible operation of the (vertical) image format in film. In this context the square is the form that can comprise all other forms. See Sergej M. Eisenstein: "The Dynamic Square" (1931). In: *Selected Works, Vol. 1: Writings 1922–1935*. London: British Film Institute 1988: 206–18.

2 The seminal works on this topic and the origin of further contributions to the debate is Frederick Jackson Turner's *The Frontier in American History*. London: Dover 1996 [orig. 1893]. Applications of this concept to cinema can be found in Jim Kitses: *Horizons West: Anthony Mann, Budd Boetticher, Sam Peckinpah: Studies of Authorship within the Western*. London: Thames & Hudson 1969; Edward Buscombe (ed.): *The BFI Companion to the Western*. London: Deutsch 1988.

3 See for a strong structuralist account of the Western as genre, Will Wright: *Sixguns & Society: a Structural Study of the Western*. Berkeley, CA: University of California Press 1975.

4 More on the fundamental process of drawing borders can be found in Niklas Luhmann: *Social Systems*. Stanford, CA: Stanford University Press 1995 [orig. German *Soziale Systeme* 1984]; Niklas Luhmann: *Art as a Social System*. Stanford, CA: Stanford University Press 2000 [orig. German *Die Kunst der Gesellschaft* 1995].

5 Edgar Morin: *The Cinema, or The Imaginary Man*. Minneapolis, MN: University of Minnesota Press 2005 [orig. French *Le cinéma ou le homme imaginaire: Essai d'anthropologie sociologique* 1956].

6 The concept of liminality was introduced in the 1960s by ethnologist Victor Turner, who drew inspiration from Arnold van Gennep, for whom this term designates an unstable state of in-betweenness "betwixt and between the positions assigned and arrayed by law, custom, convention and ceremonial". See Victor Turner: *The Forest of Symbols*. Ithaca, NY: Cornell University Press 1967.

7 For more on the film poster as advertising material and aesthetic object, see Wolfgang Beilenhoff and Martin Heller (eds.): *Das Filmplakat*. Zürich, Berlin, New York: Scalo 1995.

8 For more on the trailer as an aesthetic object, economic object and cultural component of the cinematographic institution, see Lisa Kernan: *Coming Attractions: Reading American Movie Trailers*. Austin, TX: University of Texas Press 2005 (Texas Film and Media Studies); Vinzenz Hediger: *Nostalgia for the Coming Attraction: American Movie Trailers and the Culture of Film Consumption* (New York: Columbia University Press 2009).

9 Alexander Böhnke et al. (eds.): *Das Buch zum Vorspann: "The Title Is a Shot"*. Berlin: Vorwerk 8 2006. More on contemporary developments can be found in Deborah Allison: "Catch Me If

You Can: Auto Focus and the Art of Retro Title Sequences". At: www.sensesofcinema.com/contents/03/26/retro_titles.html (accessed 30 August 2006) and a comprehensive survey and appreciation of title sequences in French: www.generique-cinema.net (30 August 2006).

10 Gerard Genette: Paratexts: *Thresholds of Interpretation*. Cambridge: Cambridge University Press 1997 [orig. French 1987]. The French original, it should be noted, uses the term "seuils", i.e. "threshold", so that our description of the "thresholds of film" indirectly harks back to Genette. More on various approaches to cinema loosely inspired by Genette can be found in Veronica Innocenti and Valentina Re (eds.): *Limina: Le soglie des film/Film's Thresholds*. Udine: Forum 2004.

11 See Hoberman and Rosenbaum: *Midnight Movies*. New York: da Capo 1991.

12 More on various reading modes and on the communicational contract between spectator and film can be found in Roger Odin: "For a Semio-Pragmatics of Film" and "A Semio-Pragmatic Approach to the Documentary Film". In: Warren Buckland (ed.): *The Film Spectator: From Sign to Mind*. Amsterdam: Amsterdam University Press 1995: 213–26, 227–35, as well as Odin: *De la fiction*. Brussels: De Boeck 2000.

13 Kristin Thompson: *Breaking the Glass Armour: Neoformalist Film Analysis*. Princeton, NJ: Princeton University Press 1988: 26. The following quotations in the text refer to this edition.

14 The origin of the concepts "syuzhet" and "fabula" lies in Russian Formalism. On the applications of this paradigm to film, see David Bordwell: *Narration in the Fiction Film*. Methuen/Madison, WI: University of Wisconsin Press 1985; Edward Branigan: *Narrative Comprehension and Film*. London, New York: Routledge 1992. For a theoretical foundation of this narrative theory in a wider context, see Kristin Thompson: *Breaking the Glass Armour: Neoformalist Film Analysis*. Princeton, NJ: Princeton University Press 1988.

15 David Bordwell: "The Classical Hollywood Style". In: David Bordwell, Janet Staiger and Kristin Thompson: *The Classical Hollywood Cinema: Film Style and Mode of Production to 1960*. London: Routledge & Kegan Paul 1985: 1–84, here 37.

16 Edward Branigan: *Narrative Comprehension and Film*. London, New York: Routledge 1992. His earlier discussion of point-of-view in film can be found in *Point of View in the Cinema*. The Hague: Mouton 1984.

17 See Murray Smith: *Engaging Characters: Fiction, Emotion, and the Cinema*. Oxford: Clarendon Press 1995; Ed Tan: *Film as an Emotion Machine: Emotion as a Structure of Narrative Film*. Mahwah, NJ: Erlbaum 1996; Torben Grodal: *Moving Pictures: a New Theory of Film Genres, Feelings and Cognition*. Oxford: Clarendon Press 1997.

18 A theoretical frame is provided by Kristin Thompson: *Breaking the Glass Armour: Neoformalist Film Analysis*. Princeton, NJ: Princeton University Press 1988; case studies are her *Storytelling in the New Hollywood: Understanding Classical Narrative Technique*. Cambridge, MA: Harvard University Press 1999; *Herr Lubitsch Goes to Hollywood: German and American Film After World War I*. Amsterdam: Amsterdam University Press 2005.

19 Robert Stam: *Subversive Pleasure: Bakhtin, Cultural Criticism, and Film*. Baltimore, MD: Johns Hopkins University Press 1989: 187.

20 See the chapter "From Dialogism to ZELIG". In: Robert Stam: *Subversive Pleasure: Bakhtin, Cultural Criticism, and Film*. Baltimore, MD: Johns Hopkins University Press 1989: 187–218.

21 See Raymond Bellour: *The Analysis of Film* (edited by Constance Penley). Bloomington, IN: Indiana University Press 2002; Stephen Heath: *Questions of Cinema*. London: Macmillan/Bloomington, IN: Indiana University Press 1981; Colin MacCabe: *Tracking the Signifier: Theoretical Essays: Film, Linguistics, Literature*. Minneapolis, MN: University of Minnesota Press 1985. For Stam, see notes 19 and 20.

22 See, for instance, Arthur M. Eckstein and Peter Lehman (eds.): THE SEARCHERS. Detroit, MI: Wayne State University Press 2004; Edward Buscombe: THE SEARCHERS. London: BFI Classics 2008 for bibliographies.

23 Garrett Stewart: *Framed Time: Toward a Postfilmic Cinema*. Chicago, IL, and London: University of Chicago Press 2007: 17.

24 See Thierry Kuntzel: "The Film Work". In: *Enclitic*, 2.1, 1978: 38–61 [orig. French 1972] and "The Film Work, 2". In: *Camera Obscura*, 1980: 7–68 [orig. French 1975].

25 Thierry Kuntzel: "The Film Work, 2". In: *Camera Obscura*, No. 5, 1980: 8ff.

26 Thierry Kuntzel: "The Film Work, 2". In: *Camera Obscura*, No. 5, 1980: 9f.

27 See "System of a Fragment" (on THE BIRDS) and "Symbolic Blockage" (on NORTH BY NORTHWEST) in Raymond Bellour: *The Analysis of Film* (edited by Constance Penley). Bloomington, IN: Indiana University Press 2002: 28–68, 77–192; Stephen Heath: "Film and System" (two parts). In: *Screen*, Vol. 16, No. 1: 7–77 and Vol. 16, No. 2: 91–113; editors of *Cahiers du Cinéma*: "John Ford's YOUNG MR. LINCOLN". In: *Screen*, Vol. 13, No. 5, autumn 1972 [orig. French 1970]. Reprinted in Bill Nichols (ed.): *Movies and Methods, Vol. 1*. Berkeley, CA: University of California Press 1976: 493–529.

28 David Bordwell: "Historical Poetics". In: *The Poetics of Cinema*. New York: Routledge 2008.

29 See Elena Dagrada: "Through the Keyhole: Spectators and Matte Shots in Early Cinema". In: *Iris*, Vol. 6, No. 2 [Nr. 11], 1990: 95–106.

30 There is an extensive literature on films and film-scenes that make the screen seem permeable, starting with the so-called "Rube" films from around 1900. For a recent reconsideration of this tradition and its current relevance, see Thomas Elsaesser in W. Strauven (ed.): *The Cinema of Attractions Reloaded*. Amsterdam: Amsterdam University Press 2006: 205–25. A detailed discussion of SHERLOCK JUNIOR can be found in Linda Haverty Rugg: "Keaton's Leap: Self-Projection and Autobiography in Film". In: *Biography*, Volume 29, Number 1, Winter 2006: v–xiii.

3 Cinema as mirror and face

1 Gilles Deleuze cites Ingmar Bergman's joke that this confusion of identities was something the actresses themselves had to grapple with: "We left the film on the editing table, and then Liv said: 'Did you see how ugly Bibi is!,' whereupon Bibi said: 'It's not me that's ugly, it's you...'". Gilles Deleuze: *Cinema 1: the Movement-Image*. Minneapolis, MN: Minnesota University Press 1986: 103 [orig. French 1983].

2 More on the importance and accumulation of faces/close-ups in the films of Ingmar Bergmann can be found in Gilles Deleuze: *Cinema 1: the Movement-Image*. Minneapolis, MN: University of Minnesota Press 1986: 99f., 105 [orig. French 1983].

3 Christian Metz: "Mirror Construction in Fellini's 8½". In: *Film Language: a Semiotics of the Cinema*. New York 1974: 228–34 [orig. "La construction 'en abyme' dans 8½ de Fellini". In: *Revue d'Esthetique*, xix–1, janvier–mars 1966: 96–101].

4 It is precisely this alternating perception of the alter as ego and vice-versa that makes communication, intersubjectivity and, hence, society possible in the first place. More on the "double contingency" can be found in Niklas Luhmann: *Social Systems*. Stanford: Stanford University Press 1995: 103–36 [orig. German 1984].

5 Dudley Andrew: *Concepts in Film Theory*. Oxford: Oxford University Press 1984: 134.

6 A late example is Sergej Eisenstein's famous essay from 1944, "Dickens, Griffith, and the Film Today". In: *Film Form: Essays in Film Theory and The Film Sense* (ed. and trans. Jay Leyda). New Haven, CT: Meridian Books 1957: 195–255.

7 Béla Balázs, preface to *Visible Man*, cited from the translation by Erica Carter and Rodney Livingstone, in Béla Balázs: "Visible Man, or the Culture of Film" (1924). In: *Screen*, 48, 1, 2007: 91–108.

8 More resources on Balázs' tumultuous life in the unpredictable flow of European history during the first half of the twentieth century can be found in Joseph Zsuffa: *Béla Balázs: the Man and the Artist*. Berkeley, CA: University of California Press 1987; Hanno Loewy: *Béla Balázs: Märchen, Ritual und Film*. Berlin: Vorwerk 8 2003.

9 Béla Balázs: *Der sichtbare Mensch oder die Kultur des Films*. Frankfurt/Main: Suhrkamp 2001 [orig. German 1924].

10 Unfortunately, Balázs' Eurocentric perspective occasionally gives way to open racism, most

notably when he excludes "non-white people" from participating in this universal culture and postulates a kind of Social Darwinist selection:

> Correspondingly, a certain normal psychology of the white race has also developed, which provides the basis for every cinematic fable. [. . .] Hidden herein is the first living sprout of that white normal man who will one day be born as a synthesis of various races and peoples. The cinematograph is a machine which, in its own way, establishes a lively and concrete internationalism: the only common psyche of white people. Furthermore, by proposing a unitary ideal of beauty as the general goal of breed selection, film will bring forth a unitary species of the white race.
>
> (22, emphasis in the original)

11 Béla Balázs, preface to *Visible Man*, cited from the translation by Erica Carter and Rodney Livingstone, in: Béla Balázs: "Visible Man, or the Culture of Film" (1924). *Screen*, 48, 1, 2007: 91–108. Further quotations in the text are from this source.

12 For more on the parallel between early cinema and hieroglyphs, as well as on modern forms of pictorial language, see Miriam Hansen: *Babel and Babylon: Spectatorship in American Silent Film*. Cambridge, MA: Harvard University Press 1991. This idea of film as modern Esperanto had already been circulated by Vachel Lindsay: *The Art of the Moving Picture*. New York: Macmillan 1915 (reprint 2000).

13 See among the countless publications on this topic that have appeared in the last 15 years, three books by important protagonists with somewhat different accentuations – W.J.T. Mitchell: *Picture Theory: Essays on Verbal and Visual Representation*. Chicago: University of Chicago Press 1994; Nicholas Mirzoeff: *an Introduction to Visual Culture*. London: Routledge 1999; Marita Sturken and Lisa Cartwright (eds.): *Practices of Looking: an Introduction to Visual Culture*. Oxford: Oxford University Press 2007, 2nd edition.

14 See here Lotte Eisner: *The Haunted Screen*. Berkeley, CA: University of California Press 1969 [orig. French 1952].

15 Gilles Deleuze: *Cinema 1: the Movement-Image*. Minneapolis, MN: University of Minnesota Press 1986: 87 (italics in original) [orig. French 1983]. The following quotes in the text are from this edition.

16 Jacques Aumont: *Du visage au cinéma*. Paris: Éditions de l'Étoile 1992: 85. As Mary-Ann Doane, who also cites this passage, comments:

> The close-up transforms whatever it films into a quasi-tangible thing, producing an intense phenomenological experience of presence, and yet, simultaneously, that deeply experienced entity becomes a sign, a text, a surface that demands to be read. This is, inside or outside of the cinema, the inevitable operation of the face as well.
>
> ("The Close-Up: Scale and Detail in the Cinema". In: *differences*, 14, 3, 2003: 89–111, here 94)

17 See Therese Davis: *The Face on the Screen: Death, Recognition and Spectatorship*. Bristol: Intellect 2004; Christa Blümlinger and Karl Sierek (eds.): *Das Gesicht im Zeitalter des bewegten Bildes*. Wien: Sonderzahl 2002; Joanna Barck and Petra Löffler (eds.): *Gesichter des Films*. Bielefeld: transcript 2005.

18 M.H. Abrams: *The Mirror and the Lamp: Romantic Theory and the Critical Tradition*. Oxford: Oxford University Press 1953.

19 Michel Foucault: *The Order of Things*. London & New York: Routledge 2002: 17–19.

20 This school of theory came under heavy attack, especially by Neoformalist and cognitivist critics. For more on this, see for instance Noël Carroll: *Philosophical Problems of Classical Film Theory*. Princeton, NJ: Princeton University Press 1988; David Bordwell and Noël Carroll (eds.): *Post-Theory: Reconstructing Film Studies*. Madison, WI: University of Wisconsin Press 1996 (Wisconsin Studies in Film). A more neutral, though still very critical, discussion can be found in Richard Allen: *Projecting Illusion: Film Spectatorship and the Impression of Reality*. New York: Cambridge University Press 1995. A consistently amiable presentation from an

internal perspective can be found in Judith Mayne: *Cinema and Spectatorship*. London, New York: Routledge 1995 (Sightlines).

21 For concise introductions to Metz's thinking/ideas, see Dudley Andrew: *The Major Film Theories: an Introduction*. London: Oxford University Press 1976: 212–41 (limited to the first phase of Metz's thinking); Robert T. Eberwein: "Christian Metz". In: Peter Lehman (ed.): *Defining Cinema*. London: Athlone Press 1997: 189–206.

22 This phase would fall by and large under our first ontology of cinema as frame and window, since his two main works of this period – *Essai sur le signification au cinéma*. Paris: Klincksieck 1968, 1972 (two parts) (English edition: *Film Language: a Semiotics of Cinema*. Oxford: Oxford University Press 1974 [reprint University of Chicago Press 2000]) and *Langage et cinéma*. Paris: Larousse 1971 (English edition: *Language and Cinema*. The Hague: Mouton 1974) – deal with the paradigm of film as language. In both works Metz takes issue with the extremely loose way in which his teacher Jean Mitry had employed the language metaphor.

23 Christian Metz: "Problems of Denotation in the Fiction Film". In: *Film Language* (trans. Michael Taylor). New York: Oxford University Press, 1974: 145.

24 One could further distinguish a third phase in Metz's work in which he focused on filmic enunciation, i.e. on the act of bringing forth an enunciation as Roland Barthes understood it. See *L'énonciation impersonelle, ou le site de film*. Paris: Klincksieck 1991.

25 Christian Metz: *The Imaginary Signifier: Psychoanalysis and the Cinema*. Indianapolis, IN: Indiana University Press 1986: 45 [orig. French 1975].

26 Jacques Lacan: *The Mirror Stage as Formative of the Function of the I as Revealed in Psychoanalytic Theory* (1949). In: *Écrits: a Selection*. London: Tavistock Publications 1977.

27 Christian Metz: *The Imaginary Signifier: Psychoanalysis and the Cinema*. Indianapolis, IN: Indiana University Press 1986: 45 [orig. French 1975].

28 Jacques Lacan: *The Mirror Stage as Formative of the Function of the I as Revealed in Psychoanalytic Theory* (1949). In: *Écrits: a Selection*. London: Tavistock Publications 1977.

29 Christian Metz: *The Imaginary Signifier: Psychoanalysis and the Cinema*. Indianapolis, IN: Indiana University Press 1986: 46 [orig. French 1975].

30 Christian Metz: *The Imaginary Signifier: Psychoanalysis and the Cinema*. Indianapolis, IN: Indiana University Press 1986: 49 [orig. French 1975].

31 Jean-Louis Baudry: "The Apparatus: Metapsychological Approaches to the Impression of Reality in the Cinema" (1975). In: Philip Rosen (ed.): *Narrative, Apparatus, Ideology*. New York: Columbia University Press 1986: 313.

32 Jean-Louis Baudry: "The Apparatus: Metapsychological Approaches to the Impression of Reality in the Cinema" (1975). In: Philip Rosen (ed.): *Narrative, Apparatus, Ideology*. New York: Columbia University Press 1986: 303.

33 Jean-Louis Baudry: "The Apparatus: Metapsychological Approaches to the Impression of Reality in the Cinema" (1975). In: Philip Rosen (ed.): *Narrative, Apparatus, Ideology*. New York: Columbia University Press 1986: 313.

34 Constance Penley: "The Avant-Garde and its Imaginary". In: *Camera Obscura*, No. 2, Fall 1977: 3–33; Constance Penley: "Feminism, Film Theory, and the Bachelor Machines". In: *m/f*, 10, 1985, 39–59.

35 Jonathan Crary: *Techniques of the Observer: On Vision and Modernity in the 19th Century*. Cambridge, MA: MIT Press 1992. Crary adopts a Foucauldian perspective to complicate the genealogy of "optical" vision and voyeurism, pointing to the history of a more embodied theory of perception, and reminding his readers of the popularity of stereoscopy. Both displace any linear descent of the cinema from the central perspective and the *camera obscura*.

36 For more on this, see Thomas Elsaesser: "Wie der frühe Film zum Erzählkino wurde". In: Irmbert Schenk (ed.). *Erlebnisort Kino*. Marburg: Schüren 2000: 34–54.

37 Tom Gunning: "The Cinema of Attraction". In: Thomas Elsaesser (ed.): *Early Cinema: Space, Frame, Narrative*. London: British Film Institute 1990: 56–62 [orig. 1986].

38 Linda Williams: "Film Body: an Implantation of Perversions". *Cine Tracts*, 12, Vol. 3, No. 4, Winter 1981: 19–35.

39 See Lucy Fisher: "The Lady Vanishes: Women, Magic and the Movies". *Film Quarterly*, Vol. 33, No. 1, Autumn 1979: 30–40; Noël Burch's TV-documentary CORRECTION PLEASE, OR HOW WE GOT INTO PICTURES (GB, 1979).

40 One only has to think of films such as THE OTHER (DER ANDERE, GE, 1913, Max Mack), THE STUDENT OF PRAGUE (DER STUDENT VON PRAG, GE, 1913, Stellan Rye/Paul Wegener), THE CABINET OF DR CALIGARI (DAS CABINET DES DR. CALIGARI, GE, 1920, Robert Wiene), THE GOLEM (DER GOLEM, WIE ER IN DIE WELT KAM, GE, 1920, Carl Boese/Paul Wegener), NOS-FERATU (GE, 1921, F.W. Murnau) and WAXWORKS (DAS WACHSFIGURENKABINETT, GE, 1924, Paul Leni).

41 See Thomas Elsaesser: "Too Big and Too Close: Alfred Hitchcock and Fritz Lang". In: *Hitchcock Annual*, Vol. 12, 2003: 1–41. For questions of scale and dimensions, see also Mary Ann Doane: "The Close-Up: Scale and Detail in the Cinema". In: *differences: a Journal of Feminist Cultural Studies*, Vol. 14, No. 3, Fall 2003: 89–111.

42 See, for examples of this discussion, Gabriel Teshome: *Third Cinema in the Third World*. Ann Arbor, MI: UMI Research Press 1982; Jim Pines and Paul Willemen (eds.): *Questions of Third Cinema*. London: British Film Institute 1989. For more on the feminist appropriation of this stance, see Chapter 4.

43 Gilles Deleuze: *Foucault* (trans. Sean Hand). Minneapolis, MN: University of Minnesota Press 1988: 96–97; Gilles Deleuze: *The Fold – Leibniz and the Baroque*. London: Continuum 2006.

44 See Yuri Tsivian on mirror shots in early (Russian) cinema in *Immaterial Bodies: a Cultural Anatomy of Early Russian Films* (CD-Rom, University of Southern California, 2000).

45 For a recent overview of the debate on mirror neurons, see C. Keysers and V. Gazzola: "Towards a Unifying Neural Theory of Social Cognition". In: A. Anders *et al.* (eds.): *Progress in Brain Research*, Vol. 156, Elsevier, 2006: 379–401.

46 US scientist V.S. Ramachandran even goes so far as to base the existence of language and culture on the existence of mirror neurons. See V.S. Ramachandran and Sandra Blakeslee: *Phantoms in the Brain: Probing the Mysteries of the Human Mind*. New York: William Morrow & Company 1999. See also the popular scientific contribution to this theme available under: www.pbs.org/wgbh/nova/sciencenow/3204/01.html (accessed 12 January 2007).

47 Ed Tan delivered a lecture entitled "Why people are very good at 'einfühlen', but do not do it all the time" on 8 December 2006 at the conference *Einfühlung: On the History and Present of an Aesthetic Concept* organized at the Freie Universität Berlin within the SFB "Cultures of the Performative"; publication of texts will follow in 2009 at Fink under the editorship of Robin Curtis, Marc Gloede and Gertrud Koch.

48 Linda Haverty Rugg: "Self-Projection and Still Photography in the Work of Ingmar Bergman: Persona". In: M. Koskinen (ed.): *Ingmar Bergman Revisited*. London: Wallflower Press 2007.

4 Cinema as eye – look and gaze

1 At least this is what the so-called "director's cut" suggests, i.e. the supposedly authentic version edited by director Ridley Scott and released theatrically in 1992 (a second "more authentic" version has recently been published on the home market). More about the genesis, analysis and interpretation of BLADE RUNNER can be found in Scott Bukatman: BLADE RUNNER. London: British Film Institute 2000 (BFI Modern Classic); Will Brooker (ed.): *The* BLADE RUNNER *Experience: the Legacy of a Science Fiction Classic*. London: Wallflower 2005.

2 For the interrelation of cinema and modernity see Stephen Kern: *The Culture of Time and Space, 1880–1918*. Cambridge, MA: Harvard University Press 1983; Leo Charney and Vanessa R. Schwartz (eds.): *Cinema and the Invention of Modern Life*. Berkeley, CA: University of California Press 1995; Francesco Casetti: *Eye of the Century: Film, Experience, Modernity*. New York: Columbia University Press 2008.

3 Cinema gave women access to public entertainment, which had previously been reserved for men alone – an important factor in the appeal of early cinema to female spectators. More on

this topic can be found in Heide Schlüpmann: "Early German Cinema – melodrama: social drama". In: Richard Dyer and Ginette Vincendeau (eds.): *Popular European Cinema*. London, New York: Routledge 1992: 206–19; Heide Schlüpmann: "Cinema as Anti-Theater: Actress and Female Audiences in Wilhelminian Germany". In: *Iris*, No. 11, Summer 1990 (reprinted in Richard Abel (ed.): *Silent Film*. New Brunswick, NJ: Rutgers University Press 1996: 125–41); Miriam Hansen: *Babel and Babylon: Spectatorship in American Silent Film*. Cambridge, MA: Harvard University Press 1991.

4 For more on the "phantom rides", see Tom Gunning: "An Unseen Energy Swallows Space: the Space in Early Film and its Relation to American Avant-Garde Film". In: John A. Fell (ed.): *Film Before Griffith*. Berkeley, Los Angeles, CA: University of California Press 1983: 355–66.

5 See Lev Manovich: *The Language of New Media*. Cambridge, MA: MIT Press 2001; Yuri Tsivian: "Man with a Movie Camera, Reel One: a Selective Glossary". In: *Film Studies: an International Review*, Issue 2, Spring 2000: 51–76, as well as Tsivian's audio commentary to the DVD version published by the BFI, and Jonathan Beller: "Dziga Vertov and the Film of Money". In: *Boundary*, No. 2, 26.3, 1999: 151–99.

6 Dziga Vertov: "Kinoks: a Revolution" [orig. Russian 1923]. In: Annette Michelson (ed.): *Kino-Eye: the Writings of Dziga Vertov* (trans. Kevin O'Brien). Berkeley, CA: University of California Press 1984: 11–21, here 21.

7 Walter Benjamin: "The Work of Art in the Age of Mechanical Reproduction". In: *Illuminations* (ed. Hannah Arendt, trans. Harry Zohn). New York: Schocken 1969: 217–52, here 236.

8 An attempt to identify a distinct body of film theory around the mobile eye is made in Malcolm Turvey: *Doubting Vision: Film and the Revelationist Tradition*. New York: Oxford University Press 2008.

9 See note 18 and the discussion of Laura Mulvey's influential theory below (pp. 93–100).

10 A seminal essay in this context was Jacques Alain Miller's "La suture". In: *Cahiers pour l'analyse*, No. 1, 1966. Published in English, not accidentally, in a film-theoretical context: "Suture: Elements of the Logic of the Signifier". In: *Screen*, Vol. 18, No. 4, 1977: 24–34.

11 Stephen Heath: "Narrative Space" [orig. 1976]. In: *Questions of Cinema*. London: Macmillan 1981: 19–75, here 32, italics in original.

12 A central text is Jean-Pierre Oudart: "Notes on Suture". In: *Screen*, Vol. 18, No. 4, Winter 1977–8: 35–47 [orig. French: "La suture". In: *Cahiers du Cinéma*, No. 211, 1969: 36–9; and in No. 212, 1969: 50–5]. Influential in the 1970s was Daniel Dayan: "The Tutor-Code of Classical Cinema". In: *Film Quarterly*, Fall 1974, pp. 22–31. This latter text preceded the publication in English of Oudart's text but narrowed the discussion unnecessarily to the shot–countershot technique. Another seminal text of this debate is Stephen Heath: "Notes on Suture". In: *Screen*, Vol. 18, No. 4, Winter 1977–8: 48–79 (available online at www.lacan. com/symptom8_articles/heath8.html, accessed 23 February 2007). Retrospective overviews and further elaborations can be found in Kaja Silverman: "Suture". In: *The Subject of Semiotics*. New York: Oxford University Press 1983: 194–236; as well as in the paradigm of the Slovenian Neo-Lacanian scholar Slavoj Žižek: "Back to the Suture". In: *The Fright of Real Tears: Krzysztof Kie lowski Between Theory and Post-Theory*. London: BFI Publishing 2001: 35–54.

13 See Gregory Currie: *Image and Mind: Film, Philosophy and Cognitive Science*. Cambridge: Cambridge University Press 1995.

14 See Gilles Deleuze: *Cinema 1: the Movement-Image* (trans. Hugh Tomlinson). Minneapolis, MN: University of Minnesota Press 1986 [orig. 1983]; *Cinema 2: the Time-Image* (trans. Hugh Tomlinson). Minneapolis, MN: University of Minnesota Press 1989 [orig. 1985].

15 For an early critique of the idea of suture, see William Rothman: "Against 'The System of the Suture'". In: *Film Quarterly*, Vol. 29, No. 1, 1975: 45–50. A major polemic against suture theory specifically can be found in Noël Carroll: *Mystifying Movies: Fads and Fallacies in Contemporary Film Theory*. New York: Columbia University Press 1988: 183–99.

16 This is in principle no different than the so-called "Kuleshov effect". Kuleshov had alternated one and the same shot of actor Ivan Mozjukin with various other shots – a bowl of soup, a woman's face and a child's coffin. Spectators took the first sequence to represent hunger, the second to be love and the third mourning.

17 David Bordwell: *Narration in the Fiction Film*. Methuen/Madison, WI: University of Wisconsin Press 1985; Edward Branigan: *Narrative Comprehension and Film*. London, New York: Routledge 1992; Slavoj Žižek: *The Fright of Real Tears: Krzysztof Kieslowski Between Theory and Post-Theory*. London: BFI 2001.

18 Laura Mulvey: "Visual Pleasure and Narrative Cinema". In: *Screen*, Vol. 16, No. 3, 1975: 6–18. The text has been re-printed in numerous anthologies. We will be quoting from Gerald Mast *et al.* (eds.): *Film Theory and Criticism: Introductory Readings* (fourth edition). New York, Oxford: Oxford University Press 1992: 746–57. All further citations in the text will be from this version.

19 Mulvey believes that this can be changed only on the level of film practice through a film form that denies any scopophilic pleasure and any spectator satisfaction that might be derived from a narcissistic ego-identification (in the case of men) or from fetishism and castration anxiety (in the case of women). In that period, Mulvey has put this into practice, most notably in her film RIDDLES OF THE SPHINX (GB, 1977, together with Peter Wollen). The relationship between theory and practice was generally an important aspect of feminism in the 1970s and 1980s – see for instance the two influential magazines *Women and Film* (1972–5) in the US and *Frauen und Film* in Germany (since 1974).

20 Probably the most important study on this topic published shortly before Mulvey's polemic was Molly Haskell: *From Reverence to Rape: the Treatment of Women in the Movies*. New York: Holt, Rinehart and Winston 1974.

21 Mary Ann Doane: *The Desire to Desire: the Woman's Film of the 1940s*. Bloomington, IN: Indiana University Press 1987; Teresa de Lauretis: *Alice Doesn't: Feminism, Semiotics, Cinema*. Bloomington, IN: Indiana University Press 1984; Kaja Silverman: *The Acoustic Mirror: the Female Voice in Psychoanalysis and Cinema*. Bloomington, IN: Indiana University Press 1988 (see also Chapter 6 on the ear); Tania Modleski: *The Women Who Knew Too Much: Hitchcock and Feminist Theory*. London, New York: Methuen 1988; Sandy Flitterman-Lewis: *To Desire Differently: Feminism and the French Cinema*. Urbana, IL: University of Illinois Press 1990; Barbara Klinger: *Melodrama and Meaning: History, Culture, and the Films of Douglas Sirk*. Bloomington, IN: Indiana University Press 1994.

22 The classical studies in this field are Marjorie Rosen: *Popcorn Venus: Women, Movies & the American Dream*. New York: Coward, McCann & Geoghegan 1973; Molly Haskell: *From Reverence to Rape: the Treatment of Women in the Movies*. New York: Holt, Rinehart and Winston 1974; Joan Mellen: *Women and their Sexuality in the New Film*. New York: Horizon 1974.

23 Claire Johnston: "Women's Cinema as Counter Cinema". In: Claire Johnston (ed.): *Notes on Women's Cinema*. London: Society for Education in Film and Television 1972: 25.

24 Pam Cook and Claire Johnston: "The Place of Woman in the Cinema of Raoul Walsh". In: Patricia Erens (ed.): *Issues in Feminist Film Criticism*. Bloomington and Indianapolis, IN: Indiana University Press 1990: 19–27.

25 On this topic, see the exemplary analyses by Raymond Bellour, available in *The Analysis of Film* (ed. Constance Penley). Bloomington, IN: Indiana University Press 2002; see also Stephen Heath: *Questions of Cinema*. London: Macmillan/Bloomington, IN: Indiana University Press 1981.

26 For more on this, see the special issue "The Spectratrix" (edited by Mary Ann Doane and Janet Bergstrom) of *Camera Obscura*, No. 20/21, 1990.

27 Laura Mulvey: "Afterthoughts on Visual Pleasure". In: *Framework*, 15–17 (1981): 12–15.

28 See Gaylyn Studlar: *In the Realm of Pleasure: Von Sternberg, Dietrich, and the Masochistic Aesthetic*. New York: Columbia University Press 1988.

29 See Linda Williams: "Melodrama Revised". In: Nick Browne (ed.): *Refiguring American Film Genres: History and Theory*. Berkeley, CA: University of California Press 1998: 42–88; Joan

Copjec: *Read My Desire: Lacan Against the Historicists*. Cambridge, MA: MIT Press 1994; Mary Ann Doane: "The Clinical Eye: Medical Discourses in the 'Woman's Film' of the 1940s". In: Susan Rubin Suleiman (ed.): *The Female Body in Western Culture: Contemporary Perspectives*. Cambridge, MA: Harvard University Press 1986: 152–74.

30 See Carol Clover: *Men, Women, and Chainsaws: Gender in the Modern Horror Film*. London: British Film Institute 1992.

31 See E. Ann Kaplan (ed.): *Women in Film Noir*. London: British Film Institute 2005 (new edition).

32 Janet Staiger: "Taboos and Totems: Cultural Meanings of THE SILENCE OF THE LAMBS". In: Jim Collins *et al.* (eds.): *Film Theory Goes to the Movies*. New York, London: Routledge 1993 (AFI Film Reader): 142–54.

33 For more on reception studies and film, see Janet Staiger: *Perverse Spectators: the Practices of Film Reception*. New York: New York University Press 2000.

34 Several of these position can be found cogently argued in Richard Allen: *Projecting Illusion: Film Spectatorship and the Impression of Reality*. New York: Cambridge University Press 1995; see also Murray Smith: *Engaging Characters: Fiction, Emotion, and the Cinema*. Oxford: Clarendon Press 1995.

35 See, for example, Laurent Mannoni: *The Great Art of Light and Shadow: Archaeology of the Cinema* (trans. Richard Crangle). Exeter: University of Exeter Press 2000; Stephen Herbert: *A History of Pre-Cinema* (3 vols.). London, New York: Routledge 2000.

36 By way of a short introduction, see Thomas Elsaesser: "The New Film History". In: *Sight and Sound*, Vol. 55, No. 4, Autumn 1986: 246–51. A monographic application/implementation is offered by Robert C. Allen and Douglas Gomery: *Film History: Theory and Practice*. New York: Knopf 1985.

37 For a recent overview, see Jennifer M. Bean and Diane Negra (eds.): *A Feminist Reader in Early Cinema*. Durham, NC and London: Duke University Press 2002. See also the work by Miriam Hansen and Heide Schlüpmann cited in note 3.

38 What comes to mind in this context are the works of Hayden White or the New Historicism advocated by Stephen Greenblatt and others. For applications to cinema, see Vivian Sobchack (ed.): *The Persistence of History: Cinema, Television and the Modern Event*. London, New York: Routledge 1996 (AFI Film Reader).

39 For further elaborations of this position as well as for alternatives, see Marijke de Valck and Malte Hagener (eds.): *Cinephilia: Movies, Love, and Memory*. Amsterdam: Amsterdam University Press 2005.

40 Alexander Mitscherlich: *Society Without a Father*. New York: Schocken Books 1970. With specific reference to cinema:

> Might not the perverse pleasure of fascism, its fascination have been less the sadism and brutality of SS officers, but that of being seen, of placing oneself in view of the all-seeing eye of the State? [...] Fascism in its social imaginary encouraged a moral exhibitionism, as it encouraged denunciation and mutual surveillance. Hitler appealed to the *Volk*, but he always pictured the German nation as standing there, observed by "the eyes of the world". The massive specularisation of public life, famously diagnosed by Walter Benjamin as the "aestheticisation of politics", might be said to have helped institutionalise that structure of "to be is to be perceived" which Fassbinder's cinema never ceases to interrogate.
>
> (Thomas Elsaesser: *Fassbinder's Germany: History – Identity – Subject*. Amsterdam: Amsterdam University Press 1996: 93)

41 The painting is situated in the National Gallery in London. For more about the painting, see Susan Foister, Ashok Roy and Martin Wyld: *Holbein's Ambassadors*. London: Yale University Press 1998.

42 See, for instance, the debate between the mutually antagonizing forces of Žižek and David Bordwell. Žižek has taken Bordwell to task for what he understands as Bordwell's advocacy

of "post-theory" in *The Fright of Real Tears: Krzysztof Kieslowski Between Theory and Post-Theory*. London: British Film Institute 2001. Bordwell replies on his blog: "Slavoj Žižek: Say Anything" (posted April 2005): www.davidbordwell.com/essays/zizek.php (accessed 22 January 2009).

43 Slavoj Žižek, *Everything You Always Wanted to Know About Lacan But Were Afraid to Ask Hitchcock*. London: Verso 1992.

44 For an overview, see Rex Butler: *Slavoj Žižek: Live Theory*. New York: Continuum 2005.

45 Slavoj Žižek: *Organs Without Bodies: On Deleuze and Consequences*. London, New York: Routledge 2004: 151–62, here 154.

46 Slavoj Žižek: *The Fright of Real Tears: Krzysztof Kie lowski Between Theory and Post-Theory*. London: BFI Publishing 2001: 34.

47 Michel Foucault: *Discipline and Punish: the Birth of the Prison* (trans. Alan Sheridan). New York: Vintage 1979: 217.

48 Gilles Deleuze: *Foucault*. Minneapolis, MN: University of Minnesota Press 1988: 111.

49 Niklas Luhmann: *Art as a Social System* (trans. Eva M. Knodt). Stanford, CA: Stanford University Press 2000: 93 [orig. German 1995].

50 See here Gilles Deleuze: "Postscript on Control Societies". In: *Negotiations, 1972–1990* (trans. Martin Joughin). New York: Columbia University Press 1995: 177–82.

5 Cinema as skin and touch

1 Vivian Sobchack: "What My Fingers Knew: the Cinesthetic Subject, or Vision in the Flesh". In: *Carnal Thoughts: Embodiment and Moving Image Culture*. Berkeley, CA: University of California Press 2004: 53–84, here 55ff. The text can, in a different version, also be found online at www.sensesofcinema.com/contents/00/5/fingers.html (accessed 29 January 2007).

2 Steven Connor: *The Book of Skin*. London: Reaktion Books 2004.

3 Claudia Benthien: *Skin: On the Cultural Border Between Self and the World*. New York: Columbia University Press 2002 [orig. German 1999].

4 More about this complex can be found in Noël Carroll: "The Future of Allusion: Hollywood in the Seventies (and Beyond)". In: *October*, No. 20, Spring 1982; Dan Harries: *Film Parody*. London: British Film Institute 2000; and, under the heading of post-modernism, in various essays from Jürgen Felix (ed.): *Die Postmoderne im Kino: Ein Reader*. Marburg Schüren 2002. See also, conceptualized as a cinephilic practice, Marijke de Valck and Malte Hagener (eds.): *Cinephilia: Movies, Love, and Memory*. Amsterdam: Amsterdam University Press 2005.

5 See here also the analysis in Warren Buckland and Thomas Elsaesser: *Studying Contemporary American Film: a Guide to Movie Analysis*. London: Arnold 2002: 249–83.

6 Vivian Sobchack: "What My Fingers Knew: the Cinesthetic Subject, or Vision in the Flesh". In: *Carnal Thoughts: Embodiment and Moving Image Culture*. Berkeley, CA: University of California Press 2004: 53–84, here 63.

7 Vivian Sobchack: *The Address of the Eye: a Phenomenology of Film Experience*. Princeton, NJ: Princeton University Press 1992: 3.

8 Vivian Sobchack: *The Address of the Eye: a Phenomenology of Film Experience*. Princeton, NJ: Princeton University Press 1992: 5.

9 Vivian Sobchack: "What My Fingers Knew: the Cinesthetic Subject, or Vision in the Flesh". In: *Carnal Thoughts: Embodiment and Moving Image Culture*. Berkeley, CA: University of California Press 2004: 53–84, here 63.

10 Vivian Sobchack: "Beating the Meat/Surviving the Text, or How to Get Out of the Century Alive". In: *Carnal Thoughts: Embodiment and Moving Image Culture*. Berkeley, CA: University of California Press 2004: 165–78.

11 Steven Shaviro: *The Cinematic Body*. Minneapolis, MN and London: University of Minnesota Press 1993: 255f.

12 See, for instance, Joe McElhaney: "Fritz Lang and the Cinema of Tactility". In: Alice Autelitano *et al.* (eds.): *I cinque sensi dei cinema: The Five Senses of Cinema*. Udine: Forum 2005:

299–314. There are also numerous films on the topic of the hand as representation, for instance HÄNDE (DE, 1928/29, Hans Richter), THE BEAST WITH FIVE FINGERS (US, 1946, Robert Florey), THE HAND (US, 1981, Oliver Stone), DER AUSDRUCK DER HÄNDE (DE, 1997, Harun Farocki).

13 Jan Sahli: *Filmische Sinneserweiterung: László Moholy-Nagys Filmwerk und Theorie*. Marburg: Schüren 2006 (Zürcher Filmstudien 14): 24.

14 http://thegalleriesatmoore.org/publications/valie/valietour3.shtml and www.valieexport. at/en/werke/werke/?tx_ttnews%5Btt_news%5D=1956&tx_ttnews%5BbackPid%5D=4& cHash=6d9b20c733; see also Wanda Strauven: "Touch, Don't Look". In: Alice Autelitano *et al.* (eds.): *I cinque sensi dei cinema: The Five Senses of Cinema*. Udine: Forum 2005: 283–97.

15 Joachim Jäger *et al.* (eds.): *Beyond Cinema: the Art of Projection. Films, Videos and Installations from 1963 to 2005*. Ostfildern: Hatje Crantz 2006: 130.

16 Linda Williams: "Film Bodies: Gender, Genre, and Excess". In: *Film Quarterly*, Vol. 44, No. 4, Summer 1991: 2–13, here 4.

17 Linda Williams: "Film Bodies: Gender, Genre, and Excess". In: *Film Quarterly*, Vol. 44, No. 4, Summer 1991: 5.

18 Barbara Creed: *The Monstrous Feminine: Film, Feminism, Psychoanalysis*. London, New York: Routledge 1993: 14.

19 See Thomas Elsaesser: *Filmgeschichte und frühes Kino: Archäologie eines Medienwandels*. München: edition text + kritik 2002: 71–4; Wanda Strauven: "Touch, Don't Look". In: Alice Autelitano *et al.* (eds.): *I cinque sensi dei cinema: The Five Senses of Cinema*. Udine: Forum 2005: 283–97; Miriam Hansen: *Babel and Babylon: Spectatorship in American Silent Film*. Cambridge, MA: Harvard University Press 1991: 25–30.

20 Laura U. Marks: *The Skin of Film: Intercultural Cinema, Embodiment and the Senses*. Durham, NC and London: Duke University Press 2000, as well as *Touch: Film and Multisensory Theory*. Minneapolis, MN: University of Minnesota Press 2002.

21 Laura U. Marks: *The Skin of Film: Intercultural Cinema, Embodiment, and the Senses*. Durham, NC and London: Duke University Press 2000: xi. Further citations are from this book.

22 Antonia Lant: "Haptical Cinema". In: *October*, 74, 1995: 45–73; David Trotter: "Stereoscopy: Modernism and the 'Haptic'". In: *Critical Quarterly*, 46, 4, 2004: 38–58. The term "haptic" has also famously been applied by Gilles Deleuze in: *Francis Bacon: the Logic of Sensation* (trans. Daniel W. Smith). London: Continuum 2003 [orig. French 1983].

23 Claire Perkins: "This Time, It's Personal". In: *Senses of Cinema*, No. 33, October–December 2004: http://archive.sensesofcinema.com/contents/books/04/33/touch_laura_marks. html (accessed 29 January 2009).

24 Hamid Naficy: *Accented Cinema: Exilic and Diasporic Filmmaking*. Princeton, NJ and Oxford: Princeton University Press 2001: 28–30.

25 Robert Stam: *Film Theory: an Introduction*. Malden, MA, Oxford: Blackwell 2000: 272.

26 See Drehli Robnik: "Körper-Erfahrung und Film-Phänomenologie". In: Jürgen Felix (ed.): *Moderne Film Theorie*. Mainz: Bender 2002: 246–80.

27 Siegfried Kracauer: *Theory of Film: the Redemption of Physical Reality*. New York: Oxford University Press 1960: xi, 158, 297; see also Gertrud Koch: *Siegfried Kracauer: an Introduction* (trans. Jeremy Gaines). Princeton, NJ: Princeton University Press 2000; Miriam Hansen: "With Skin and Hair: Kracauer's Theory of Film, Marseille 1940". In: *Critical Inquiry*, Vol. 19, No. 3, Spring 1993: 437–69.

6 Cinema as ear – acoustics and space

1 For a number of critical approaches to the film, see Steve Cohan: "Case Study: interpreting SINGIN' IN THE RAIN". In: Christine Gledhill and Linda Williams (eds.): *Reinventing Film Studies*. London: Arnold 2000: 53–75. See also Peter Wollen: SINGIN' IN THE RAIN. London: British Film Institute 1992.

2 Whereas SINGIN' IN THE RAIN presents the introduction of sound film as a comedy, ÉTOILE

SANS LUMIÈRE (FR, 1946, Marcel Blistène), starring Edith Piaf, tells the same story in a tragic vein.

3   For new research on synesthesia, see Richard E. Cytowic: *Synesthesia: a Union of the Senses* (second edition). Cambridge, MA: MIT Press (Bradford Books) 2002; Lynn C. Robertson and Noam Sagiv (eds.): *Synesthesia: Perspectives from Cognitive Neuroscience*. Oxford: Oxford University Press 2004; Robin Curtis *et al.* (eds.): *Synästhesie-Effekte: Zur Intermodalität der ästhetischen Wahrnehmung*. Paderborn: Fink 2009.

4   Mirjam Schaub: *Bilder aus dem Off: Zum philosophischen Stand der Kinotheorie*. Weimar: VDG 2005: 76.

5   For the sake of consistency and normal language use, we will stick to the term "spectator" in this chapter, even though "audiovisual perceiver" or something along those lines might be more fitting.

6   See Martin Marks: *Music and the Silent Film: Contexts and Case Studies, 1895–1924*. Oxford: Oxford University Press 1997 (Film and Culture); Richard Abel and Rick Altman (eds.): *The Sounds of Early Cinema*. Bloomington, IN: Indiana University Press 2001; Rick Altman: *Silent Film Sound*. New York: Columbia University Press 2004 (Film and Culture).

7   A theoretical perspective on sound which focuses on performativity, materiality and variability is offered by Rick Altman: "Cinema as Event". In: Rick Altman (ed.): *Sound Theory, Sound Practice*. London, New York: Routledge 1992: 1–15.

8   Rudolf Arnheim: "Der tönende Film". In: *Die Weltbühne*, No. 42, 16 October 1928: 601–4; cited from the collection: *Die Seele in der Silberschicht: Medientheoretische Texte. Photographie – Film – Rundfunk* (with an introduction by Helmut H. Diederichs). Frankfurt/Main: Suhrkamp 2004: 67–70, here 68.

9   See introductory textbooks for examples of this type of analysis, e.g. David Bordwell and Kristin Thompson: *Film Art: an Introduction*. New York: MacGraw-Hill 1993 (fourth edition): 292–332.

10 Within different theoretical frameworks, this is the conclusion reached by both David Bordwell: *Narration in the Fiction Film*. Methuen/Madison, WI: University of Wisconsin Press 1985 and Steve Neale: *Cinema and Technology: Image, Sound, Color*. Bloomington, IN: Indiana University Press 1985.

11 James Lastra: *Sound Technology and the American Cinema: Perception, Representation, Modernity*. New York: Columbia University Press 2000; Sarah Kozloff: *Invisible Storytellers: Voice-over Narration in American Fiction Film*. Berkeley, CA: University of California Press 1988.

12 Many early musicals dramatize this shift, but there are also horror films that stress the uncanny nature of sound, as well as such musical dramas as THE GREAT GABBO (US, 1929, James Cruze). For similar readings along these lines, see Tom Gunning: *The Films of Fritz Lang: Allegories of Vision and Modernity*. London: British Film Institute 1999.

13 The increasing commodification and marketing of (pop) music in Hollywood since the 1950s is examined in Jeff Smith: *The Sounds of Commerce: Marketing Popular Film Music*. New York: Columbia University Press 1998.

14 James Lastra: *Sound Technology and the American Cinema: Perception, Representation, Modernity*. New York: Columbia University Press 2000.

15 Good introductions and overviews are offered by Claudia Gorbman: *Unheard Melodies: Narrative Film Music*. Bloomington, IN, London: Indiana University Press/British Film Institute 1987; Caryl Flinn: *Strains of Utopia: Gender, Nostalgia, and Hollywood Film Music*. Princeton, NJ: Princeton University Press 1992; Royal S. Brown: *Overtones and Undertones: Reading Film Music*. Berkeley, CA: University of California Press 1994.

16 Michel Chion: *The Voice in Cinema*. New York: Columbia University Press 1999: 18.

17 Michel Chion: *Audiovision: Sound on Screen*. New York: Columbia University Press 1994: 129.

18 Barbara Flückiger: *Sound Design: Die virtuelle Klangwelt des Films*. Marburg: Schüren 2001 (Zürcher Filmstudien 6): 56.

19 For an informative discussion see Michael Ondaatje: *The Conversations: Walter Murch and the Art of Editing Film*. New York: Knopf 2002.

20 Renate Salecl and Slavoj Žižek (eds.): *Gaze and Voice as Love Objects*. Durham, NC, London: Duke University Press 1996.
21 Walter Murch: "Foreword". In: Michel Chion: *Audiovision: Sound on Screen*. New York: Columbia University Press 1994: vii–xxiv, here vii.
22 Mary Ann Doane: "The Voice in the Cinema: the Articulation of Body and Space" [orig. 1980]. In: Bill Nichols (ed.): *Movies and Methods, Vol. 2*. Berkeley, CA: University of California Press 1985: 565–76, here 567.
23 Kaja Silverman: *The Acoustic Mirror: the Female Voice in Psychoanalysis and Cinema*. Bloomington, IN: Indiana University Press 1988: ix.
24 Kaja Silverman: *The Acoustic Mirror: the Female Voice in Psychoanalysis and Cinema*. Bloomington, IN: Indiana University Press 1988: 72ff.
25 Michel Chion: *The Voice in Cinema*. New York: Columbia University Press 1999: 79.
26 Slavoj Žižek: *The Art of the Ridiculous Sublime: On David Lynch's* LOST HIGHWAY. Seattle: Walter Chapin Centre for the Humanities 2000; Michel Chion: *David Lynch*. London: BFI 1995 [orig. French 1992].
27 More about the Walkman can be found in Paul Du Gay: *Doing Cultural Studies: the Story of the Sony Walkman*. London: SAGE 1997.

7 Cinema as brain – mind and body

1 Sergej M. Eisenstein: "The Fourth Dimension in Cinema" (1929). In: *Selected Works, Vol. 1: Writings 1922–1934* (ed. and trans. Richard Taylor). London: British Film Institute/Bloomington, IN: Indiana University Press 1988: 181–94, here 183.
2 See Oksana Bulgakowa: "Eisensteins Vorstellung vom unsichtbaren Bild oder: Der Film als Materialisierung des Gedächtnisses". In: Thomas Koebner and Thomas Meder (eds.): *Bildtheorie und Film*. München: edition text + kritik 2006: 36–51.
3 Hugo Münsterberg: *The Photoplay: a Psychological Study*. New York, London: Appleton 1916. Reprinted with an introduction by Richard Griffith, New York: Dover 1970.
4 Hugo Münsterberg: "Warum wir ins Kino gehen?". In: Dimitri Liebsch (ed.): *Philosophie des Films: Grundlagentexte*. Paderborn: Mentis 2005: 27–36, here 36.
5 Friedrich A. Kittler: "Romanticism—Psychoanalysis—Film: a History of the Double". In: *Literature, Media, Information Systems: Essays* (ed. John Johnston, trans. Stefanie Harris). Amsterdam: G+B Arts International 1997: 85–100, here 99–100 [translation modified].
6 Friedrich A. Kittler: *Austreibung des Geistes aus den Geisteswissenschaften: Programme des Poststrukturalismus*. Paderborn 1980. One should note that the humanities in German are called "Geisteswissenschaft" (literally "mind sciences" or "spirit sciences").
7 See the analyses in Tom Gunning: *The Films of Fritz Lang: Allegories of Vision and Modernity*. London: British Film Institute 2000; Stefan Andriopoulos: *Possessed: Hypnotic Crimes, Corporate Fiction, and the Invention of Cinema* (trans. Peter Jansen and Stefan Andriopoulos). Chicago: Chicago University Press 2008.
8 See Thomas Elsaesser: "The Mind-Game Film". In: Warren Buckland (ed.): *Puzzle Films: Complex Storytelling in Contemporary Cinema*. Malden, MA, Oxford: Blackwell 2009: 13–41.
9 Thomas Elsaesser: "Was wäre, wenn du schon tot bist? Vom, 'postmodernen' zum 'postmortem'-Kino am Beispiel von Christopher Nolans MEMENTO". In: Christine Rüffert et al. (eds.): *ZeitSprünge: Wie Filme Geschichte(n) erzählen*. Berlin: Bertz 2004: 115–25.
10 See Patricia Pisters: "The Universe as Metacinema". In: *The Matrix of Visual Culture: Working with Deleuze in Film Theory*. Stanford, CT: Stanford University Press 2003: 14–44.
11 Esquenazi, Pisters.
12 Gilles Deleuze: *Cinema 1: the Movement-Image* and *Cinema 2: the Time-Image* (trans. Hugh Tomlinson). Minneapolis, MN: University of Minnesota Press 1986 and 1989 [orig. 1983 and 1985].
13 For such an approach, see Mary M. Litch: *Philosophy Through Film*. London, New York: Routledge 2002.

14 Gilles Deleuze: "On *The Movement-Image*". In: *Negotiations, 1972–1990* (trans. Martin Joughin). New York: Columbia University Press 1995: 46–56, here 51.

15 Gilles Deleuze: "On *The Time-Image*". In: *Negotiations, 1972–1990* (trans. Martin Joughin). New York: Columbia University Press 1995: 57–61, here 59.

16 Annette Michelson: "Bodies in Space: Film as 'Carnal Knowledge' ". In: *Art Forum*, 7, No. 6, February 1969: 54–63, here 58. Further citations in the text in brackets are from this article.

17 Torben Kragh Grodal: "Art Film, the Transient Body, and the Permanent Soul". In: *Aura*, Vol. 6, No. 3, 2000: 33–53.

18 See Linda Williams: "Discipline and Fun: PSYCHO and Postmodern Cinema". In: Christine Gledhill and Linda Williams (eds.): *Reinventing Film Studies*. London: Arnold 2000: 351–78; Thomas Elsaesser: "Discipline through Diegesis". In: Wanda Strauven (ed.): *The Cinema of Attractions Reloaded*. Amsterdam: Amsterdam University Press 2006: 205–25.

19 Thomas Elsaesser, "The Mind-Game Film", 31–2.

20 See, for example, Steven Johnson: *Everything Bad Is Good for You: How Popular Culture Is Making Us Smarter*. London: Penguin 2006; Malcolm Gladwell: *Blink: the Power of Thinking Without Thinking*. London: Penguin 2006.

21 Joseph D. Anderson: *The Reality of Illusion: an Ecological Approach to Cognitive Film Theory*. Carbondale and Edwardsville, IL: Southern Illinois University Press 1996: 12.

22 For further considerations along these lines, see Joseph D. Anderson and Barbara Fisher Anderson (eds.): *Moving Image Theory: Ecological Considerations*. Carbondale, IL: Southern Illinois University Press 2005.

23 Noël Carroll: "The Cinematic Image". In: *Mystifying Movies: Fads and Fallacies in Contemporary Film Theory*. New York: Columbia University Press 1988: 89–146.

24 See Kendall Walton: *Mimesis as Make-Belief: On the Foundations of the Representational Arts*. Cambridge, MA: Harvard University Press 1990.

25 Christopher S. Wood: "Theories of Reference". In: *The Art Bulletin*, 3 January 1996. Available online at www.encyclopedia.com/doc/1G1–18394854.html (8 June 2007).

Conclusion: digital cinema – the body and the senses refigured?

1 See the essay on digital cinema at: www.manovich.net/TEXT/digital-cinema.html. More generally, his *Language of New Media* (Cambridge, MA: MIT Press 2001) has become a central text in the debate around the relationship between cinema and new media.

2 Sean Cubitt: *The Cinema Effect*. Cambridge, MA: MIT Press 2004.

3 Vivian Sobchack: "Introduction". In: *Meta-Morphing: Visual Transformation and the Culture of Quick-Change*. Minneapolis, MN, London: University of Minnesota Press 2000: xi–xxiii, here xii. See also Vivian Sobchack: " 'At the Still Point of the Turning World'. Meta-Morphing and Meta-Stasis". In: *Meta-Morphing: Visual Transformation and the Culture of Quick-Change*. Minneapolis, MN, London: University of Minnesota Press 2000: 131–58.

4 Jay David Bolter and Richard Grusin: *Remediation: Understanding New Media*. Cambridge, MA, London: MIT Press 1999.

5 See, for some examples, the websites of David Bordwell, Roger Ebert, Jonathan Rosenbaum and Henry Jenkins: www.davidbordwell.net/, http://rogerebert.suntimes.com/, www.jonathanrosenbaum.com and www.henryjenkins.org/ (accessed 10 December 2008).

6 A sketch of this position can be found in Tom Gunning: "An Aesthetic of Astonishment: Early Film and the (In)Credulous Spectator". In: Linda Williams (ed.): *Viewing Positions*. New Brunswick, NJ: Rutgers University Press 1995. For a recent (philosophical) overview of positions, see Gertrud Koch and Christiane Voss (eds.): *... kraft der Illusion*. München: Wilhelm Fink 2006.

7 See special issue "Indexicality: Trace and Sign", edited by Mary Ann Doane, in *Differences: a Feminist Journal of Cultural Studies*, 18, 1, 2007. See also Robin Curtis: "Deixis and the Origo

of Time-based Media: Blurring the 'here and now' from the Dickson Experimental Sound Film of 1894 to Janet Cardiff's Installation Ghost Machine". In: *Möglichkeitsräume: Zur Performativität von sensorischer Wahrnehmung*. Berlin: Erich Schmidt Verlag 2007: 255–66.

8 Alexander R. Galloway: *Gaming: Essays on Algorithmic Culture*. Minneapolis, MN, London: University of Minnesota Press 2006: 8f.

9 Anne Friedberg: *The Virtual Window: From Alberti to Microsoft*. Cambridge, MA: MIT Press 2006.

10 Real-live action films with actors "may become merely the default values of the system cinema, in the future, all kinds of other options are possible, so that both narrative and live action may seem to be options rather than constitutive features of cinema". Lev Manovich, "Digital Cinema" (www.jupiter/ucsd.edu/~manovich).

11 See Bruno Latour and Peter Weibel (eds.): *Making Things Public – Atmospheres of Democracy*. Cambridge, MA: MIT Press, 2005; Justin Clement and Dominic Pettman: *Avoiding the Subject: Media, Culture and the Object*. Amsterdam: Amsterdam University Press 2005.

12 For two recent discussions of these transformations from different angles, see Barbara Klinger: *Beyond the Multiplex: Cinema, New Technologies and the Home*. Berkeley, CA: University of California Press 2006; Janine Marchessault and Susan Lord (eds.): *Fluid Screens, Expanded Cinema*. Toronto, Buffalo, NY, London: University of Toronto Press 2007.

13 Lev Manovich: *The Language of New Media*. Cambridge, MA: MIT Press 2001.

14 Certainly Gilles Deleuze's cinema books have led to a boom in a field one could label "film and philosophy" which is too broad to characterize in a few lines. See, for overviews from different perspectives: Cynthia A. Freeland and Thomas E. Wartenberg (eds.): *Philosophy and Film*. London, New York: Routledge 1995; Noel Carroll and Jinhee Choi (eds.): *Philosophy of Film and Motion Pictures: an Anthology*. Malden, MA, London: Blackwell 2005; Daniel Shaw: *Film and Philosophy: Taking Movies Seriously*. London, New York: Wallflower 2008. See also the well-kept website *Film-Philosophy* (www.film-philosophy.com; accessed 19 December 2008).

Bibliography

Richard Abel and Rick Altman (eds.): *The Sounds of Early Cinema*. Bloomington, IN: Indiana University Press 2001.

Richard Allen: *Projecting Illusion: Film Spectatorship and the Impression of Reality*. New York: Cambridge University Press 1995.

Richard Allen and Murray Smith (eds.): *Film Theory and Philosophy*. New York: Oxford University Press 1999.

Rick Altman: *Silent Film Sound*. New York: Columbia University Press 2004 (Film and Culture).

Rick Altman (ed.): *Sound Theory, Sound Practice*. London, New York: Routledge 1992.

Joseph D. Anderson: *The Reality of Illusion: an Ecological Approach to Cognitive Film Theory*. Carbondale, Edwardsville, IL: Southern Illinois University Press 1996.

Joseph D. Anderson and Barbara Fisher Anderson (eds.): *Moving Image Theory: Ecological Considerations*. Carbondale, IL: Southern Illinois University Press 2005.

Dudley Andrew: *André Bazin*. New York: Oxford University Press 1978.

Dudley Andrew: *Concepts in Film Theory*. Oxford: Oxford University Press 1984.

Dudley Andrew: *The Major Film Theories: an Introduction*. New York: Oxford University Press 1976.

Rudolf Arnheim: *Film as Art*. London: Faber & Faber 1958 [orig. German 1932].

Rudolf Arnheim: *Film Essays and Criticism* (trans. Brenda Benthien). Madison, WI: University of Wisconsin Press 1997.

Jacques Aumont: *Montage Eisenstein*. Bloomington, IN: Indiana University Press 1987 [orig. 1979].

Jacques Aumont, Michel Marie and Alain Bergala: *Aesthetics of Film*. Austin, TX: University of Texas Press 1992 [orig. 1983].

Béla Balázs: *Der sichtbare Mensch oder die Kultur des Films*. Frankfurt/Main: Suhrkamp 2001 [orig. German 1924].

André Bazin: *What Is Cinema? 2 Vols.* (trans. Hugh Gray). Berkeley, CA: University of California Press 1967, 2005 [orig. 1958–62; first published in English in 1971].

Jennifer M. Bean and Diane Negra (eds.): *A Feminist Reader in Early Cinema*. Durham, NC, London: Duke University Press 2002.

Wolfgang Beilenhoff (ed.): *Poetika Kino: Theorie und Praxis des Films im russischen Formalismus*. Frankfurt/Main: Suhrkamp 2005.

Raymond Bellour: *The Analysis of Film*. Bloomington, IN: Indiana University Press 2002.

David Bordwell: *The Cinema of Eisenstein*. Cambridge, MA: Harvard University Press 1993.

David Bordwell: *Narration in the Fiction Film*. London: Methuen/Madison, WI: University of Wisconsin Press 1985.

David Bordwell: *Poetics of Cinema*. New York: Routledge 2008.

David Bordwell and Noël Carroll (eds.): *Post-Theory: Reconstructing Film Studies*. Madison, WI: University of Wisconsin Press 1996.

David Bordwell, Janet Staiger and Kristin Thompson: *The Classical Hollywood Cinema: Film Style and Mode of Production to 1960*. London: Routledge & Kegan Paul 1985.

Edward Branigan: *Narrative Comprehension and Film*. London, New York: Routledge 1992.

Edward Branigan: *Projecting a Camera: Language Games in Film Theory*. New York: Routledge 2006.

Leo Braudy: *The World in a Frame: What We See in Films*. Garden City, NY: Anchor Press/Doubleday 1976.

Leo Braudy and Marshall Cohen (eds.): *Film Theory and Criticism: Introductory Readings* (sixth edition). New York: Oxford University Press 2004.

Royal S. Brown: *Overtones and Undertones: Reading Film Music*. Berkeley, CA: University of California Press 1994.

Warren Buckland (ed.): *The Film Spectator: From Sign to Mind*. Amsterdam: Amsterdam University Press 1995.

Warren Buckland (ed.): *Puzzle Films: Complex Storytelling in Contemporary Cinema*. Malden, MA, Oxford: Blackwell 2009.

Bert Cadullo (ed.): *Bazin at Work: Major Essays and Reviews from the Forties and Fifties* (trans. Alain Piette and Bert Cadullo). London, New York: Routledge 1997.

Noël Carroll: *Mystifying Movies: Fads and Fallacies in Contemporary Film Theory*. New York: Columbia University Press 1988.

Noël Carroll: *Philosophical Problems of Classical Film Theory*. Princeton, NJ: Princeton University Press 1988.

Noël Carroll: *The Philosophy of Motion Pictures*. London: Blackwell 2008.

Noël Carroll and Jinhee Choi (eds.): *Philosophy of Film and Motion Pictures: an Anthology*. Malden, MA: Blackwell 2005.

Francesco Casetti: *Eye of the Century: Film, Experience, Modernity*. New York: Columbia University Press 2008.

Francesco Casetti: *Theories of Cinema, 1945–1995*. Austin, TX: University of Texas Press 1999 [orig. Italian 1993].

Stanley Cavell: *Contesting Tears: the Hollywood Melodrama of the Unknown Woman*. Chicago, IL: University of Chicago Press 1996.

Stanley Cavell: *Pursuits of Happiness: the Hollywood Comedy of Remarriage*. Cambridge, MA: Harvard University Press 1981.

Stanley Cavell: *The World Viewed: Reflections on the Ontology of Film*. Cambridge, MA: Harvard University Press 1979.

Leo Charney and Vanessa R. Schwartz: *Cinema and the Invention of Modern Life*. Berkeley, CA: University of California Press 1995.

Michel Chion: *Audiovision: Sound on Screen*. New York: Columbia University Press 1994 [orig. Paris 1990].

Michel Chion: *The Voice in the Cinema*. New York: Columbia University Press 1999 [orig. Paris 1982].

Carol Clover: *Men, Women, and Chainsaws: Gender in the Modern Horror Film*. London: British Film Institute 1992.

Jim Collins, Hilary Radner and Ava Preacher Collins (eds.): *Film Theory Goes to the Movies*. New York, London: Routledge 1993.

Pam Cook (ed.): *The Cinema Book*. London: British Film Institute 2008 (third edition; first published in 1985).

Jonathan Crary: *Techniques of the Observer: On Vision and Modernity in the 19th Century*. Cambridge, MA: MIT Press 1992.

Barbara Creed: *The Monstrous Feminine: Film, Feminism, Psychoanalysis*. London, New York: Routledge 1993.

Sean Cubitt: *The Cinema Effect*. Cambridge, MA: MIT Press 2004.

Gregory Currie: *Image and Mind: Film, Philosophy and Cognitive Science*. Cambridge: Cambridge University Press 1995.

Robin Curtis and Gertrud Koch (eds.): *Einfühlung: Zu Geschichte und Gegenwart eines ästhetischen Konzeptes*. München: Fink 2007.

Therese Davis: *The Face on the Screen: Death, Recognition and Spectatorship*. Bristol: Intellect 2004.

Teresa de Lauretis: *Alice Doesn't: Feminism, Semiotics, Cinema*. Bloomington, IN: Indiana University Press 1984.

Marijke de Valck and Malte Hagener (eds.): *Cinephilia: Movies, Love, and Memory*. Amsterdam: Amsterdam University Press 2005.

Gilles Deleuze: *Cinema 1: the Movement-Image* (trans. Hugh Tomlinson). Minneapolis, MN: University of Minnesota Press 1986 [orig. 1983].

Gilles Deleuze: *Cinema 2: the Time-Image* (trans. Hugh Tomlinson). Minneapolis, MN: University of Minnesota Press 1989 [orig. 1985].

Mary Ann Doane: *The Desire to Desire: the Woman's Film of the 1940s*. Bloomington, IN: Indiana University Press 1987.

Mary Ann Doane: *The Emergence of Cinematic Time: Modernity, Contingency, the Archive*. Cambridge, MA, London: Harvard University Press 2002.

James Donald and Michael Renov (eds.): *The Sage Handbook of Film Studies*. London: Sage 2008.

Sergej Eisenstein: *Selected Works* (four volumes; edited by Richard Taylor). London: British Film Institute/Bloomington, IN: Indiana University Press 1988, 1991, 1995, 1996.

Thomas Elsaesser (ed.): *Early Cinema: Space, Frame, Narrative*. London: British Film Institute 1990.

Thomas Elsaesser and Warren Buckland: *Studying Contemporary American Film: a Guide to Movie Analysis*. London: Arnold 2002.

Thomas Elsaesser and Kay Hoffmann (eds.): *Cinema Futures: Cain, Abel or Cable?* Amsterdam: Amsterdam University Press 1997.

Patricia Erens (ed.): *Issues in Feminist Film Criticism*. Bloomington and Indianapolis, IN: Indiana University Press 1990.

Caryl Flinn: *Strains of Utopia: Gender, Nostalgia, and Hollywood Film Music*. Princeton, NJ: Princeton University Press 1992.

Sandy Flitterman-Lewis: *To Desire Differently: Feminism and the French Cinema*. Urbana, Chicago, IL: University of Illinois Press 1990.

Daniel Frampton: *Filmosophy*. London, New York: Wallflower 2006.

Cynthia A. Freeland and Thomas E. Wartenberg (eds.): *Philosophy and Film*. London, New York: Routledge 1995.

Anne Friedberg: *The Virtual Window: From Alberti to Microsoft*. Cambridge, MA: MIT Press 2006.

Anne Friedberg: *Window Shopping: Cinema and the Postmodern*. Berkeley, CA: University of California Press 1993.

Alexander R. Galloway: *Gaming: Essays on Algorithmic Culture*. Minneapolis, MN, London: University of Minnesota Press 2006.

Christine Gledhill and Linda Williams (eds.): *Reinventing Film Studies*. London: Arnold 2000.

Claudia Gorbman: *Unheard Melodies: Narrative Film Music*. Bloomington, IN, London: Indiana University Press/British Film Institute 1987.

Lee Grieveson and Haidee Wasson (eds.): *Inventing Film Studies*. Durham, NC: Duke University Press 2008.

Torben Grodal: *Moving Pictures: a New Theory of Film Genres, Feelings, and Cognition*. Oxford: Clarendon Press 1997.

Miriam Hansen: *Babel and Babylon: Spectatorship in American Silent Film*. Cambridge, MA: Harvard University Press 1991.

Molly Haskell: *From Reverence to Rape: the Treatment of Women in the Movies*. New York: Holt, Rinehart and Winston 1974.

Susan Hayward: *Cinema Studies: the Key Concepts*. London, New York: Routledge 2000.

Stephen Heath: *Questions of Cinema*. London: Macmillan/Bloomington, IN: Indiana University Press 1981.

John Hill and Pamela Church Gibson (eds.): *The Oxford Guide to Film Studies*. New York: Oxford University Press 1998.

Barbara Klinger: *Beyond the Multiplex: Cinema, New Technologies and the Home*. Berkeley, CA: University of California Press 2006.

Barbara Klinger: *Melodrama and Meaning: History, Culture, and the Films of Douglas Sirk*. Bloomington, IN: Indiana University Press 1994.

Sarah Kozloff: *Invisible Storytellers: Voice-over Narration in American Fiction Film*. Berkeley, CA: University of California Press 1988.

Siegfried Kracauer: *Theory of Film: the Redemption of Physical Reality*. New York: Oxford University Press 1960.

James Lastra: *Sound Technology and the American Cinema: Perception, Representation, Modernity*. New York: Columbia University Press 2000.

Peter Lehman (ed.): *Defining Cinema*. London: Athlone Press 1997.

Vachel Lindsay: *The Art of the Moving Picture*. New York: Macmillan 1915 (reprint 2000).

Colin MacCabe: *Tracking the Signifier: Theoretical Essays: Film, Linguistics, Literature*. Minneapolis, MN: University of Minnesota Press 1985.

Lev Manovich: *The Language of New Media*. Cambridge, MA: MIT Press 2001.

Janine Marchessault and Susan Lord (eds.): *Fluid Screens, Expanded Cinema*. Toronto, Buffalo, NY, London: University of Toronto Press 2007.

Laura Marks: *The Skin of Film: Intercultural Cinema, Embodiment and the Senses*. Durham, NC, London: Duke University Press 2000.

Laura Marks: *Touch: Film and Multisensory Theory*. Minneapolis, MN: University of Minnesota Press 2002.

Judith Mayne: *Cinema and Spectatorship*. London, New York: Routledge 1995.

Christian Metz: *Film Language: a Semiotics of Cinema*. New York, Oxford: Oxford University Press 1974 (reprint University of Chicago Press 2000) [orig. 1968].

Christian Metz: *The Imaginary Signifier: Psychoanalysis and the Cinema*. Indianapolis, IN: Indiana University Press 1986 [orig. 1975].

Christian Metz: *Language and Cinema*. The Hague: Mouton 1974 [orig. 1971].

Annette Michelson (ed.): *Kino-Eye: the Writings of Dziga Vertov* (trans. Kevin O'Brien). Berkeley, CA: University of California Press 1984.

Toby Miller and Robert Stam (eds.): *A Companion to Film Theory*. Malden, MA: Blackwell 1999.

Tania Modleski: *The Women Who Knew Too Much: Hitchcock and Feminist Theory*. London, New York: Methuen 1988.

Edgar Morin: *The Cinema, or The Imaginary Man*. Minneapolis, MN: University of Minnesota Press 2005 [orig. 1956].

Laura Mulvey: *Death 24× a Second: Stillness and the Moving Image*. London: Reaktion Books 2006.

Laura Mulvey: *Visual and Other Pleasures*. Bloomington, IN: Indiana University Press 1989.

Hugo Münsterberg: *The Photoplay: a Psychological Study*. New York, London: Appleton 1916. Reprinted with an introduction by Richard Griffith, New York: Dover 1970.

Hamid Naficy: *Accented Cinema: Exilic and Diasporic Filmmaking*. Princeton, NJ, Oxford: Princeton University Press 2001.

Steve Neale: *Cinema and Technology: Image, Sound, Color*. Bloomington, IN: Indiana University Press 1985.

Bill Nichols (ed.): *Movies and Methods: Volumes I & II*. Berkeley, CA: University of California Press 1976, 1985.

Patricia Pisters: *The Matrix of Visual Culture: Working with Deleuze in Film Theory*. Stanford, CT: Stanford University Press 2003.

Dana Polan: *Scenes of Instruction: the Beginnings of the US Study of Film*. Berkeley, CA: University of California Press 2007.

Jacques Rancière: *Film Fables*. Oxford: Berg 2006.

David Rodowick: *The Difficulty of Difference: Psychoanalysis, Sexual Difference and Film Theory*. London: Routledge 1991.

Marjorie Rosen: *Popcorn Venus: Women, Movies & the American Dream*. New York: Coward, McCann & Geoghegan 1973.

Philip Rosen: *Change Mummified: Cinema, Historicity, Theory*. Minneapolis, MN: University of Minnesota Press 2001.

Philip Rosen (ed.): *Narrative, Apparatus, Ideology*. New York: Columbia University Press 1986.

Steven Shaviro: *The Cinematic Body*. Minneapolis, MN, London: University of Minnesota Press 1993.

Daniel Shaw: *Film and Philosophy: Taking Movies Seriously*. London, New York: Wallflower 2008.

Kaja Silverman: *The Acoustic Mirror: the Female Voice in Psychoanalysis and Cinema*. Bloomington, IN: Indiana University Press 1988.

Kaja Silverman: *The Threshold of the Visible World*. New York, London: Routledge 1996.

Murray Smith: *Engaging Characters: Fiction, Emotion, and the Cinema*. Oxford: Clarendon Press 1995.

Vivian Sobchack: *The Address of the Eye: a Phenomenology of Film Experience*. Princeton, NJ: Princeton University Press 1992.

Vivian Sobchack: *Carnal Thoughts: Embodiment and Moving Image Culture*. Berkeley, CA: University of California Press 2004.

Vivian Sobchack (ed.): *Meta-Morphing: Visual Transformation and the Culture of Quick-Change*. Minneapolis, MN, London: University of Minnesota Press 2000.

Vivian Sobchack (ed.): *The Persistence of History: Cinema, Television and the Modern Event*. London, New York: Routledge 1996.

Janet Staiger: *Perverse Spectators: the Practices of Film Reception*. New York: New York University Press 2000.

Robert Stam: *Film Theory: an Introduction*. Malden, MA, Oxford: Blackwell 2000.

Robert Stam: *Subversive Pleasure: Bakhtin, Cultural Criticism, and Film*. Baltimore, MD: Johns Hopkins University Press 1989.

Robert Stam, Robert Burgoyne and Sandy Flitterman-Lewis: *New Vocabularies in Film Semiotics: Structuralism, Post-Structuralism and Beyond*. London, New York: Routledge 1992.

Garrett Stewart: *Between Film and Screen: Modernism's Photo Synthesis*. Chicago, IL: Chicago University Press 1999.

Garrett Stewart: *Framed Time: Toward a Postfilmic Cinema*. Chicago, IL, London: University of Chicago Press 2007.

Wanda Strauven (ed.): *The Cinema of Attractions Reloaded*. Amsterdam: Amsterdam University Press 2006.

Gaylyn Studlar: *In the Realm of Pleasure: Von Sternberg, Dietrich, and the Masochistic Aesthetic*. New York: Columbia University Press 1988.

Ed Tan: *Film as an Emotion Machine: Emotion as a Structure of Narrative Film*. Mahwah, NJ: Erlbaum 1996.

Kristin Thompson: *Breaking the Glass Armour: Neoformalist Film Analysis*. Princeton, NJ: Princeton University Press 1988.

Kristin Thompson: *Storytelling in the New Hollywood: Understanding Classical Narrative Technique*. Cambridge, MA, London: Harvard University Press 1999.

Linda Williams (ed.): *Viewing Positions*. New Brunswick, NJ: Rutgers University Press 1995.

Slavoj Žižek: *The Fright of Real Tears: Krzysztof Kieslowski Between Theory and Post-Theory*. London: British Film Institute 2001.

Index

26016320 45